TATTOOFINDER.COM'S

Tattoo-Pedia

CHOOSE FROM OVER 1,000 OF THE **HOTTEST** TATTOO DESIGNS FOR YOUR NEW INK!

From the Editors of TattooFinder.com

HarperCollins*Publishers*

HarperCollins*Publishers*
77–85 Fulham Palace Road
Hammersmith, London W6 8JB

www.harpercollins.co.uk

First published by HarperCollins*Publishers* 2012

10 9 8 7 6 5 4 3 2 1

The Editors at TattooFinder.com assert the moral right to be identified as the authors of this work

A catalogue record of this book is available from the British Library

ISBN 978-0-00-745703-8

Printed and bound in China

Cover tattoo artwork:
Gary Davis (Winding Cobra, front cover)
Rand Johnson (Bound by Love 02, spine)
Rand Johnson (Angered Red Dragon, back cover)
Rand Johnson (Pefliter, back cover)
Rand Johnson (Butterfly Over Rose, back cover)

Contents

Dedication

We'd like to dedicate this book to tattooist Rachael Bardach, cofounder of Flash2xs.com and TattooFinder.com, who has now retired after twenty-five incredible years in the field. We could never have done this book without you, Rachael, and we're sending you loving energy through every page.

Special Thanks

Special thanks go out to all the Flash2xs.com employees, particularly Bryan, Steph, and Kathleen. We're extremely grateful for your hard work and dedication in putting together this book while still managing to keep the business running in tip-top shape! Also thanks to Jeannine Dillon at HarperCollins*Publishers* for spearheading the project and Running Feet Design for brilliantly refining the book into a work of art. Thanks also to the TattooFinder.com customers and the readers who enjoyed our first book, *The Tattoo Sourcebook*. Your continuing support and valuable feedback allow us to grow and improve every single day. And finally, of course, we must thank our incredibly talented artists. They are the cornerstone of both the TattooFinder.com Web site and this amazing book. It is their art that inspires the creativity in our customers who ultimately wear their designs with pride and affection.

Note from TattooFinder.com

Tattoo-Pedia showcases a range of the most incredible tattoo artwork created by some of the best artists in the world and provides all the important information you need to know when getting tattooed. This book is an extension of our company's Web site, TattooFinder.com (launched in 2003), which has so far helped hundreds of thousands of people find the design reference they need to get their perfect tattoo. Our hope is that this book will inspire and guide you in your next great tattoo adventure!

There are, of course, many places you can go for tattoo inspiration. You could scour general art books or browse a myriad of internet Web sites and search engines for tattoo ideas. And, the truth is, you could actually take any picture you find, bring it into a tattoo studio, and eventually get a tattoo based on it. However, this route usually involves painstaking work for your tattooist to make the lines, colors, and shading in the design work, with the limitations of modern tattoo equipment, inks, and your skin. Just as important, the tattooist will need to generate the stencil ("blueprint" for the tattoo), which can be a labor-intensive process. Once all that work is done, there's still the possibility that the design you wanted won't translate to exactly the tattoo you hoped for.

At TattooFinder.com, we've refined our design product over the years, developing new Tattoo Friendly™ quality standards that allow for the best possible translation from design reference to skin. Our comprehensive system of quality controls and modifications ensure that:

- we start with only the best artwork and scan these originals at high resolution in order to preserve the artist's intent to the highest possible degree.

- we size the artwork to its "Minimum Tattooable Size"—the smallest that a design can be tattooed without having to remove any detail. You can always tattoo our designs larger, but go too small and your tattooist will have to make significant alterations to the design.

- we perform color correction and clean-up to match industry-standard inks and ensure the artwork is free of blemishes and other imperfections.

Most importantly, the corresponding stencil is similarly processed and always included with the designs we sell on TattooFinder.com. Tattoo Friendly™ design reference puts you and your tattooist on the same page before you even walk in the shop, getting you the tattoo you actually want and saving you both time and money in the process.

While the artwork in this book is not technically Tattoo Friendly™ "as is," due to limitations of the book-publishing format (space limitations prohibit the inclusion of stencils, for example), all designs contained in *Tattoo-Pedia* are derived directly from our Tattoo Friendly™ artwork. Plus, most designs in this book (as well as tens of thousands of additional designs) can be found on the TattooFinder.com Web site, with their exact size, dimensions, and corresponding stencils available. However you choose to approach your next tattoo, our goal is simply that you have the best possible tattoo experience and end up with ink on your skin that you love!

Lou Bardach, CEO—Flash2xs.com, LLC
& the Editors at TattooFinder.com

A Word on Size in Tattoo-Pedia

Does size matter? When it comes to tattoo designs, it absolutely does! Most people run into trouble when they want a tattoo smaller than the size of the original design. You can always tattoo the design larger, but go too small and your tattooist will have to make significant alterations to the piece. You can use any of the designs in this book for your new ink, but just make sure you take a look at the size designation underneath each one. It will give you a general size designation that is the smallest that a design can be tattooed without having to remove any detail. If you want the exact "minimum tattooable size" of the original tattoo design, you can go directly to www.TattooFinder.com, and we'll provide you with the precise measurements there.

Size Designations in Tattoo-Pedia

Extra Small is generally 2 inches or smaller (less than 5cm)

Small is approximately 2 to 3.25 inches (5–8cm)

Medium is approximately 3.25 to 6 inches (8–15cm)

Large is approximately 6 to 8 inches (15–20cm)

Extra Large is generally 8 inches (20cm) or larger

Introduction

If you think getting a tattoo seems more common and acceptable in today's Western culture than ever before, then you're absolutely right. Over the past twenty years, the popularity of getting inked in the United States and across Europe has soared exponentially—and there isn't any sign of the enthusiasm waning.

So just how popular are tattoos today? Well, in 1936, *Life* magazine cited that ten million Americans (about 6 percent) had at least one tattoo. In April 2006, the U.S. Food and Drug Administration calculated that more than 45 million Americans, or 15 percent, had at least one tattoo. And a 2007 Pew Research Center study found that 36 percent of eighteen- to twenty-five-year-olds had at least one tattoo.

While the Eastern world has dabbled in body art for centuries, the tattoo craze really began to catch on in the West during the 1970s, and by the 1990s, there was a definite "Tattoo Renaissance" underway, as people began looking differently at tattoos and those getting tattooed. Tattoos were no longer solely the territory of bikers, sailors, and "bad boys"—or even men in general; the number of women with tattoos actually quadrupled from 1960 to 1980. By 2007 tattooing had soared in popularity to become the sixth-fastest-growing business in the United States, according to U.S. News and World Report.

If the sheer number of tattooed individuals isn't compelling enough evidence, tattoos have now entered the mainstream consumer marketplace. In fact, in 2011 famed toy company Mattel released, for adults, a limited-edition Tokidoki Barbie, which sported pink hair and elaborate tattoos snaking around her body. With only 7,400 dolls made, it retailed for $50; it purportedly starting going for upward of $200 on eBay.com, after it sold out!

But even with this popularity, there still remains a certain amount of backlash. The Tokidoki Barbie, for example, was met with outrage by parents' groups, angered that this tattooed Barbie was a poor role model for growing girls, particularly noting her elaborate

Did You Know?

- 16 percent of all adults have at least one tattoo
- 31 percent of gay, lesbian, or bisexual people report having tattoos
- 36 percent of those with tattoos are between 25–29 years old
- 34 percent of people with tattoos feel sexier because they are tattooed
- 29 percent of adults with tattoos feel more rebellious
- 17 percent of those with tattoos regret getting them
- In the United States, Democrats are more likely to have tattoos than Republicans

Original source: Harris Interactive Poll, October 2003

"garland" tattoo necklace and back tattoos (among others), her leopard-print leggings, and her heart-and-crossbones T-shirt. However, this wasn't the first time Barbie sported tattoos. There was also controversy over the Barbie Totally Stylin' Tattoos Doll (released in 2008), which actually came with a Tattoo Stamper, and a limited-edition Harley Davidson Barbie (1999), which some stores refused to shelve because of Barbie's eagle-wing back art.

Tattoo: Then and Now

As we explained in our first book, *The Tattoo Sourcebook*, the word "tattoo" can be traced back to the journal of Joseph Banks, the naturalist on board Captain Cook's ship, the *HMS Endeavour*, in 1769. He noted the tattoos of the people he encountered during the exploration of the South Pacific in 1769: "I shall now mention the way they mark themselves indelibly, each of them is so marked by their humor or disposition." The word he used to describe the markings was "tattoo," and it was the first written use of the word, most likely drawing from the Samoan word *tatau* (*ta*, meaning "to strike;" *tau* meaning "to reach a conclusion").

Evidence of the practice of tattooing the skin has been found in almost every culture dating back to the Bronze Age, circa 3000 B.C. While the first tattoos probably came about by accident—a sharpened spit used to roast meat may have left a charcoaled mark on the skin—they soon became deliberate. If this mark left behind could be a reminder of a successful kill, what other events could be commemorated on the skin? Battles fought and won were definitely up there. Spears and daggers may have been dusted with charcoal or color, so when they penetrated the skin, the recipient would be left with more than a simple "war scar." In fact, the mark left behind became a symbol of valor, bravery, and survival—an emotional connection between body and experience, common to tattoo seekers today.

The ancient art has since developed in sophistication and meaning, but, as evidenced with Barbie, that hasn't necessarily made tattoos universally accepted. Tattooing wasn't even legal in New York City until 1997, and it remained illegal in other parts of the United States as late as 2006, when Oklahoma finally relented.

Today, a tattoo may be called "Ink," "Tat," "Art," "Piece," or "Work," and the reasons people get tattoos now are as varied as the designs chosen. People get tattoos for anything from immortalizing a union or celebrating the arrival of a child to commemorating a lost loved one. A tattoo can illustrate a firmly held spiritual belief or it could be a tribute to a favorite celebrity. It can be playful, showing affection for a beloved childhood cartoon character or a sports fan's loyal tribute to his or her favorite team. Tattoos, of course, can also be menacing—a nonverbal way to communicate "stand back" to others.

Aside from the random impulse tattoo inked on a crazy night of partying, we've found that people are spending more time these days choosing their tattoo designs, due in large part to the emotional connection that goes along with the ink—a symbolic expression that is, well, *more* than skin deep. And while impulse tattoos can be cherished, too, it's probably more likely that the average person will have less to regret if they've put careful, thoughtful consideration into their ink.

Welcome to Tattoo-Pedia!

At TattooFinder.com, we feature tens of thousands of designs from artists all over the world, and we're adding more all the time. Besides the incredible artwork, though, we're also committed to helping people get as much information as they can about getting tattooed—from figuring out if they're ready to ink to choosing the perfect design—and beyond. If you bought our first book, *The Tattoo Sourcebook*, don't worry—the artwork here in *Tattoo-Pedia* is all brand-new and even features some popular new tattoo categories, like "Geek" and "Baroque." And since we have tattoo artist contacts all over the world, we're providing you with the latest trends in tattoo—from tattoo cover-ups to the latest in tattoo removal.

Tattoo-Pedia is first and foremost a book of incredible tattoo art. We've provided over a thousand of the hottest new tattoo designs to spur your own imagination and creativity. But more than just a cool collection of art, it's also a smart, handy reference that will help you make the most educated decisions every step of the way in your tattoo experience—from deciding whether getting a tattoo is really for you to choosing a design and location for your new ink; from selecting the right tattooist to what level of pain you can expect during the procedure; from caring for your new ink to removing it, if need be. With *Tattoo-Pedia*, you'll find inspiration for your new tattoo, and information to make the whole process much less painful . . . and much more rewarding!

If you're sitting down with this book, you already have a sense that you want a tattoo and you may already have some idea of what that tattoo will be. We can help you decide on a tattoo that you are likely to cherish and enjoy for a lifetime.

At TattooFinder.com, we know that getting a tattoo is a unique and personal experience. Our purpose here is not to tell you what to do, but to give you all the information you need to make the best tattoo decisions. By the time you finish this book, you will have all the tools you need to get the perfect tattoo for you!

Section 1:

Think Before You Ink:

What You Should Know Before Getting a Tattoo

"In New Guinea, a swirl of tattoos on a Tofi woman's face indicates her family lineage. The dark scrawls on a Cambodian monk's chest reflect his religious beliefs. A Los Angeles gang member's sprawling tattoos describe his street affiliation, and may even reveal if he's committed murder. Whether the bearer is a Maori chief in New Zealand or a Japanese mafia lord, tattoos express an indelible identity."

—From "Looking at the World's Tattoos: Photographer Chris Rainier travels the globe in search of tattoos and other examples of the urge to embellish our skin," by Abigail Tucker, Smithsonian.com

Getting a tattoo is not something that should be taken lightly. Remember, this isn't a T-shirt with a pithy message than can be removed at the end of the day, tucked in a drawer, or tossed in the trash if the sentiment has been played out. It will be as much a permanent part of you as your limbs. In other words, while removal is possible—it's never desirable!

So Why Do You Want a Tattoo?

There are as many reasons to get a tattoo as there are designs. Okay, maybe that's a slight exaggeration, but the reasons are numerous—and they go well beyond an impulse made on a crazy night out. While some people get tattoos for the shock value, others use the medium as a way to memorialize something or someone special to them. Some just like the way it looks and get tattooed as a way to beautify their bodies with permanent artwork. Others use tattoos to tell the stories of their life.

For many, tattoos can act as a "totem." Just as totem poles in Native American culture can represent or identify lineage, cultural beliefs, or notable events (among other things), so too can your tattoos. Let's face it, you're not going to be the same person at forty that you may have been at eighteen (when you decided to get your first tattoo), but if you've chosen well, your ink helps convey the story of your own personal evolution. You might be more accepting of your eighteen-year-old-self's choice if you see that tattoo as your totem or a representation of who you were back then.

As a craft and an art form, tattoos can provide a physically intimate way to express your individuality, but they're not right for everyone. And before you begin to tackle the inevitable barrage of design questions ("Does this purple koi fish truly express my identity?"), you should educate yourself and weigh your options and preferences ("Do I even like purple?").

Learn more about why you want a tattoo and what you'll experience in getting one, and you'll be better able to answer the big question: "Am I ready to get inked?"

Ten Questions: Is a Tattoo Right for You?

Before you take the first step in your tattoo process, you need to sit back and ask yourself ten important questions, which will help you decide if getting a tattoo really is for you.

1. Are you okay with your tattoo becoming a permanent part of you?

We're not going to sugarcoat this: a tattoo is a permanent "wound" on your body; a deep one that penetrates right down into the second layer of your skin, otherwise known as the dermis. A healthy body can heal most wounds, and typically anything that penetrates your skin at that level will be broken down and flushed out of the body by the bloodstream, but the ink molecules in tattoos are too big to discharge. A healthy immune system recognizes that the ink is not poisonous or harmful and allows most of the ink to stay there . . . forever. Are you sure you fully understand the true extent of the tattoo commitment? The decision you make now will be with you in your next relationship, at your future children's high-school graduations, and with you as you rock on the front porch many decades from now.

If you feel okay about making such a long-term, permanent commitment, a tattoo may be right for you.

2. Are you confident your tattoo will stand the test of time?

It's so important that you are one hundred percent honest with yourself about why you want a tattoo, and make sure that you're really comfortable with that reason before you go through with it. Are you looking to commemorate a loved one or a special event in your life? Are you sure that in ten years what you want to celebrate today will still resonate? Can you even imagine yourself in ten years? Is there a particular image or symbol that you identify with and want to express? Are you a spiritual person who wants a reminder of something greater than yourself? Are you like Mark Wahlberg and want to tattoo your name on your arm to remind yourself of your own greatness?

The fact of the matter is that there is no right reason to go under the needle. It's an individual choice that has to be made by the person getting the tattoo—which means you'll never need to justify it to anyone. If you are true to yourself when you decide on your ink, and honest about why you want one or why you chose a particular design, then you'll be confident as you get older that the tattoo is an honest expression of the person you once were . . . even if you're different now.

If you can be comfortable with your reasons for getting this tattoo later in your life, you might be ready to get a tattoo.

3. Is getting a tattoo your idea or someone else's?

Your tattoo should not reflect the desires, views, passions, feelings, thoughts, or worldview of anyone but you. We can't stress this enough. No one else will have to live with your tattoo as closely and as intimately as you will. No one else should be able to decide, or influence you in deciding, what your tattoo should be, and no one should be making you feel either that you need to get a tattoo or that you had better not get one. Friends may pressure you to get one. Family may disown you if you have one. Regardless of external pressure, it's all up to you. Everyone you know will have their own opinions about tattoos, including how big it should be and where you should get it. But while trusted people can provide useful advice, if you don't put *your* opinions first when weighing the factors and making final decisions, you're going to end up disappointed.

If you know beyond a shadow of a doubt that you're getting this tattoo for you—not for or in spite of someone else—you may be ready to get a tattoo.

4. Are you willing to do all the required research before getting a tattoo?

Like any type of learning process, getting a proper tattoo education can take some time and effort. Between researching the design you want and speaking with different tattooists, there is much to learn, and we'll cover what you need to know in this book. Also, running your ideas by trusted friends and family can be a good idea, provided they can give you objective views and not force their opinions on you. Just be prepared from the outset that you're going to need to invest time and energy in order to get the best results.

If you're ready to make a time commitment to study up on all you need to know about getting inked, you might be ready to get a tattoo.

5. Are you okay with experiencing some level of pain?

Getting tattooed doesn't tickle. For most it isn't excruciating, like breaking a leg or childbirth, but there is an element of pain involved. If you're sensitive to pain, even minor pain, a tattoo may not be right for you. Getting tattooed is like "art surgery." There are rubber gloves involved, some blood and bandages and needles, and the process can take several hours or even a few days across multiple sessions. While the pain associated with each tattoo varies, and everyone experiences pain differently, there is almost always some level of discomfort. After all, your skin is being punctured thousands of times by little needles. Even if you're okay with the direct pain, you still need to consider that you may be sitting in a very uncomfortable position for an extended amount of time.

If you're sure you can withstand some minor to moderate levels of pain and temporary discomfort, a tattoo may be for you.

6. Do you understand that even under the best conditions, there can be health risks involved?

As we said, getting tattooed is like art surgery. As with any procedure that involves breaking the skin, when getting a tattoo, you must have the utmost trust that the person working on you is doing so with sterile instruments in a clean environment. If you know what you want and the right questions to ask (we'll help you with that), then it could be as simple as going to one tattooist and making sure you're satisfied. If they don't meet your requirements, then check out a few different places until you are. Higher demand for tattooing could potentially create more unsafe conditions for tattooing than ever before. We'll get into this more when we discuss choosing a tattooist (see pages 159–165), but keep this in mind: anyone can pick up a tattoo machine and go to town on your skin if you let them. In many states, you don't need a license or any professional training. Also, all the equipment needed to start tattooing can be acquired for less than a thousand dollars!

It's a sad fact that not all tattooists are reputable. Some adhere to local health regulations (if any even exist), while others may not. Enforcement of regulations through official inspections (again, if they actually exist) also isn't guaranteed. Some cities, counties, and states in the United States have health mandates on tattoo shops, but not all, and

Experts Know . . .

If you have special health considerations such as diabetes, hemophilia, epilepsy, or immunity deficiency problems, you should speak with your health-care provider prior to being tattooed. You will also need to notify your tattooist of any conditions that could complicate the application or healing of your tattoo.

in general, the tattoo industry isn't strictly regulated. Poor sanitation or misuse of tattoo equipment can lead to more serious and even life-endangering blood diseases like hepatitis. And, while you can be tattooed in a safe, reputable tattoo studio with little health risk, the greatest risks often occur after you've gotten your new tattoo. Improper healing and aftercare can lead to infection and long-term skin conditions, not to mention unsightly damage to your new artwork (see pages 301–302).

If you're comfortable about taking a risk (made less risky by educating yourself about tattoo safety and finding the right person to ink you), a tattoo may be right for you.

7. Are you okay with the idea of people not liking your tattoo—even openly criticizing you for it?

How well do you deal with being the center of attention? Perhaps more important: how well do you deal with being the center of scorn? Some people despise tattoos, and they're very vocal about it. They might be appalled that people would "deface" their bodies, and they won't be shy about letting you know their opinions. On the other hand, there will probably be those who feel as though they share a common bond with you because you both have ink. Some may simply be interested in your tattoo, while others may feel like it's okay to roll up your sleeve or push away other articles of clothing to get a better view—and they might do so without asking you. For better or worse, by getting a tattoo, especially if it's going to be highly visible to others, you will be drawing attention to yourself and, whether you like it or not, potentially being labeled and stereotyped. Sometimes you need to have some patience and a thick skin to wear your tattoo with pride.

If you're okay with others openly expressing their views on your tattoo (whether they're positive or negative), then a tattoo may be for you.

8. Are you willing to take full responsibility for how your tattoo turns out?

The design you choose, the artist, and the studio that you decide to work with . . . all of these decisions are yours. With the potential of getting bad work or a health complication, it's important that you are prepared to take full responsibility for the ultimate outcome. There may be other people involved, like friends and family or your tattooist, but you're the one calling the shots and the ultimate success of the tattoo experience is up to you. Educate yourself and make smart decisions about your design reference, placement, tattooist, and aftercare. The choices you make will have permanent rewards and consequences, ultimately determining whether you'll have the best possible tattoo experience.

If you're willing to accept full responsibility for how your tattoo comes out, you may be ready to get a tattoo.

9. Do you understand that as your body changes over time, so, most likely, will the appearance of your tattoo?

Like your body, tattoos are going to change as they age. The skin is the largest organ in the body, and it reproduces itself. Your body will slowly break down some of the ink pigment of your tattoo, making it look dull, faded, and blurred over time. Your artwork may also stretch or sag, which will make it appear much different than it did when new. There are ways to increase the staying power of your tattoo, which we'll look at later in the Tattoo Friendly™ section of this book (see pages 149–152), including choosing design references best suited to hold up well over time. Whatever happens, it's definitely possible to get your tattoo touched up, rescued, covered, or removed—all topics we'll cover in Section 3 (see pages 298–313). The results will vary, but it's important to know from the beginning that your tattoo will age with you and may eventually need more work to keep it looking good (see pages 304–305 for information on tattoo maintenance).

If you accept that, like the rest of you, your tattoo will not look the same in five, ten, or forty years, you may be ready to get a tattoo.

10. Is there an alternative to getting a tattoo that may be more in line with what you're really after?

If you are not sure you're ready to make such a huge commitment but still like the idea of skin decoration, there are other options. Henna art, widely used in India, is the usage of natural ink (from the henna plant) applied in decorative patterns, essentially "staining" the skin and lasting for as long as three weeks. Celebrities like Madonna and Uma Thurman have reportedly used henna for temporary skin decoration. Other options include adult temporary tattoos, which you apply using water; latex skin paint, which doesn't rub off on your clothes or absorb into your skin; or tattoo clothing, which are articles of clothing you can actually wear, like T-shirts or tattoo "sleeves" that give the wearer the appearance of being tattooed.

If you're interested in the idea of having a tattoo and just not 100 percent sure about going through with it, take the time to think through your options. Your skin isn't going anywhere.

Checklist of Top Ten Questions to Ask Yourself Before Getting a Tattoo

1. Are you okay with your tattoo becoming a permanent part of you?
2. Are you confident that you want a tattoo for all the right reasons?
3. Is getting a tattoo your idea, or is it someone else's?
4. Are you willing to do all the required research before meeting the needle?
5. Are you okay with experiencing some level of pain?
6. Do you understand that, even under the best conditions, there can be health risks involved?
7. Are you okay with the idea of people not liking your tattoo—even openly criticizing you for it?
8. Are you willing to take full responsibility for how your tattoo comes out?
9. Do you understand that as your body changes over time, so, likely, will the appearance of your tattoo?
10. Is there an alternative to getting a tattoo that may be more in line with what you're really after?

Experts Know . . .

Whether you decide to modify an existing tattoo design or go with the original artwork reference because you think it's perfect "as is," your ultimate result should be a tattoo that you really treasure. Don't cave to suggestions or even pressure that you might get from others if you're happy with your tattoo choice. Your opinion matters most.

Did You Know?

- 43 percent of people polled say they get tattooed to represent something personal
- 38 percent of people say they choose a tattoo because it has special meaning to them
- 32 percent say the quality of the artwork is how they choose their tattoo
- 32 percent say they get tattooed because they are addicted to ink
- 27 percent of people say they choose their tattoo for its originality
- 19 percent of people say they get tattooed because they like the artwork
- 4 percent of people say they get tattooed because they enjoy the feeling of it

Original source: Flash2xs.com, LLC Online Polls

Tattoo Planning

Now that you've made your way through all the "why"s of getting a tattoo, and you firmly know that you want to get a tattoo for the right reasons, it's time to cover the "what"—namely, *what* you will have tattooed on your skin. What you choose will depend on understanding your own Tattoo Plan (see overleaf) and understanding what matters most to you.

Creativity, control, time, and money are the essential aspects of tattoo planning, and they will influence your approach to getting tattooed. As you move through this section, we'll show you how to decide on your own tattoo plan.

Your Tattoo Plan

Getting a tattoo is all about really connecting with an image or idea and wanting to make it a permanent statement in your life. To that end, you want to prepare as much as you can before the procedure takes place and know the approach you want to take to make sure that you have the resources you need to get there. A variety of factors can be influential in deciding which tattoo plan is right for you:

- **Your level of personal creativity:** How artistically creative are you and how much do you know about what makes artwork tattoo-able? Do you have resources (friends, for example) who can help in this area? Do you know of an artistically creative tattooist you can work with? While it's *always* important to find a tattooist who is an expert in the craft of applying ink to skin, it's critical to know that not all tattooists are artistically gifted (we'll talk more about this later).
- **The creative control you're comfortable having and/or relinquishing:** How important is it that you have a clear, final picture on a piece of paper of what you will have tattooed, available for you to review before it goes on your skin? Is a general sketch of the design good enough for you to give the "go-ahead" to your tattooist, or do you need to see something much more concrete?
- **The amount of time and money you are willing to invest in your new ink:** Good tattoos will always take some amount of time and money on your part—and the adage here mostly holds true: you get what you pay for. But there are ways to minimize the time that it takes to accurately communicate that tattoo vision you hold in your mind's eye to the tattooist, and there are ways to keep your costs down.

At TattooFinder.com, we have developed a framework of approaches to help you figure out a tattoo plan that works best for you based on the above criteria. We've divided them into three distinct categories: personalized, custom, and couture. A brief overview of each plan follows, but they will be referenced throughout the book as we help guide you toward getting the tattoo in the way that works best for you.

Read the following three sections closely and start thinking about which tattoo plan best suits you. Knowing your tattoo plan as you go into the tattoo process will help you identify the resources you need to get the tattoo you want—and in the way that you want to get it.

Personalized Tattoo Plan

The personalized approach is probably the most straightforward of the various tattoo plans. You probably have a very clear idea, most likely a physical, printed example of the tattoo you're looking for, and while you may want to alter elements of the design slightly, you're pretty much happy to have the piece inked on your body as it is. In fact, you may be satisfied creatively by just deciding, "Yup, this is the one!", as well as how large the tattoo will be and where on your body it will be inked.

Personalized tattoo approach:

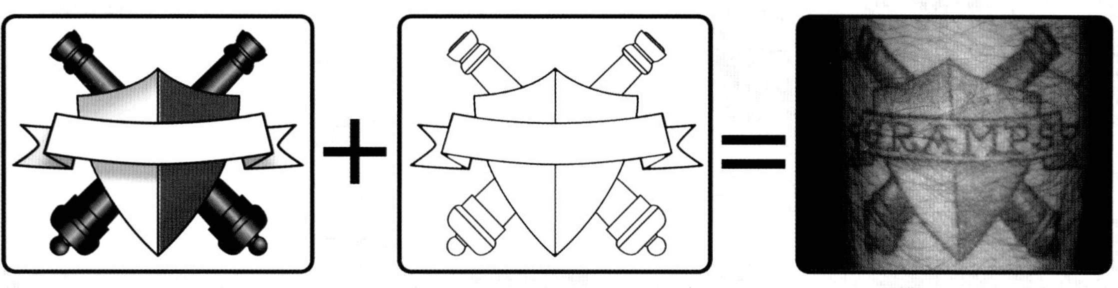

Tattoo design | Tattoo stencil | The end result on skin

One of the reasons you don't want to alter the design significantly is that you want a clear idea of what the final product will look like before it is inked on you. Paper and skin are different mediums; nothing on paper will reproduce exactly the same way on skin. With the personalized approach, the end product is as close as it can get to the design reference. Also, because you're most likely using a design reference also available to others (one you found online, in a book, etc.), you know there will probably be other people in the world with a similar tattoo to you, and you're okay with that. Keep in mind: just because someone used a similar design reference doesn't mean their tattoo will be identical to yours. You can enjoy some level of uniqueness by deciding where on your body the tattoo will go, its size, and some modifications in color and/or line thickness. Also, every tattoo is essentially an original piece of artwork just from being on your skin. The tone and texture of your skin is like no one else's, and the final tattoo won't look exactly the same on anyone else.

Please also note that finding a tattoo design isn't necessarily as easy as selecting a random image online. Some images simply aren't "tattoo friendly;" that is, they won't reproduce on your skin in the way you see them on paper or on a computer screen—they would need to be modified in order to work as a tattoo. It's recommended that you find a Tattoo Friendly™ reference piece—one that can be tattooed with the same detail you see on paper and at the size you want it on your skin.

The other factors that inform this plan are time and money. The time involved with this approach is determined primarily by how long it takes you to find your Tattoo Friendly™ design reference. Additional time will be required to select a tattooist who may not be particularly gifted artistically, since that is not necessary, but who is a skilled craftsperson in the trade (see Selecting a Tattooist and Studio, pages 159–165). You will also invest in the purchase of your Tattoo Friendly™ design reference, but that will most likely save you money overall because you won't need to pay a tattooist to create your perfect tattoo design from scratch.

Are You a Candidate for the Personalized Tattoo Plan?

If you agree with the three points below, then you might want to consider going with the personalized tattoo plan.

- The extent of your creativity is essentially finding the Tattoo Friendly™ design reference that accurately represents the tattoo vision in your mind of what it is you want.
- You want a clear representation of what your tattoo will look like *before* it goes on your skin.
- You want to keep your costs down but still get good-quality ink. You are okay with other people in the world possibly having a similar tattoo to you.

Custom Tattoo Plan

The Custom Tattoo Plan provides a lot more flexibility and is a very common trend in how people approach getting tattooed. Custom tattooing generally involves you finding multiple reference designs that represent your tattoo vision and that you want to incorporate into a single tattoo. Generally, a custom tattoo will cost more and require more time than a personalized tattoo, depending mostly on your personal level of creativity. We break the custom plan into two approaches, depending on your level of creativity.

Do-it-Yourself:

You are going to provide your tattooist with a final design of what your tattoo should look like on your skin before getting it tattooed. This is the approach that allows you to truly say, "I designed my own tattoo!" If you are a skilled artist AND you know all the criteria of what makes a design tattoo-able on skin, then you can simply draw from any reference sources you like and create your own design to get tattooed. Most people, however, do not know how to do this (which is why so much tattoo reference has been created over the years). But if you have at least some level of personal creativity (or perhaps have a friend who does), then you can definitely pull this off. By using a Tattoo Friendly™ design reference and following the rules of customization, you can select the main design parts of the tattoo that you envision and integrate those pieces together into a totally customized tattoo design. This can be done by printing out your reference, cutting it up, and pasting it together (like putting together a jigsaw puzzle). Or if you are skilled with image manipulation software, you can do this on your computer. And even if you just get the design really close to a final product, just about any tattooist can help you with final touches.

Tattooist as Assembler:

If you truly have very little faith in your artistic talent (and that's fine), you can still find the various Tattoo Friendly™ designs that you are drawn to, provide them to a tattooist, and work with that tattooist to come up with the final custom tattoo design to be tattooed. For example, tattoo artist Rachael Bardach likes the process of working with a client to compose a design, but what she needs from clients is a very specific idea of what they would like the finished product to be. "When you say 'I want a dragon tattoo,' do you mean Oriental, medieval, or fantasy dragon? Evil or good? Is the dragon flying? Is the design of the whole dragon? Is it facing forward or in another direction? Is there some type of background?"

Custom tattoo approach: An example of how multiple design references can be "assembled" to make up a single tattoo that is custom-made for the individual

In effect, the more clearly you can communicate the tattoo vision in your mind's eye, the better (and more efficiently) the tattooist can make it happen for you. If you provide a Tattoo Friendly™ design reference to your tattooist, you get the benefit of knowing that what you are communicating can be tattooed as is and won't have to be altered to make it something that can be tattooed. In essence, you could find design references for the head and body of the dragon, for the fire you want to be used as the background, and the Kanji lettering you want to incorporate that means "power." Your tattooist will take all these pieces and assemble them into a final design that should be a good representation of what your final tattoo will look like.

In either the "Do-it-Yourself" or "Tattooist as Assembler" approach to your custom plan, you can bring varying levels of your own creativity into the process of coming up with the final design to be tattooed. Those who favor the custom approach like it because it allows for differentiation. You may have started with a visual reference that others have used, but, through your creative ideas and/or through collaboration with your tattooist, you end up with something that is uniquely yours. The custom approach also allows for a high level of creative control. If you do plan on working with a tattooist and creative control is important to you, confirm that the tattooist will provide you with the final design and not just a rough "assembly sketch" before getting tattooed.

A more complex custom tattoo will generally require more time. It may take more time to find the various multiple reference designs you want to incorporate. If you are a do-it-yourself type of person, it will take time to work with the references to create your final design. If you will be providing references for your tattooist to assemble, it will take time for your tattooist to come up with the final design (and, most likely, the tattooist will charge for this work). With regard to expense, purchasing multiple Tattoo Friendly™ designs as reference will cost you more than purchasing just one design. The other additional expense will depend on the time required (if any) by the tattooist to assemble the final design—and this can turn into a long, labor-intensive (and thus, expensive) process of drafting and redrafting designs. Again, the best way to keep costs down in this area is to provide a Tattoo Friendly™ design reference that most accurately reflects the elements of the final design you want to have tattooed.

Are You a Candidate for the Custom Tattoo Approach?

If you agree with the four points below, then you might want to consider going with the Custom Tattoo Plan.

- You are artistically creative, have friends who are creative, or know of a tattooist you feel comfortable bringing into the artistic process of developing a final tattoo design.

- You want a finalized design (or at least a pretty clear representation) of what your tattoo will look like before it goes on your skin.

- You are willing to put in the time and effort to find the multiple Tattoo Friendly™ designs that will be incorporated into your final tattoo (as well as the time required to create the final design if you are doing this yourself).
- You're comfortable spending more money on purchasing multiple tattoo designs as reference, and possibly on working with a tattooist, to create the final design for a tattoo that is your personal vision—a tattoo that is unique to you.

Couture Tattoo Plan

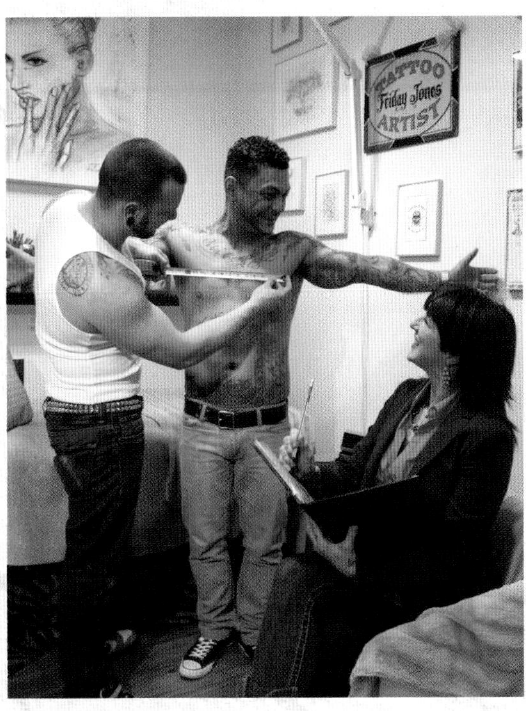

Famed celebrity tattooist Friday Jones (sketchbook in hand) consulting with a tattoo client

The couture approach essentially means handing design development over to an artistically skilled tattooist. Sometimes this involves a labor-intensive (and often expensive) consultation, drafting, and redrafting process in which, essentially, the tattooist is trying to "draw out" the tattoo vision from your mind's eye (using verbal reference) until you eventually look at a design draft and say, "Yes, that's it!" In this case, you definitely want to find a tattooist that is not only a great craftsperson, but also a highly skilled artist. And since you will be working closely with this person to develop the final design over time, you will need to feel comfortable and at ease working together. You will also need to be prepared to stand your ground if you are not happy with the direction the design is going. The last thing you want is a design you settled for simply because you didn't want to hurt someone's feelings or because the design process was taking too long and costing too much money so you cut it short. If this process goes ideally, however, you will come out of this experience with not only a great tattoo, but possibly even a new friendship.

Conversely, the couture approach can also mean the tattoo vision is primarily that of the tattooist (instead of "what you see is what you get," the process could be described as "what you get is what you see"). In a sense, you are paying someone to fill an area of your skin with ink, with you having varying levels of input on what that design will be. The tattooist will, probably be pulling from reference in his or her own mind that may get communicated to you through some basic sketches on your skin using a pen or marker. In this case, you would definitely be described as a "collector" of highly original tattoo art by a tattooist/artist whose work you have come to admire.

Either way, couture is the high-end approach to getting tattooed.

Are You a Candidate for the Couture Tattoo Approach?

If you agree with the three points below, then you might want to consider going with the Couture Tattoo Plan.

- You already know of an artistically skilled tattooist to work with and whose work you admire, or you are willing to take the time and energy to find one.
- You are prepared to enter into a time- and energy-intensive process in which the tattooist works with you to pull your tattoo ideas from your mind to produce an accurate representation of a final design on paper (or alternatively, you are willing to accept the tattooist's vision of what will be created, and will know what the final tattoo looks like only after it has been inked).
- You are willing to spend money on the most expensive approach to getting a tattoo there is and you feel that it is totally worth it.

Parlor vs. Spa: You Choose!

In recent years, particularly in larger cities like New York and Los Angeles, a new development in where and how you get tattooed has been cropping up—and it's spreading quickly! Worlds apart from the gritty tattoo parlors that still exist today are the new tattoo spas, establishments where you can get inked—and also get a facial, massage, mani-pedi, and other traditional spa services. Some tattoo spas offer full spa services (and consider this to be part of the couture tattoo experience), while others simply make certain allowances designed to help customers feel relaxed and comfortable. A tattoo spa may just consist of a serenely decorated space, relaxing New Age music, and comfortable, massaging chairs. Some people really crave the old-school, hard-edged experience and want to get tattooed in the traditional tattoo-parlor environment. For those who have hesitated getting a tattoo because they're not comfortable in this kind of environment, there are now softer options. Again, like all considerations in getting a tattoo, it really depends on the individual.

Now You Know . . .

- Getting a tattoo should not be a decision taken lightly. The more legwork you put into it beforehand, the more likely you are going to be satisfied with the result.
- Before you ink, really ask yourself why you want a tattoo. Take your time to think through the reasons and make sure it's the right decision for you.
- There are essentially three tattoo plans that encompass the tattoo needs and desires of most people. Figure out which one applies to you, as it will make the tattoo experience easier for both you and your tattooist.

America & International

Confederose
Medium

Patriotstar
Medium

USA Eagle Dagger
Medium

Eagle Engine Tribal
Extra Large

Dixie
Medium

American Inside, American out
Extra Large

Proud Flag Display Eagle
Large

Yellow Rose of Texas
Medium

Confederate Burning Skull
Large

Confederate Fire
Extra Large

Together We Fight
Large

Patriotic Army Ant
Medium

Bleeding American Skin
Medium

U.S.A. Honor Badge
Medium

Ameripenn
Large

Talons and Shield
Extra Large

9/11 In Memory
Medium

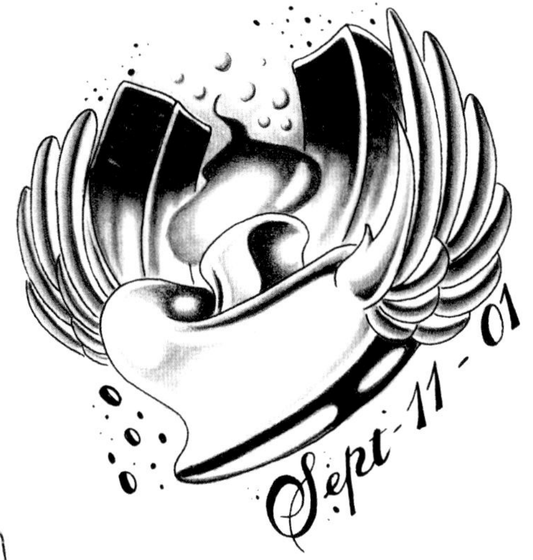

Sept 11, 2001
Medium

Stars & Stripes Eagle
Extra Large

American Made
Extra Large

Southern Girl
Medium

Confederate Grim Reaper
Large

Strength of New York City
Large

American Eagle
Large

American Made Badge
Medium

Glory Rising
Extra Large

Waving American Ribbon II
Medium

DBD
Large

USA
Medium

Made In USA Stamp
Medium

American Band
Large

Mexican Pride
Large

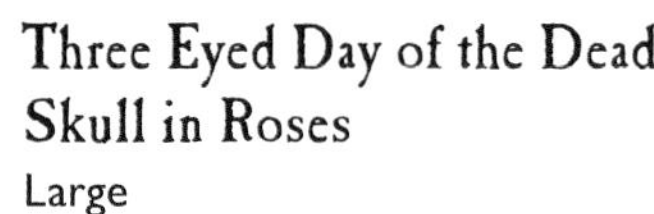

Three Eyed Day of the Dead
Skull in Roses
Large

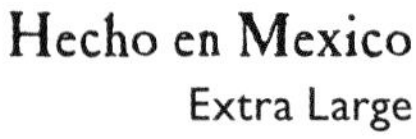

Hecho en Mexico
Extra Large

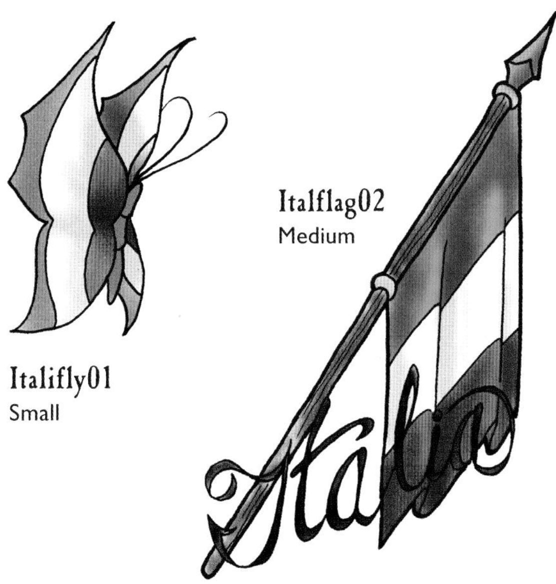

Italiflly01
Small

Italflag02
Medium

Italitrib01
Medium

Austflag01
Medium

Germflag01
Medium

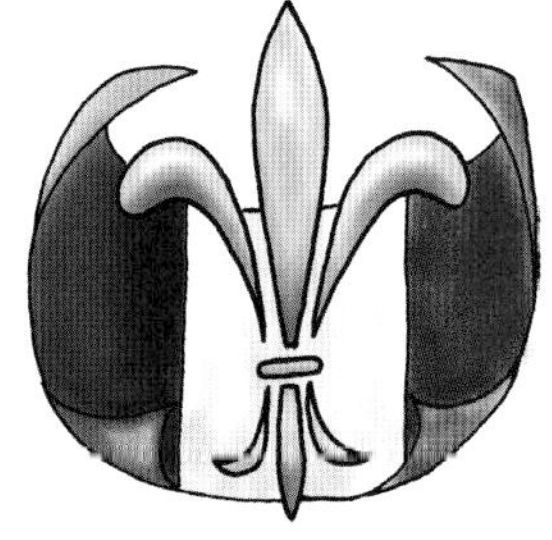

Frenflag01
Small

Canadian Maple Leaf Heart
Extra Small

Blowing Canadian Flag
Medium

Canada Tribal II
Small

Canada Tribal
Medium

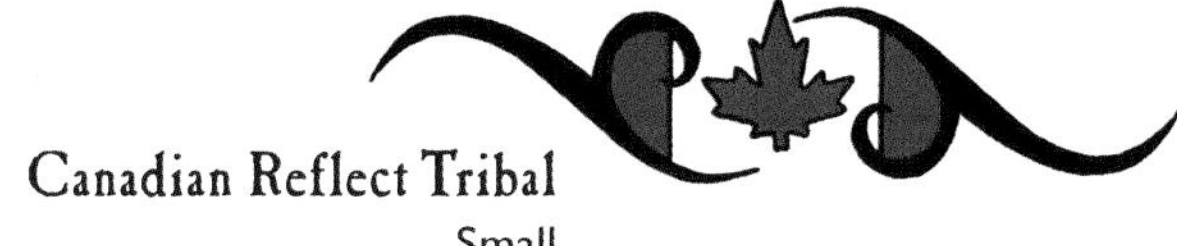

Canadian Reflect Tribal
Small

Kitana Scroll
Large

Geisha Wind
Extra Large

Garden Light
Medium

Shishi (Lion)
Large

Maple Leaf—Life
Medium

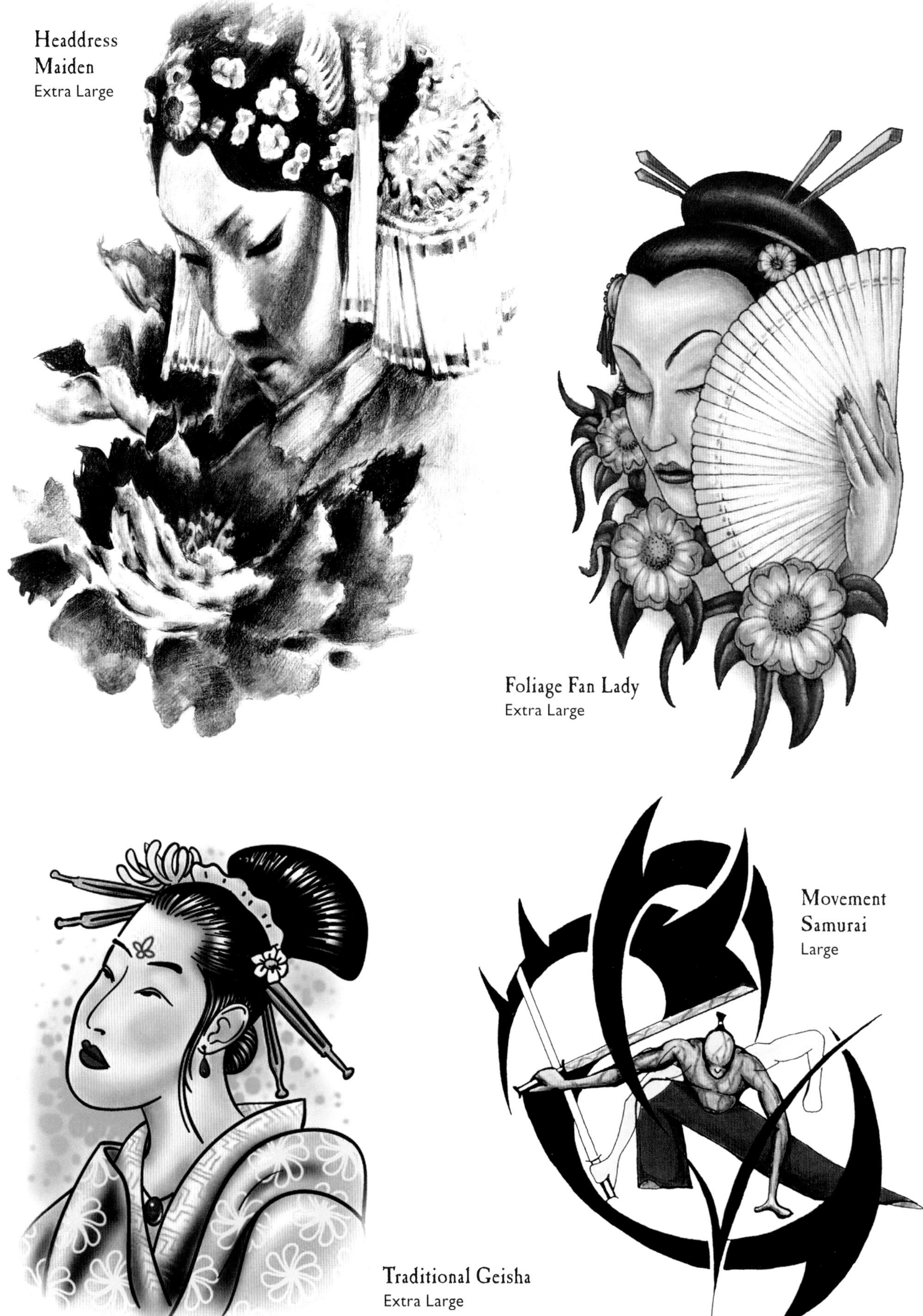

Headdress Maiden
Extra Large

Foliage Fan Lady
Extra Large

Movement Samurai
Large

Traditional Geisha
Extra Large

Ancient Cultures

Gap-Toothed Tiki
Large

Native Fire Dance
Large

Three Angry Tiki Faces
Extra Large

Circles and Circles Aztec Tribal
Small

Red Crazipelli
Medium

Portopelli
Medium

Almost Bird Aztec
Small

Blue Crazipelli
Medium

Aztec Mirror Statues
Extra Large

Chrome Chief
Medium

Native Girl & Bald Eagle
Large

Peace Time Native
Large

Enapay
Extra Large

Native Armband
Medium

He-Lush-Ka
Extra Large

Indian Portrait
Extra Large

Bugged out Native
Extra Large

Native American
Feather Butterfly
Extra Large

Askuwheteau
Extra Large

War Painted
Large

Purple Dreams
Medium

Native Skullenfeathers
Medium

Feathers on a Braid
Large

Catching Your Dreams
Extra Large

Ceremonial Flames
Extra Large

Buffalo Modern
Medium

Large Feathers
Medium

Indian Skull and Feather Profile
Medium

The Ancients Speak
Extra Large

Intently Watching
Extra Large

Winter Hunt
Large

Feather of Kind
Medium

Native Eagle Spirit
Large

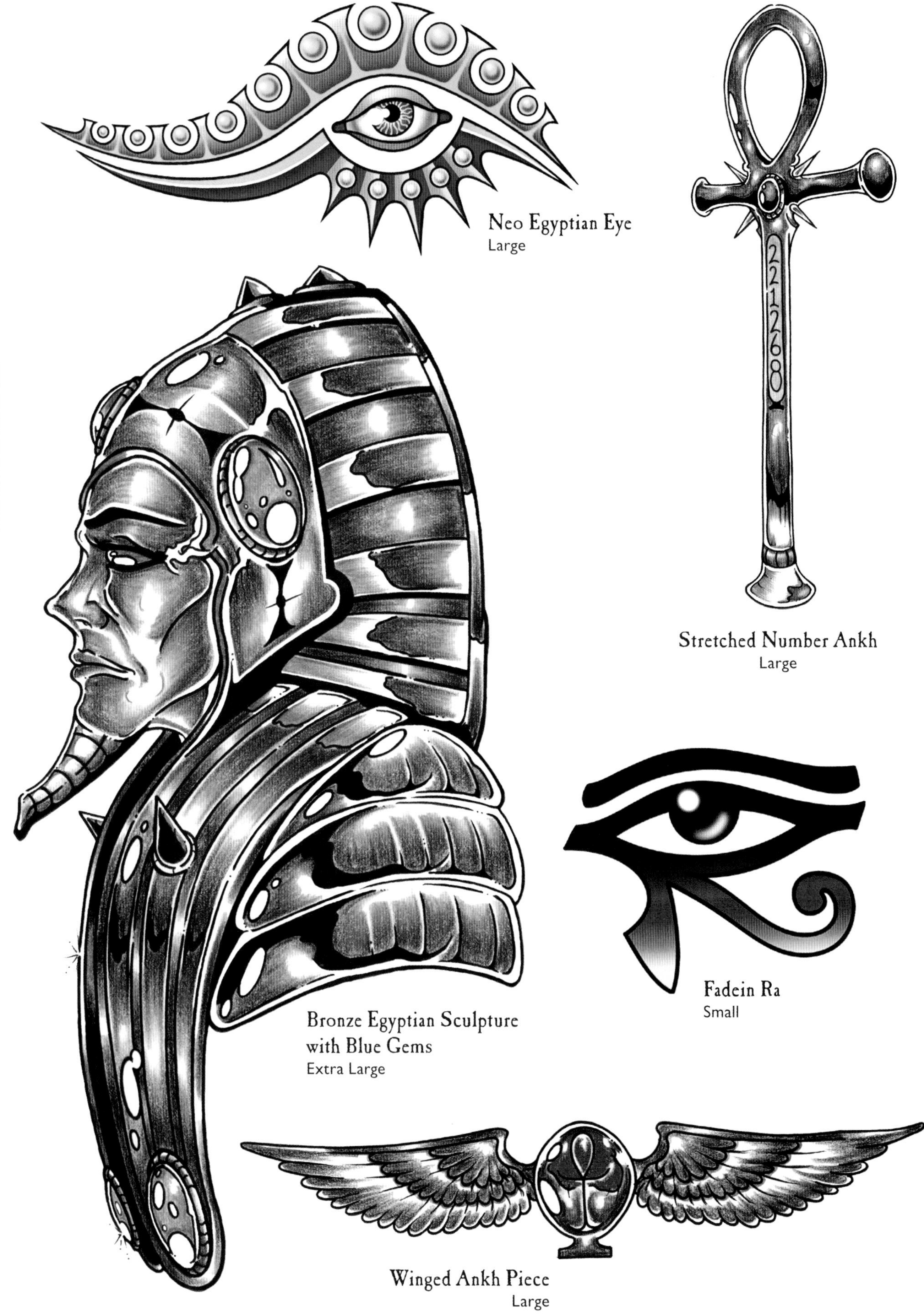

Neo Egyptian Eye
Large

Stretched Number Ankh
Large

Bronze Egyptian Sculpture with Blue Gems
Extra Large

Fadein Ra
Small

Winged Ankh Piece
Large

Womanspan
Extra Large

Talking Heads
Large

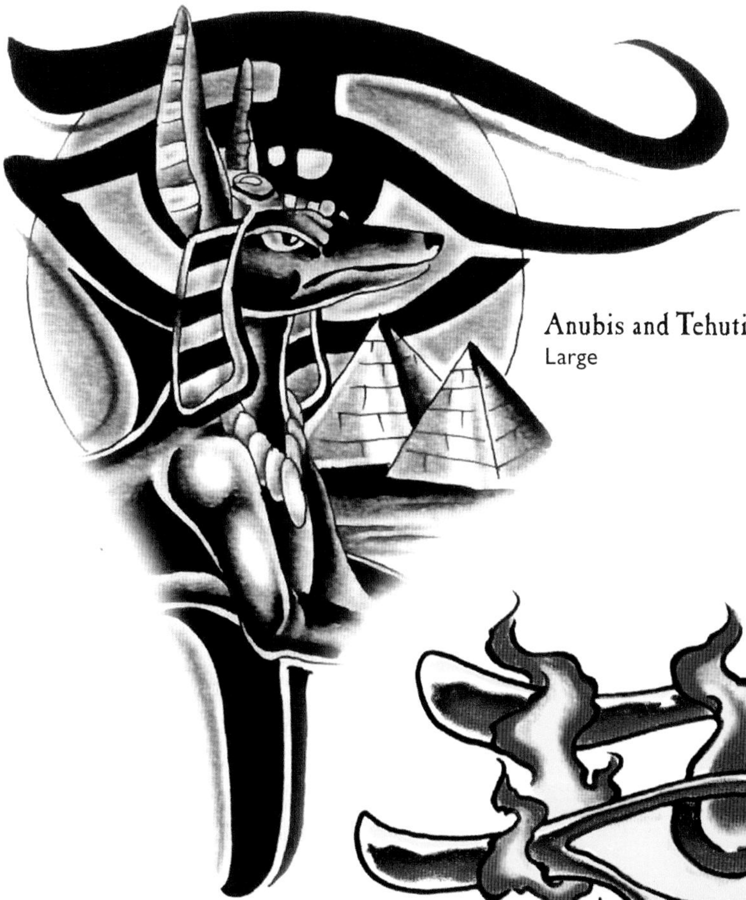

Anubis and Tehuti
Large

Ramses Bull
Medium

Burai
Medium

Bladed Red Ankh
Small

Lil Eyenpyramid
Small

Fire Pharaohskull
Extra Large

Guarding Anubis
Extra Large

Horus Falcon
Extra Large

Haida Eagle Eye
Extra Large

Ankhensnake Backtribal
Extra Large

Egyptian Eyes
Extra Large

Haida Wolf
Extra Large

Isis Back
Large

Skull Wink
Large

Skeletal Aztec Priest
Extra Large

Doesel
Extra Large

Quetzalcoatl Warrior
Extra Large

Speechless
Extra Large

Aztec Skull Crest
Large

Large Mesoamerican Stone
Extra Large

Guarded Treasure
Extra Large

Animals

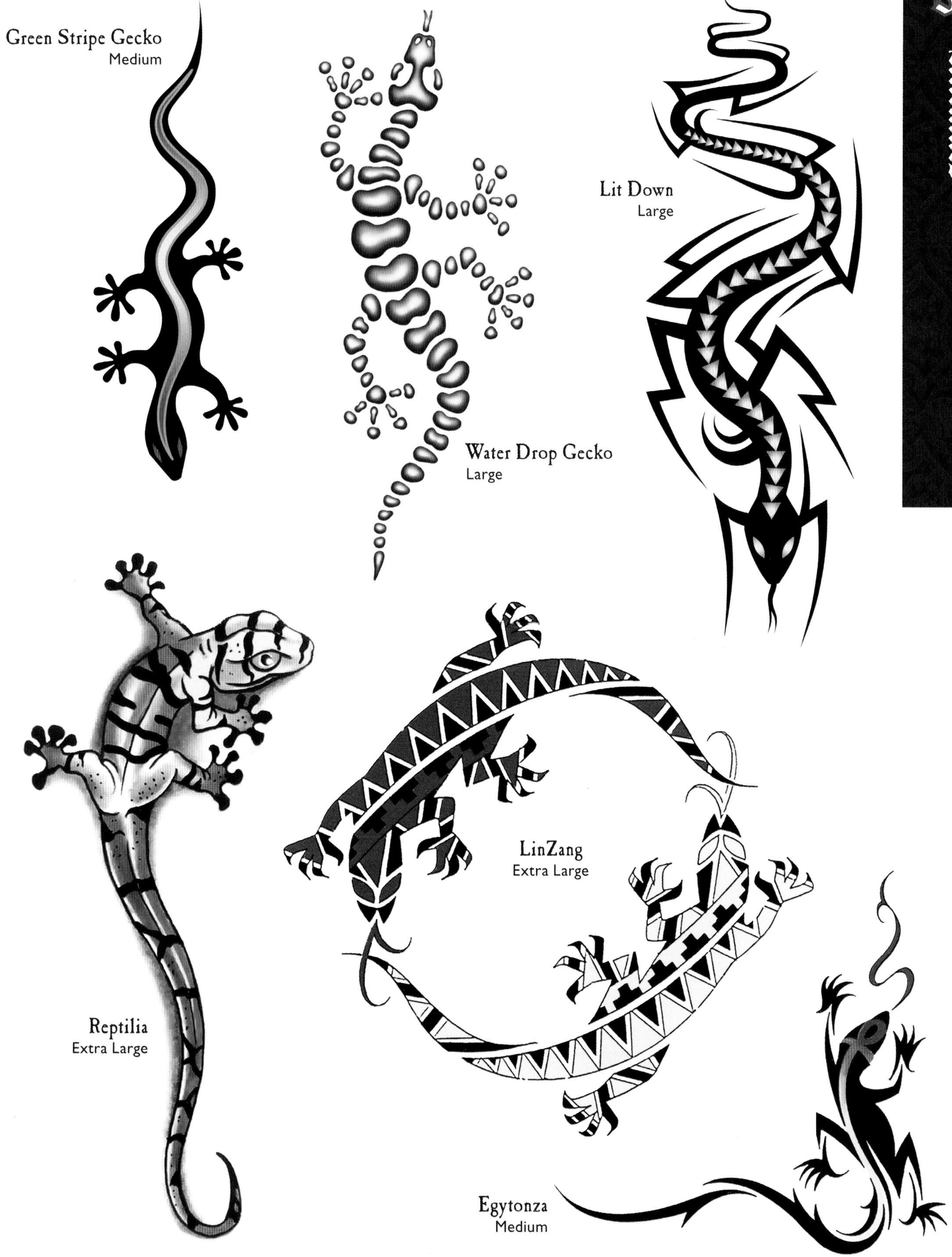
Green Stripe Gecko
Medium
Water Drop Gecko
Large
Lit Down
Large
Reptilia
Extra Large
LinZang
Extra Large
Egytonza
Medium

Daisy the Frog
Medium

Tongue Lizard 001
Large

Purple Gecko
Medium

Edge Lizard 18
Large

Black Frog
Medium

Scaling
Medium

Green Frog
Medium

Slurpee Frog
Medium

House Shopping
Medium

Climbing Frog
Medium

Bouncin'
Medium

Curious Blue Frog
Medium

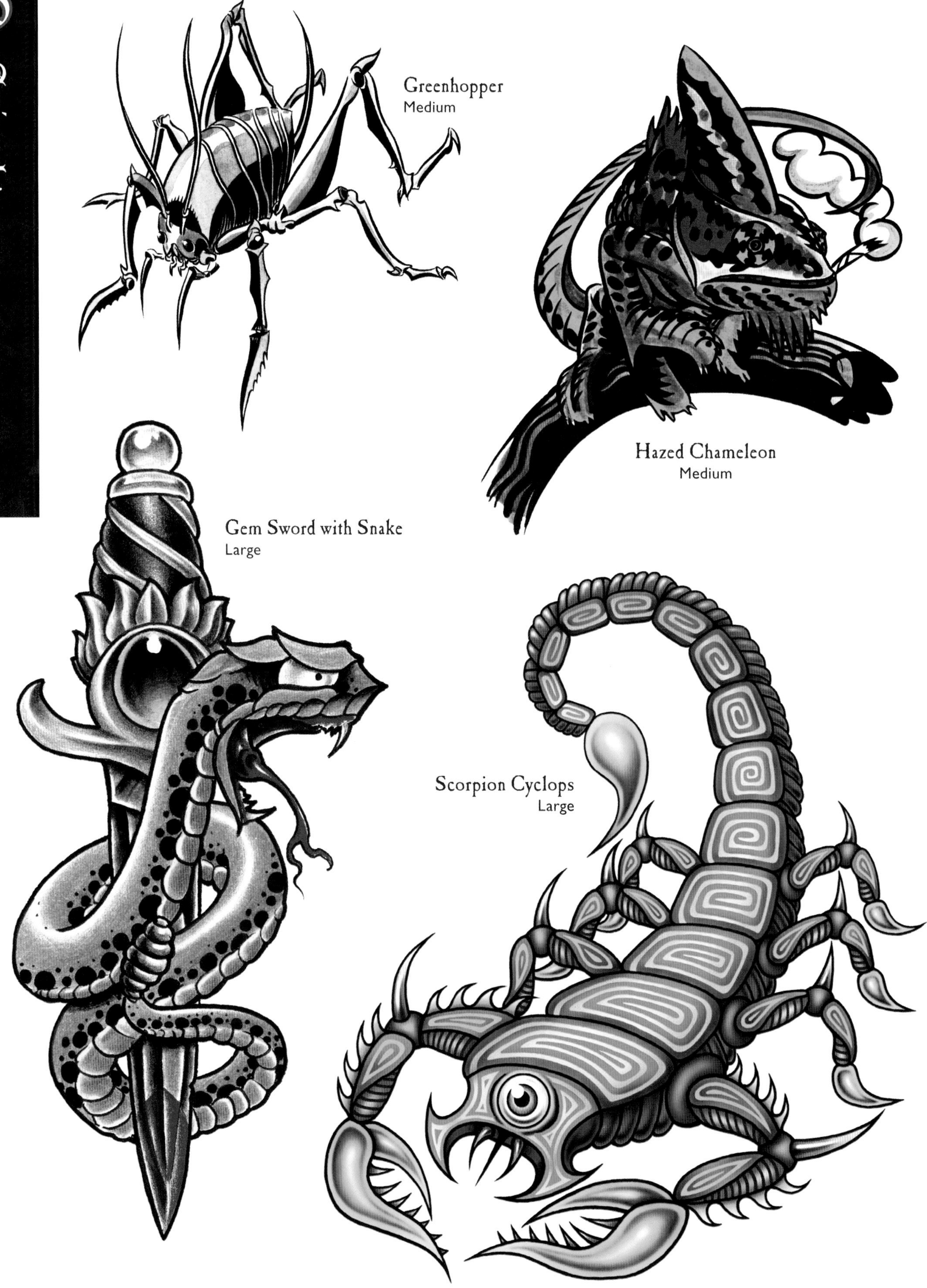

Greenhopper
Medium

Hazed Chameleon
Medium

Gem Sword with Snake
Large

Scorpion Cyclops
Large

Rattle Snake Wrapping Bull Skull
Medium

Not So Happy Camper
Extra Large

Tribal Snake
Extra Large

Green Cobra Flaming Skulls
Extra Large

Purple Cobra
Large

Hidden Swirl Tribal Snake
Extra Large

Coiled Snake Attack
Extra Large

Abankat
Medium

Vampire Bat II
Medium

Bat Pair
Smalll

Serpent Dance
Large

Lone Wolf Tribal
Medium

Brown Wolf Piece
Medium

Tribal Dream Catcher
Mountain Lion
Extra Large

Happy Bear Claws
Small

Wolf Stare Down
Extra Large

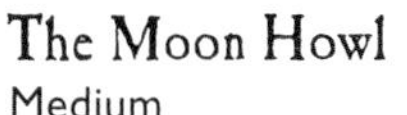

The Moon Howl
Medium

Moonlit Tribal
Extra Large

Howl at the Moon
Extra Large

Blue Lunar Wolf
Extra Large

Proud Lion Hunter
Medium

Mountain Lion Head
Medium

Vacant King
Extra Large

Slash and Shred
Extra Large

Baby Gazer
Medium

Contrast Tiger
Large

Tigertrib 02
Extra Large

Tiger Enflowers
Large

Leopard Allure
Large

Bloody Bulldog
Medium

Leaping Tribal Tiger
Extra Large

Large Fire Cat
Large

Back off
Large

BlackFire Buck
Extra Large

Devil Dog
Large

Fawn Cameo
Medium

Spike the Pit Bull
Extra Large

Little Lamb
Medium

Purple Rhino
Small

Foxxy
Medium

Great Owl
Medium

Contrasted Zoo Head
Medium

Heart 'n Seal
Medium

Baby Tortoise
Medium

Aquatic

Swirlhorse
Very Small

Baby Blue Sea Shell
Small

Seahorswirl
Medium

Tribal Pointed Seahorse
Small

Water Spout Seahorse
Large

Twist Together Seahorses
Medium

Anchor Smainchor
Small
Oh My Starfish
Extra Large
Open Mouth Fishy
Medium
Just Bubbly
Large
Green Fish One Fish
Medium

Purple Widetail Fish
Medium

Current Rider II
Medium

Underwater Angel
Large

Spout Catching
Medium

Forever Crab
Medium

Bugeye Fish
Medium

Small Stylized Koi
Small

Underliblu
Large

Fish Mischief
Extra Large

Shaded Goldfish Splash
Large

Purple Koi
Large

Jumping Koi with Flower
Large

Jumping Koi
Large

Koi Whirlpool
Extra Large

Anchors Aweigh
Large

Chest Plate
Asian Koi
Extra Large

Max
Large

Chasing Tails
Large

Fishyy
Medium

Innerphin
Small

Toxic Angler
Large

Water Walker
Extra Large

Gulf Stream Dolphin
Extra Large

Silver Surfer
Medium

Black Stencil Dolphin
Large

Dolphin Trail
Large

Bubble Shark
Large

Polar Dolphin
Small

Yin and Yang Dolphins
Medium

Lazy Dolphin
Large

Rainbow Paint Dolphin
Medium

Octoskull
Extra Large

Octowrithe
Extra Large

Octopus Overlay
Extra Large

Over Orca
Large

Banners

RIP Name Rose
Large

Good Girl Cherries
Medium

Bad Girl Nibbles
Medium

Crowned Heart Blinging
Small

Queen Mom Rose
Medium

Burning Mom & Dad Hearts
Large

Strawberry Banner
Medium

Pepper Is a Hottie
Medium

Small Inked Skull Banner
Medium

Rose Fate Heart
Medium

Name Rose Sword
Medium

Flower Sword with Banner
Medium

Naughty Devil Heart
Medium

Heart Rose Banner
Medium

Roses for Mom
Medium

Rose and Butterfly Banner
Medium

Rock 'n' Roll Karlee
Large

Such Is Love
Medium

The Horseshoe and Banner
Medium

Twins and Wings
Medium

Waiting Purple Roses
Large

Death Before Dishonor Skull Name Banner and Knife
Large

Own My Heart
Medium

Waiting Rose
Large

Leaf Name Banner Rose
Large

Three Leaf Ribbon
Small

Bald Eagle with Purple Banner
Large

Rosewrap
Small

Pride n Honor
Extra Large

Parchment Banner
Medium

Key of Passion
Medium

Brass Banner
Medium

Classic Heart
Small

Plump Heart Sword
Medium

Star Banner
Large

Pops Anchor
Medium

Wrapped up Anchor
Large

Remember the Break
Medium

Tattered but not Torn Rainbow Banner
Medium

Golden Name Banner
Medium

Triple Hearted Name Banner
Medium

Late Nighter
Large

Remember Phoenix
Large

The Key to...
Medium

Love Hurts
Extra Large

RIP Banner Cross
Medium

Butterflies and Flowers
Extra Large

Blue Scroll Lowerback
Extra Large

Glory Wings
Extra Large

Scroll Wrapped Cross
Medium

Ancient Message
Large

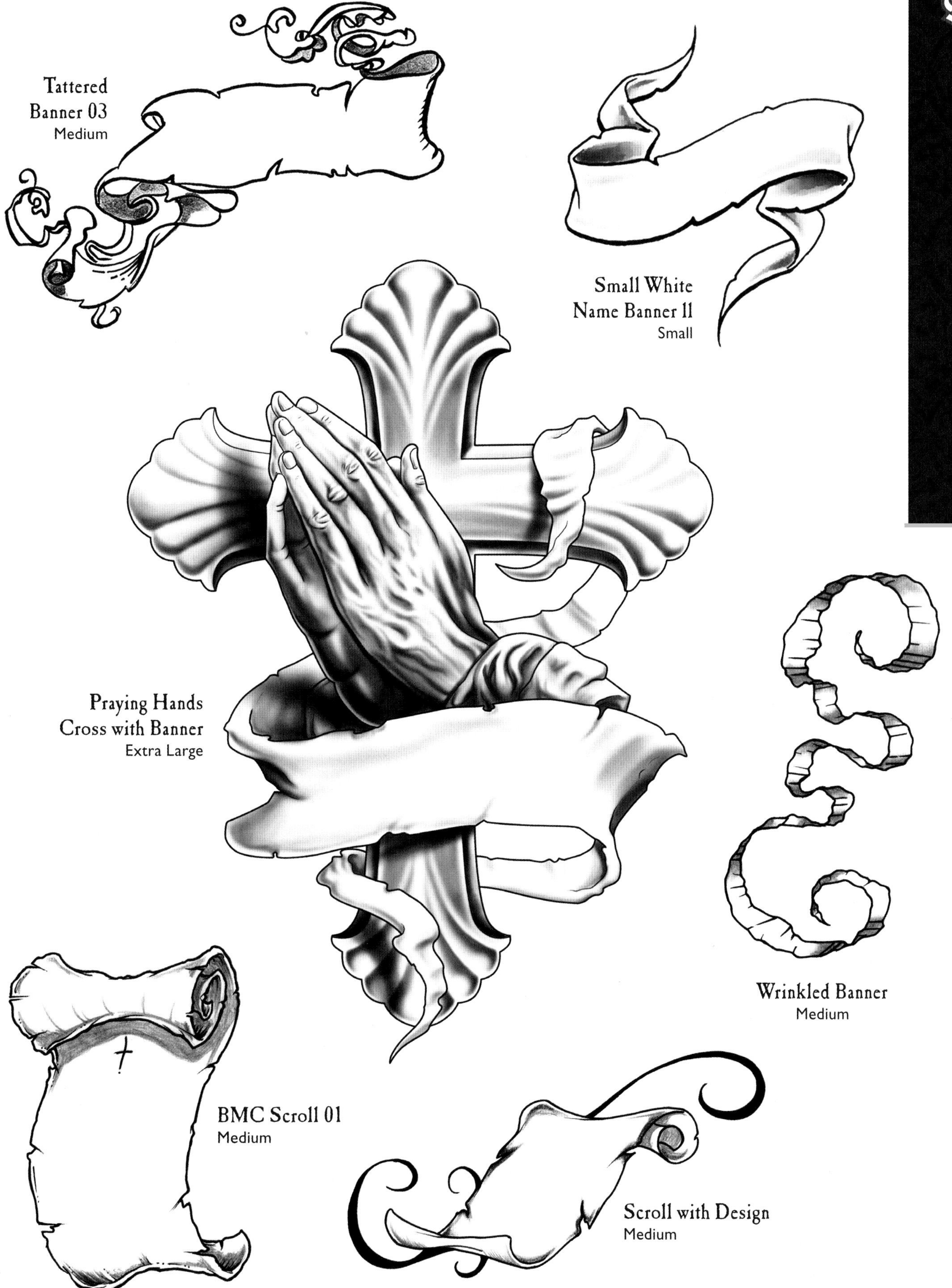

Tattered Banner 03
Medium

Small White Name Banner 11
Small

Praying Hands Cross with Banner
Extra Large

Wrinkled Banner
Medium

BMC Scroll 01
Medium

Scroll with Design
Medium

Baroque

Baroque Gold Fish
Extra Large

Elegant Memory
Large

Baroque Key
Large

Classy Owl
Extra Large

The Dead Baroque King
Extra Large

Upfrom Behinter
Medium

Ornate Tribal Black Armband
Large

Climbing Glass Bubble Flowers
Extra Large

Scrolling Lowerback
Large

Rainbow Plant
Medium

Shining Vines
Large

Falling Leaves
Medium

Right Leaf
Medium

Drapery Foliage
Extra Large

Vine Curls
Large

Terefivel
Medium

Leaves Band
Large

Vinal Leb (Lowerback)
Large

Sunset Flowers II
Medium

Medium Black Flower Design
Medium

Infinite 001
Extra Large

Slow Flow
Large

Plant
Medium

Bluefleur Filigree
Medium

Black Flower Design Large
Large

Bulporful
Extra Large
Vineband
Extra Large
Butherflay
Medium
Purple Leaves
Large
Viney Back
Extra Large
English Ivy III
Extra Large

Biker & Auto

Motorcycle Stars
Large

Full Throttle Power
Large

Heart Bike
Extra Large

Gear Shift Heart
Large

H D
Medium

Sacred Eightball Wins
Large

Skull and Crossed Checkered Flags
Large

Hot Rod Crest I
Medium

8 Is the Winning Number
Large

Bike from Front
Medium

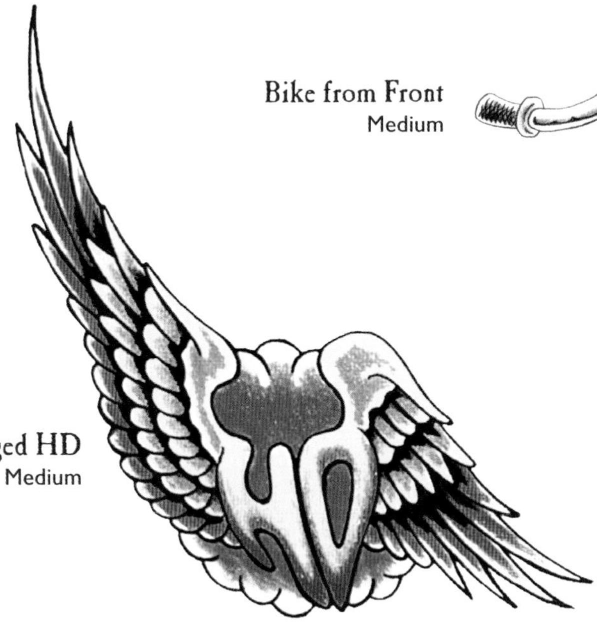

Winged HD
Medium

Pretty HD
Medium

Hippie Within
Medium

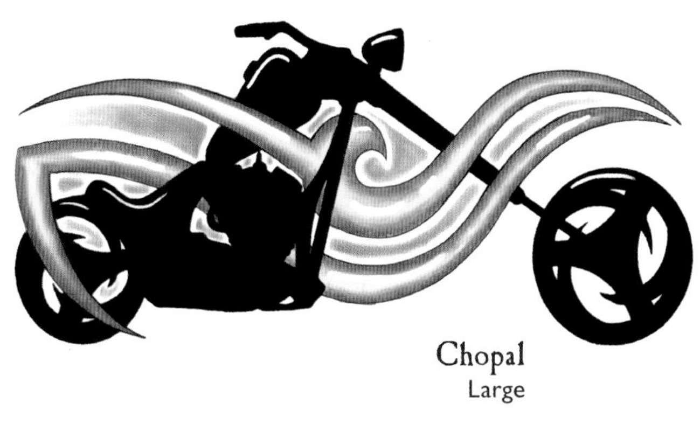

Chopal
Large

Gear Head
Large

Chrome
Medium

Orange Celti HD
Large

Burnin' Rubber
Causing Fire
Extra Large

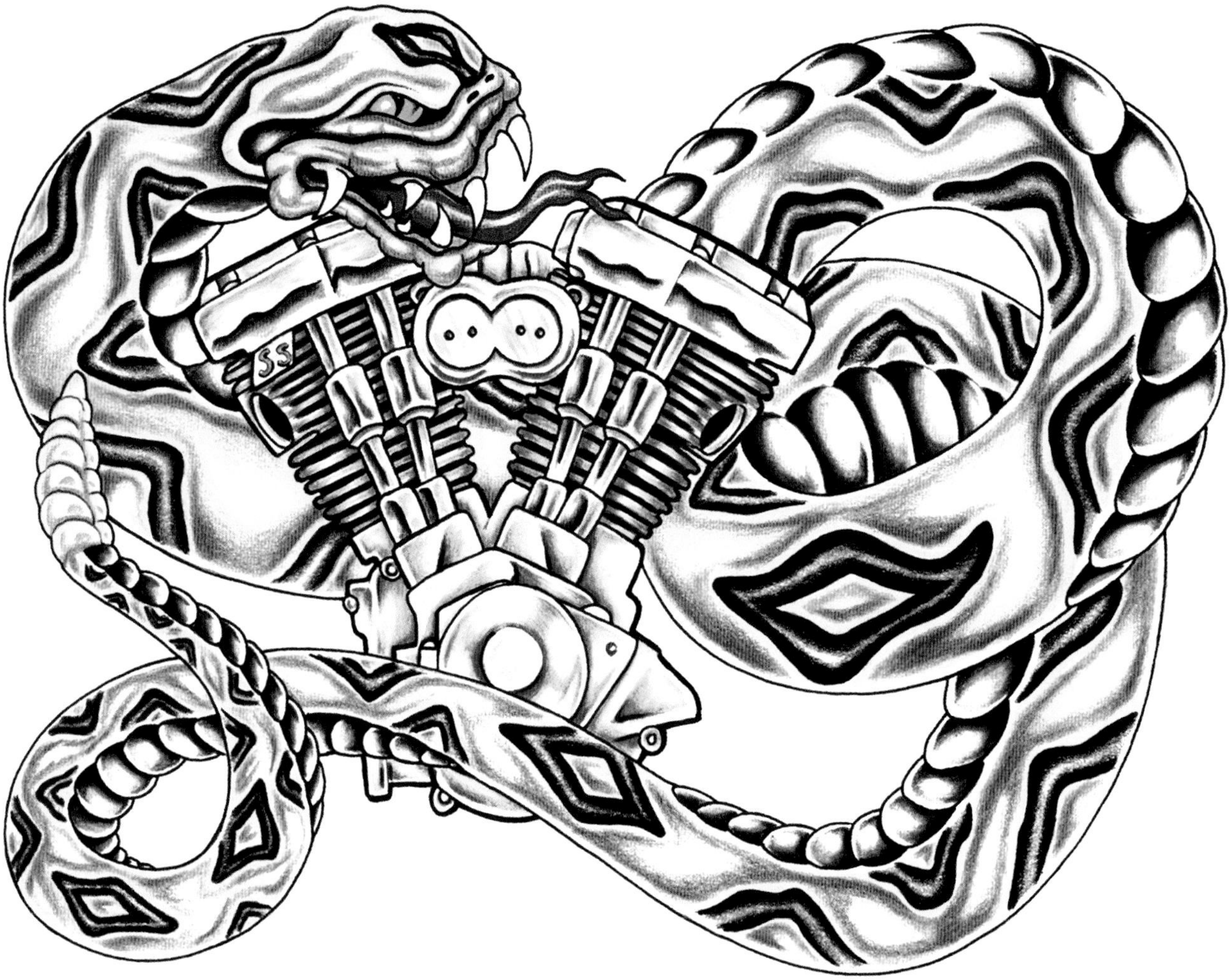

Yellow Snake with Engine
Extra Large

Shovel Head Piece
Large

Skull, Snake, and Bikes
Extra Large

Birds

Mister Cherry
Medium

Monsieur Oiseaux Bleu
Large

Circlin' Swallows
Large

Sweet Singing Sparrow
Medium

Bashful Bird
Extra Large

Swallow on a Mission
Extra Large

Bluebird
Medium

Devil Bird
Small

Sparrow with Shapes
Medium

Bearer of the Blossom
Medium

Fire Bringer
Medium

Peacock with Black Sun
Medium

Hummingbird Tail Belly
Extra Large

Crow
Medium

Two Sparrows with Three Heart
Medium

Long Tailed Humming Bird
Large

Vibrant Feast
Extra Large

Dance of the Cranes
Large

Sketched White Bird
Extra Large

Feathers to Bird Tribal
Large

Flight of the Crane
Large

Dark Plumes
Extra Large

Red-Crowned Crane
Large

Hibihumm
Medium

Toucan Bob
Large

Blue bird
Medium

The Beauty
Medium

Wide Blue Span
Medium

Feather Rufflin
Medium

Long Tailed Hummingbird
Extra Large

Tribal Hummingbird
Medium

Tail Around
Extra Large

Lyin' Toucan
Medium

Zquat
Medium

Long Tail Dove
Medium

Blue Hoot
Medium

Humming Bird Tribal Heart
Extra Large

Infinite Flight
Large

Little Bird
Large

Sight from Above
Extra Large

Owl Stare
Extra Large

Big Bald Eagle
Large

Bound in O
Large

Bald Feathers
Medium

Bald Eagle Tribal
Large

Rising Eagle
Medium

Tribalspin Eagle
Large

Bald Eagle
Extra Large

Black Eagle and Snake Fight
Large

Solid Wingspan
Extra Large

Stormcloud
Large

Skulltail Ascension
Extra Large

Patchoex
Medium

Phoenix Strength Kanji
Medium

Multicolor Phoenix
Extra Large

Peacock Ghostskull
Medium

Blazing Mad Phoenix
Large

Swoopingtail Crane
Extra Large

Water Rush Bird
Extra Large

Uplift Eagle
Extra Large

Embracing the Warmth
Extra Large

Royal Phoenix
Extra Large

Fiery Plumes
Extra Large

Body-Part Specific

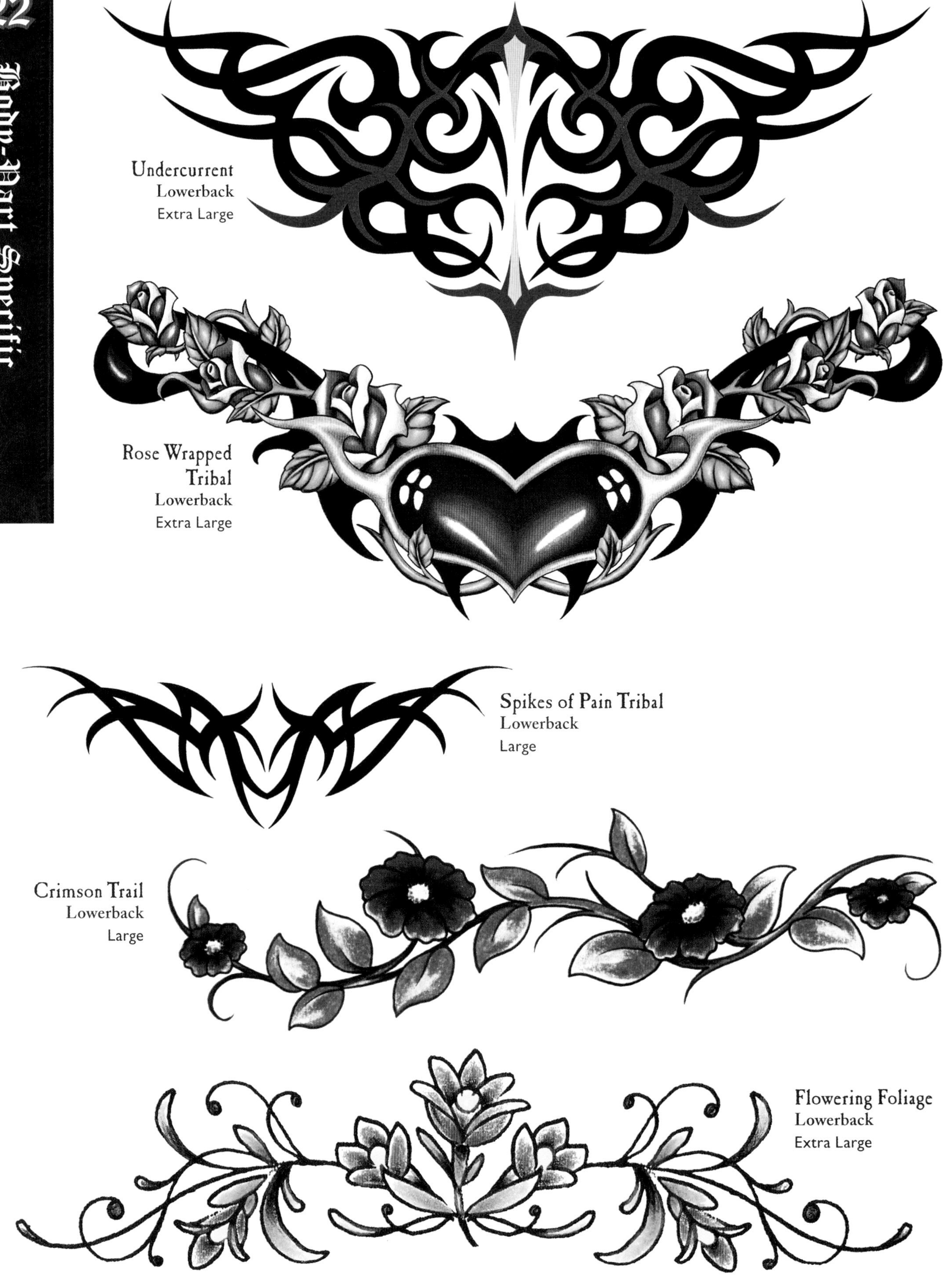

Undercurrent
Lowerback
Extra Large

Rose Wrapped Tribal
Lowerback
Extra Large

Spikes of Pain Tribal
Lowerback
Large

Crimson Trail
Lowerback
Large

Flowering Foliage
Lowerback
Extra Large

Fairy Hearts
Lowerback
Extra Large

Tribal Eyeball
Lowerback
Extra Large

Monarch
Lowerback
Extra Large

Fragile Orange Tribal
Lowerback
Extra Large

Beachcomber
Lowerback
Medium

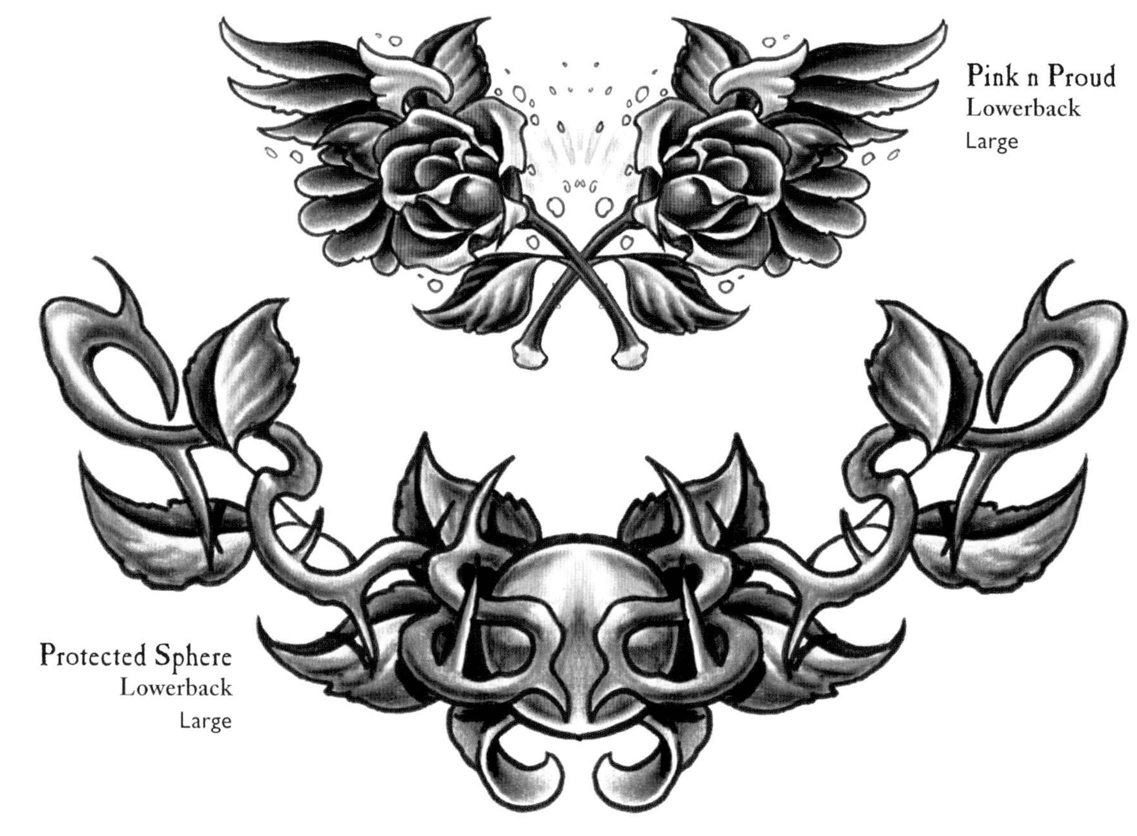

Pink n Proud
Lowerback
Large

Protected Sphere
Lowerback
Large

Orange Butterfly Cross
Lowerback
Extra Large

Inner Flower Garden
Lowerback
Large

Nestled Heart Garden
Lowerback
Extra Large

Golden Leaf Heart
Lowerback
Large

Buzz'n Around
Lowerback
Large

Sunny
Lowerback
Extra Large

Ribbony
Lowerback
Extra Large

Twodragon
Lowerback
Large

Tribal Dots
Lowerback
Extra Large

Craned out Tribal
Lowerback
Large

Bright Heart
Lowerback
Large

Heart N Scroll
Lowerback
Large

Center of Attention
Lowerback
Medium

Purlz 'n' Rozez
Lowerback
Extra Large

Blujuwel
Lowerback
Extra Large

Crystal Blue Butterfly
Lowerback
Extra Large

Butterfly Vine
Lowerback
Extra Large

Volcano Tribal
Lowerback
Extra Large

White Lily
Lowerback
Large

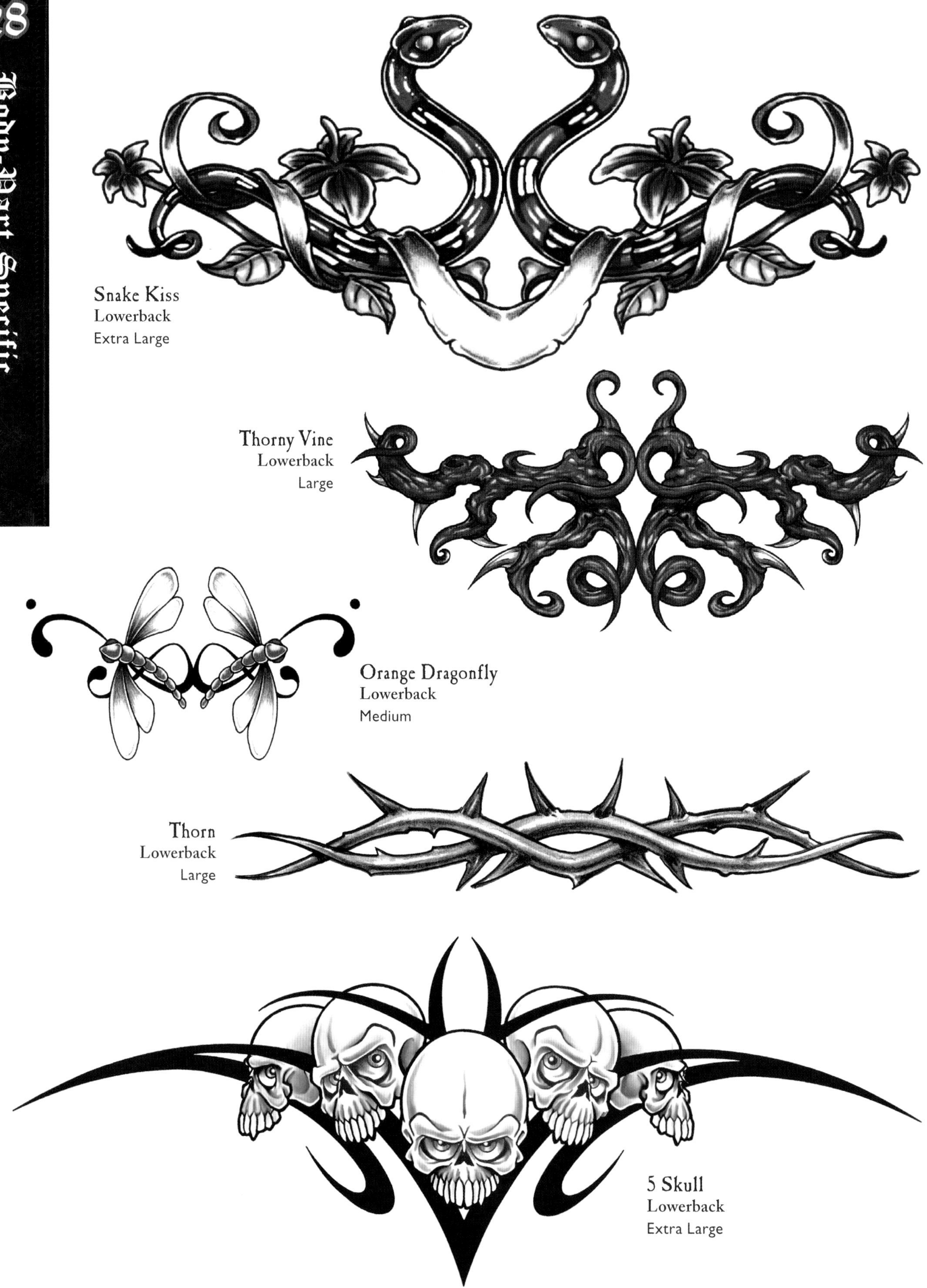

Snake Kiss
Lowerback
Extra Large

Thorny Vine
Lowerback
Large

Orange Dragonfly
Lowerback
Medium

Thorn
Lowerback
Large

5 Skull
Lowerback
Extra Large

3 Winged Skulls
Back
Extra Large

Heart Tribal
Lowerback
Large

Spine Fan Tribal
Back
Large

Blue 3-D
Lowerback
Medium

Blade Shape
Lowerback
Large

Gold Celtic Spiral Eyes
Lowerback
Extra Large

Golden Knot
Back
Extra Large

Tight Blue Bio
Lowerback
Extra Large

Lacey Sunflower
Shoulder
Extra Large

Shoulder 2
Shoulder
Extra Large

Tribal Shoulder B
Shoulder
Extra Large

Torso Tribal
Torso
Medium

Tribal Shoulder A
Shoulder
Large

Asian Floral
Chest
Extra Large

Orange Butterfly and Flowers
Navel
Extra Large

Navel Daisies
Navel
Medium

Angel Wing
Navel
Medium

Belly Swim
Navel
Small

Belly Vines
Navel
Large

Belly Barbs & Roses
Navel
Medium

Belly Phoenix
Navel
Medium

Bellymaze
Navel
Medium

Pink Blue
Belly Ring
Navel
Medium

Solar Passion
Navel
Medium

Neutered Flight
Navel
Medium

Belly Heat
Navel
Medium

Fire Spiral
Navel
Medium

Aqua Celtic Shield
Arm
Extra Large

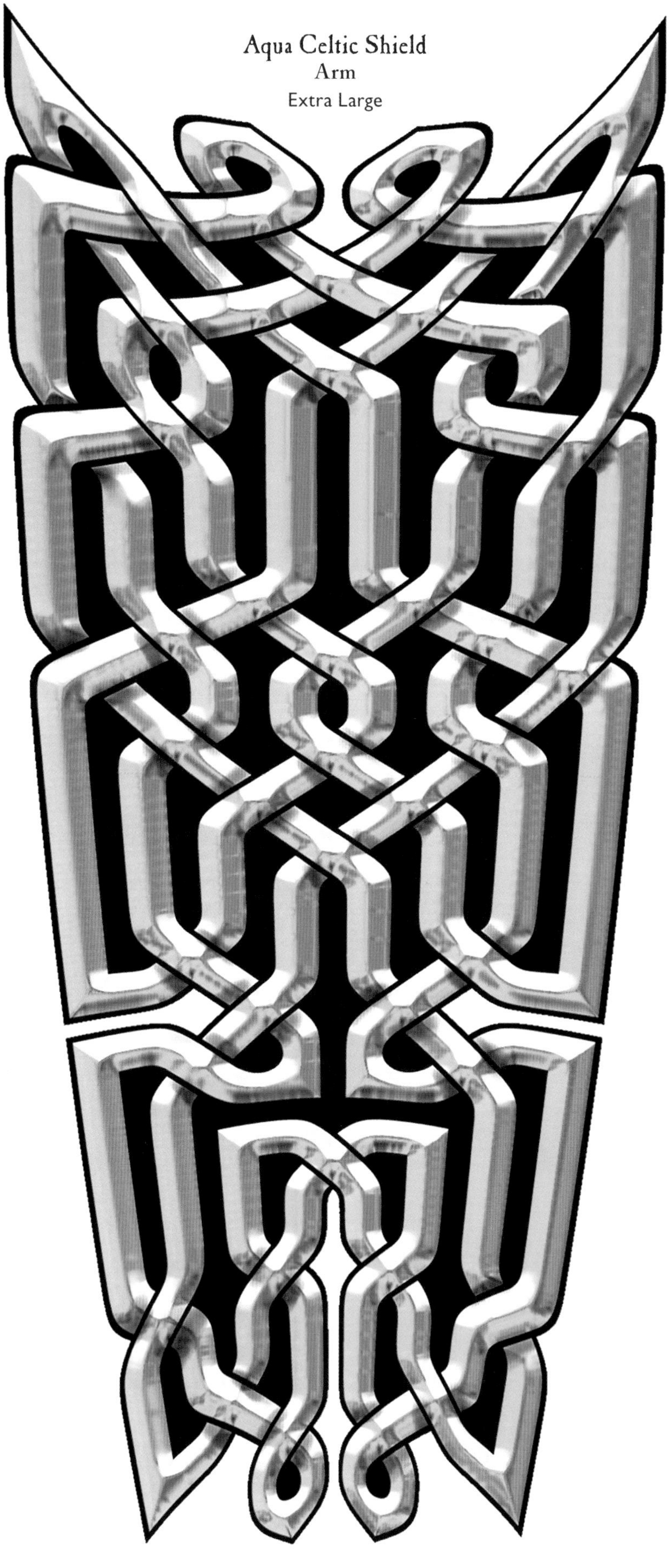

Eye Tribal
Forearm
Large

Band of Flowers
Armband
Large

Daisy Chain
Armband
Large

Carpe Diem Band
Armband
Extra Large

Armbante
Armband
Extra Large

Cogs
Armband
Extra Large

Kuwanlelenta
Armband
Extra Large

Razor Wire
Armband
Extra Large

Heartenswirl Band
Armband
Extra Large

Roses
Armband
Extra Large

Barbed Wire
Armband
Large

Thorny Band
Armband
Extra Large

Snake and Barb Wire
Armband
Extra Large

Armeblu
Armband
Medium

Thin Golden Chain
Armband
Extra Large

Curved Knotted Band
Armband
Extra Large

Maori Line
Armband
Extra Large

Blue Spikes Repeating
Armband
Large

Striking Sleeve
Arm
Extra Large

LL Tribal
Sleeve I
Arm
Extra Large

LL Tribal
Sleeve IV
Arm
Extra Large

Jesus Sleeve
Arm
Extra Large

LL Flower Sleeve I
Arm
Extra Large

LL Tribal Sleeve V
Arm
Extra Large

Celtic Bracelet
Wrist
Large

Alien Landing
Arm
Extra Large

Tribal Tiger
Arm
Extra Large

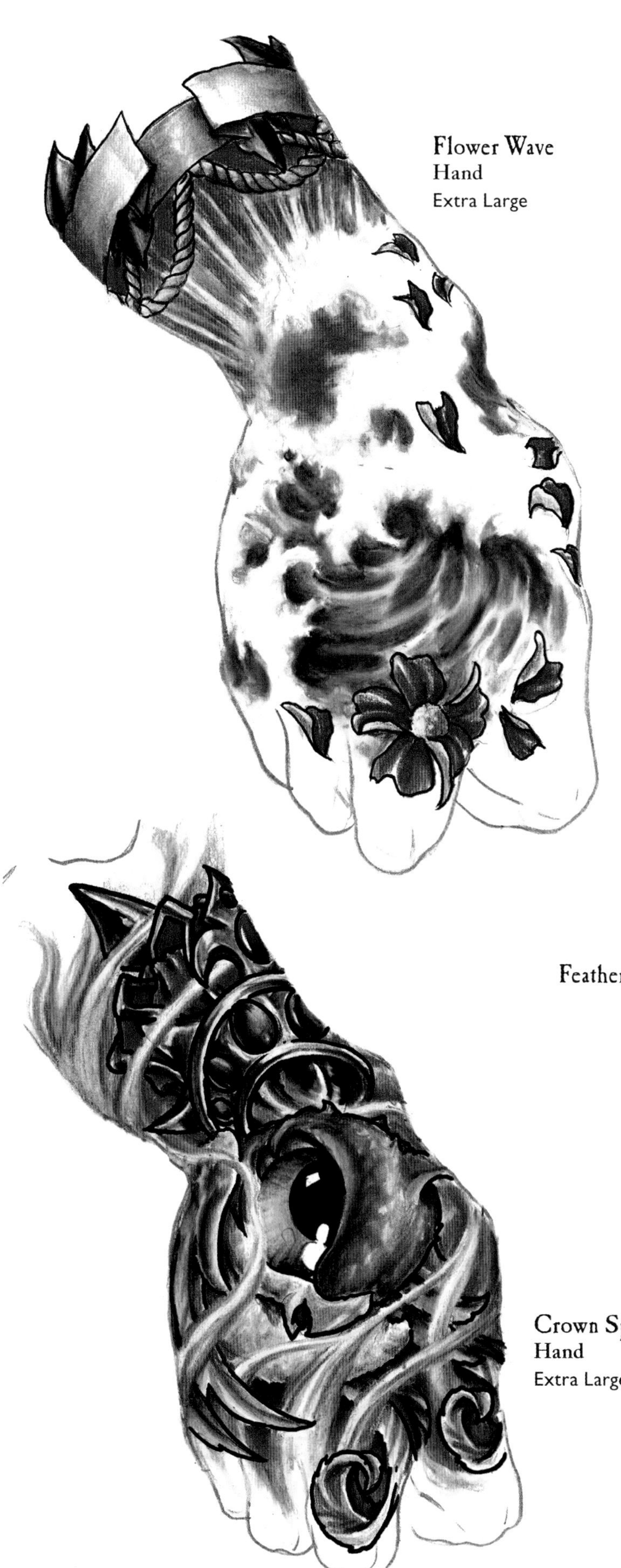

Flower Wave
Hand
Extra Large

Feather Eye Flower
Hand
Extra Large

Crown Sparrow
Hand
Extra Large

Section 2:

Developing and Communicating Your Tattoo Vision

"Tattoos are like stories—they're symbolic of the important moments in your life. Sitting down, talking about where you got each tattoo and what it symbolizes, is really beautiful."

—Pamela Anderson

Claim Your Ink, Create Your Own Vision

Now that you know getting a tattoo is right for you, and you feel confident in your approach to getting one, you need to figure out how to develop your tattoo vision and communicate this vision to a qualified tattooist. This is extremely important, since knowing what you want and getting it are two very different things in the tattoo world. It's not enough to only see what you want in your mind. You need to be able to communicate that vision as well.

We have broken down the process of finding the right tattoo for you into ten steps.

Ten Tips to Finding Your Perfect Tattoo Reference

1. Know your tattoo design references—and their limitations.
2. Be realistic about your tattoo design vision.
3. Make sure your tattoo design reflects what you really want.
4. Determine what your tattoo means to you now, later, and forever.
5. Identify your tattoo style.
6. Keep in mind the importance of finding a Tattoo Friendly™ design reference that includes a corresponding stencil.
7. Be aware of multiple interpretations of your design choice.
8. Decide the location on your body that best suits you.
9. Try to consider if this will be your one and only tattoo—or the first of many.
10. Take responsibility—and take your time!

Ten of the Most Popular Tattoo Types

Here are the tattoo types we've found to be the most common at TattooFinder.com. These are just the base categories, of course. Consider, for example, how amazingly different even a butterfly can look in various tattoo styles (an old-school-styled butterfly vs. a softer, pastel-hued butterfly).

1. Tribal tattoos
2. Butterfly tattoos
3. Celtic tattoos
4. Fairy tattoos
5. Wing tattoos
6. Cross tattoos
7. Aztec tattoos
8. Fire/flame tattoos
9. Gay tattoos
10. Kanji tattoos

1. Know your tattoo design resources—and their limitations.

Magazines, books, internet searches, and all other forms of media are full of images, but in order to avoid being disappointed by falling in love with a design that can't be tattooed "as is," you should ultimately rely on artwork that is intended to be tattooed, created by flash artists and tattooists who understand the limitations of a tattoo machine and human skin. Consider limiting your resources to those most reliable for a design-to-tattoo translation.

2. Be realistic about your tattoo design vision.

Skin is a living canvas, so there is a natural limit to what will work and what will not work as a tattoo. Be realistic about the size and complexity of your tattoo design. You don't want your tattoo to be more complex or detailed than the size or placement on your body warrants. The tattoo in your mind might be vague at first, so you just need to develop that idea and get it on paper so that it can be easily communicated to the tattooist.

3. Make sure your tattoo design reflects what you really want.

Remember why you're doing this as you work through the process of choosing a design—who or what your tattoo is commemorating, what image you're trying to convey with your tattoo, etc. If you want to create a "bad girl" look, chances are a cute butterfly tattoo won't get the response you're looking for.

4. Determine what your tattoo means to you now, later, and forever.

What meaning does this design have for you now—and how might that change later in life? This goes back to the "totem" concept discussed earlier—if you're honest with yourself about what you truly want, and you're representing yourself as you are, then you might avoid tattoo regret later in life. In other words, even if you've changed a lot since your first ink, you still see the tattoo as an honest representation of the person you were back then, and that could make all the difference in the world. So be honest with yourself. What's important to you? And how important do you think it will be in the future?

5. Identify your tattoo style.

There are probably as many styles as there are tattooists and flash artists to create them. Identify different styles of artwork you're naturally drawn to. Are you attracted to a traditional and vintage look? Are you more modern or urban? Do you like photo-realistic forms, buoyant cartoon designs, or designs that simulate watercolor, airbrush, and oils? Getting a tattoo isn't just about deciding on an image; it's how that image will be expressed on your skin.

6. Keep in mind the importance of finding a Tattoo Friendly™ design reference that includes a corresponding stencil.

Every great tattoo starts with a reference. Even if you already know what you want in your mind's eye, good design reference clearly communicates your tattoo vision to your tattooist (saving both of you a lot of time and frustration). Try and select a "stencil-ready" design. High-quality tattoo design stencils are like blueprints of your tattoo that don't include color or shading. They essentially give subtle direction to the tattooist on how to create the design on your skin—similar to how architects use blueprints to create their buildings. Providing your artist with good design references and high-quality stencils dramatically increases the likelihood that your tattoo will be an accurate representation of the original design (see pages 149–152 for more information on Tattoo Friendly™ reference).

All the tattoos available in this book have corresponding stencils available at www.TattooFinder.com. The site features tens of thousands of designs, so you can find even more Tattoo Friendly™ artwork with accompanying stencils there.

7. Be aware of multiple interpretations of your design choice.

A picture tells a thousand words—but will yours tell the one you want to convey? Remember that as you decide what your tattoo will be, and while that interpretation may be obvious to you, it may mean something else to others. You might decide to commemorate your summer in Spain with a fantastic tattoo of a black bull, but you might get a lot of people misinterpreting your tattoo as the zodiac symbol for Taurus. A tattoo of a moon and star could look celestial, but it also could resemble the symbol of Islam. While the opinions of others should not be important in your choice of design, at the very least you should considering possible alternative interpretations. Do some research and understand the various symbolic interpretations your design may take on before you commit to a permanent tattoo.

8. Decide the location on your body that best suits you.

The "what" of your tattoo will definitely be influenced by the "where." In other words, not only will your tattoo location determine how visible it is to everyone else, but it will also dictate what you can reasonably fit in the available space. Additionally, some designs simply work better aesthetically on different parts of the body. Will your design enhance the curves of your body or draw attention to (or away from) certain body parts?

Experts Know . . .

Not really sure where you want your tattoo or how big you want it? Experiment. Don't hesitate to apply some temporary tattoos or to pull out a nonpermanent marker and try out a few things so you can see how it looks and feels—and be more realistic about the limitations of your "canvas."

9. Try to consider if this will be your one and only tattoo—or the first of many.

If you think this tattoo may lead to another, put some thought into how the tattoo you're considering now will fit into your larger "tattoo future" in terms of style, theme, balance of color, and size. For example, if you think this tattoo on your forearm may someday become part of a sleeve, consider how your current tattoo will fit into that larger picture of a sleeve.

10. Take responsibility—and take your time.

You're going to have this tattoo forever, so take all the time you need to find something you love. While the final choice is ultimately your responsibility (and your prerogative), it may not hurt to get opinions from trusted people in your life. But beware: if you don't have a general idea of the tattoo you want, you may be susceptible to pressure from your friends or your tattooist. Think through all ten steps carefully and don't let yourself get talked into anything.

Tattoo Friendly™ Reference: What You See Is What You Get

Getting a tattoo is a creative and personal process, so it's no surprise that imaginations can really run wild during the search for design reference. Some artwork is just so impressive that you can't help but want to memorialize it on your skin. Unfortunately, not all of your ideas or the great artwork that inspires you will be Tattoo Friendly™—that is, possible to recreate on skin as you see it online or on paper. Frequently, designs will need to be reworked to translate onto your skin properly, and sometimes this can compromise the complexity or the quality of the initial art that you loved so much.

A Tattoo Friendly™ design is ideal for any reputable tattooist, no matter what their artistic skill level, since they won't need to take the design reference a person provides and "make it a tattoo." While tattooists *can* do this, it's a labor-intensive process to "make a design into a tattoo" and to create the accurate, corresponding stencil. What does this mean for you? More time and expense, for one thing, but you also might not be happy with the final "tattoo-able" design, since it may not look as it did on Google Images, for example.

At TattooFinder.com, we've developed a rigorous system of quality control for our designs. Every single tattoo (of the tens of thousands on our site) is a Tattoo Friendly™ reference. In order to help you better understand the complexity of what makes a design "Tattoo Friendly™," we've narrowed it down to three key aspects.

1. Tattoo Friendly™ reference includes corresponding stencils, which are the blueprint for a great tattoo.

When you acquire a piece of Tattoo Friendly™ artwork, you get two things: the design and the corresponding stencil. The stencil (also known as line art) is the tool your tattooist uses to accurately translate the artwork onto your skin.

Stencils contain the information that your tattooist needs to convert the most important subtleties of the design, such as the nuanced line work and shading. Well-drawn stencils allow for an extremely high degree of accuracy when it comes to tattooing the design onto your skin. And when you're getting something permanently inked on your body, accuracy is pretty damn important.

Tattoo Friendly™ design reference with its corresponding stencil

2. Tattoo Friendly™ reference is made to be tattooed on human skin.

Your skin is the canvas for your tattoo art, but over time your skin will change. And despite the many technological advances in the tattooing world over the years, there will always be limits to what makes an image "tattoo-able." In order for artwork to be considered Tattoo Friendly™, we must consider color usage and size and how that translates to the many varieties of human skin when tattooed. A tattoo will always have some probability of being damaged by the sun, stretched with age, and pulled by gravity, but Tattoo Friendly™ artwork has been designed to be tattooed as accurately as possible and to best withstand these changes over time.

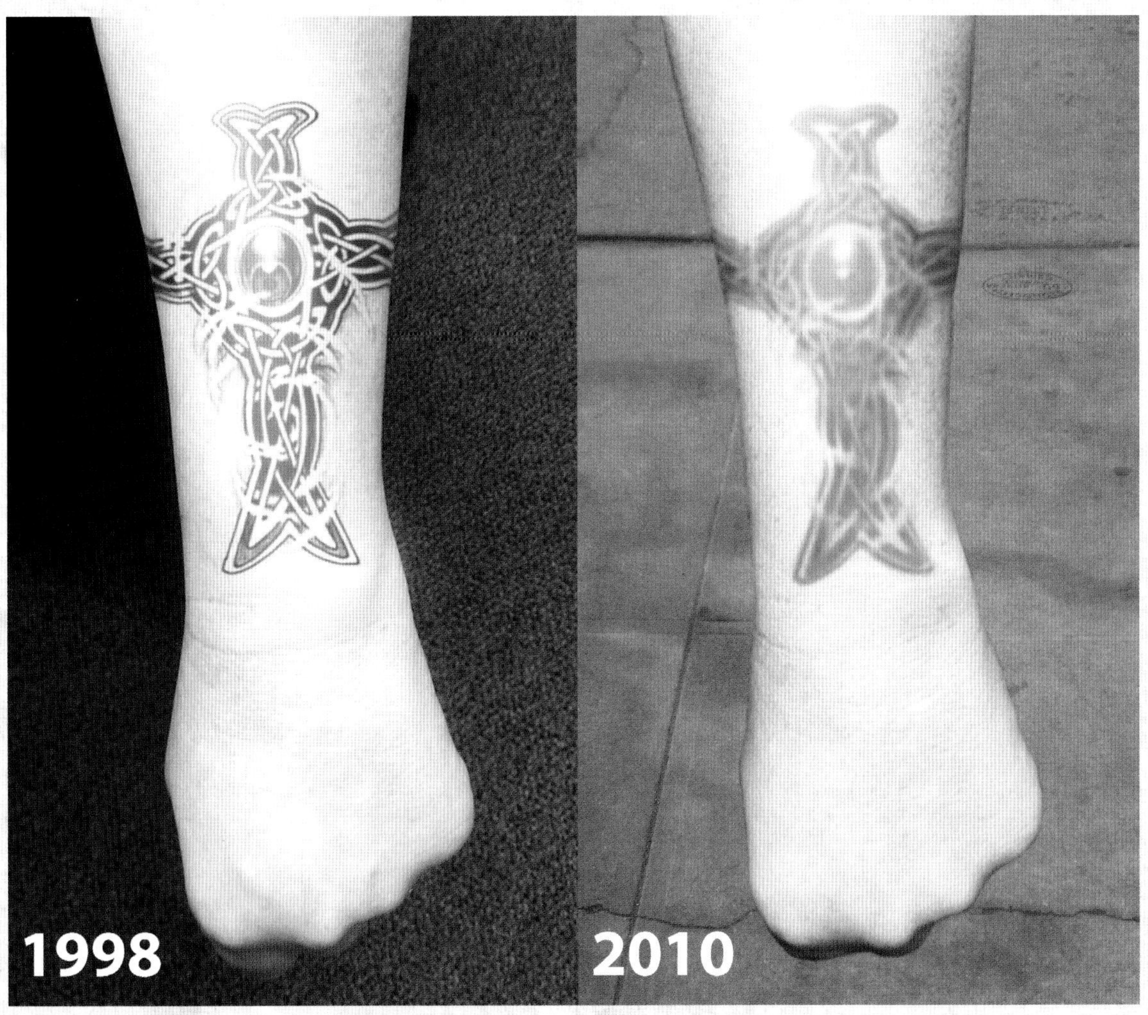

A newly inked tattoo, with the line work and colors still appearing sharp

An example of the damage that can occur to a non-Tattoo Friendly™ design over time

3. Tattoo Friendly™ reference is ready to be modified and combined.

We purposefully allow you to directly download a high-resolution, modifiable version of the tattoo design and stencil at TattooFinder.com so that you or your tattooist are free to change it in any way you see fit. We will never include any DRM (digital rights management) software, download limits, or other tricks that serve to restrict you from accessing, modifying, or combining designs. We also carefully separate our designs so that they can be easily merged together, as well as provide versions with transparent backgrounds. All of our artwork is made available at 300 DPI print resolution, offering the highest level of print quality as well, should you choose to manually combine artwork rather than do it through digital tools.

Tattoo Friendly™ references make it easy to combine images to create a unique tattoo, as shown above with this design assembled from components of three separate references

A Picture Tells a Thousand Words . . . What Will Yours Say?

When making your design choice, remember that tattoos are like words. How you say something makes as much of an impact as what you actually say.

If you decide that you want a butterfly tattoo, think about the type of butterfly you want. A butterfly tattoo could mean freedom. If depicted as a cartoonish butterfly, though, it could be a playful, whimsical display of freedom, a fun way to show off a free spirit. A butterfly that is more elaborate, intense, or with dark overtones could speak of a very specific type of freedom, perhaps an escape or release from a bad relationship. Which type better describes what you're picturing?

A dragon tattoo could be a symbol of power or fertility—or it could be a celebration of a person's passion for fantasy literature. If it's a Chinese dragon, it might stand for luck. Symbols represent different things to different people. No matter how diligently you research a symbol or design, it could still mean something different to an onlooker. The important thing is to be aware of a design's potential meanings and then to decide what it means for you.

Consider the pentagram, which is a hugely controversial symbol. Pentagrams celebrate the number five, which frequently appears in various cultures and belief systems. The Chinese Five Phases or Elements (wood, fire, earth, metal, water); the connection in medieval Christianity to the Five Wounds of Christ, and the Five Virtues of Knighthood (generosity, courtesy, chastity, chivalry, and piety); in Wiccan belief, as the four elements plus Gaia, or Mother Earth. But, inverted, the pentagram also has a connotation of Satanism (see below, right). Depending on the angle of your tattoo, how will your pentagram appear to others? This applies not only to its position, but also in its meaning—some people don't realize that the pentagram has symbolism other than Satanism. It's definitely something you want to consider before you get tattooed.

The pentagram has traditionally symbolized the elements, Mother Earth, and the virtues of medieval knighthood . . .

. . . But invert the design, and the image becomes a commonly interpreted symbol of Satanism

Nature Tattoos and Their Meanings

Below is a selection of symbols found in nature and how they might translate to a tattoo. Are you considering any of these designs? Think before you ink! There might be a few symbolic meanings on this list that you weren't aware of before, and these only represent a few of the possible interpretations. That's why it's so important for you to do your research and get the meaning right before you ink anything on your body.

Symbol	Potential symbolism
Acorn	Life, immortality
Cactus	Endurance
Cattail	Peace, prosperity
Dahlia	Dignity, elegance, good taste
Daisy	Loyalty, innocence
Forget-me-not	True, faithful love
Gardenia	Secret love
Iris	Faith, hope, wisdom, valor
Ivy	Affection, fidelity, friendship
Lily of the valley	Sweetness
Orchid	Love, beauty

Words to Live by

A popular trend today is not to tattoo a picture or symbol on the skin, but to actually spell out what you want to say—sometimes in English or your native language and sometimes in a foreign language. As careful as you should be when you choose an image to convey a message, so too will you need to be with your words—and maybe even a little *more* careful.

Pictures are open to interpretation, but words are there, spelling it out, so to speak. If you choose the wrong words, or mangle your words, disaster will result—at your expense! There are plenty of bad tattoos out there with misspellings, grammatical mistakes, and much more. We've seen "I'M AWSOME," "ONLY GOD WILL JUGE ME," and "TOO STRONG TO LOOSE." That doesn't even include all the incorrect foreign-language translations.

Wild at Heart

Make sure that you check and recheck your spelling in any tattooed text. Don't forget: Any mistakes could become mistakes for life

If you choose words, choose them carefully and make sure they mean (and are spelled) the way you intend for them to come across. If you want a foreign phrase spelled out on your body, *do not* simply consult a translation search engine on the internet. Have the phrase professionally translated. Awkward construction of phrases and sentences are bad enough in the eyes of a native speaker, but you may also be inadvertently conveying something humorous or offensive. Be extremely careful in what you say about yourself in permanent ink on your body as, again, the joke can be (indelibly) on you.

Below are some popular alternatives to standard pictorial tattoos:

- Use a word that you feel describes you—just make sure you have it spelled correctly! People have used everything, from "Awesome" and "Fearless" to "At Peace" or "Hellcat."

- Use a quote that resonates for you. Just be sure to check and double-check and get the attribution (and translation) right! You can head to the internet to search for quotes from famous people, such as authors, statesmen, and rock stars, but again, make sure the site itself is a reputable one. Lady Gaga, a self-professed "Daddy's girl," who has a tattoo on her shoulder of a heart tied in a ribbon that reads "Dad" and a "Little Monsters" tag, also has the words of Austrian-born poet and philosopher Rainer Maria Rilke tattooed on her arm. The quote translates as:

  "In the deepest hour of the night, confess to yourself that you would die if you were forbidden to write. And look deep into your heart where it spreads its roots, the answer, and ask yourself, must I write?"

- Use a word or phrase in a foreign language that has meaning for you. These can be words or expressed in characters, like Kanji, Hebrew, or Greek lettering. Many celebrities, like David Beckham, use characters to adorn their skin. Popular ones can be found in the Calligraphy chapter on pages 187–200.

Keep in mind that what's true for pictorial tattoos is also true for characters, words, and quotes: the image on your skin will become somewhat distorted over time as you age and your body changes. What will read great on young, elastic skin might get muddled in wrinkles.

"Show me a man with a tattoo and I'll show you a man with an interesting past."

—Author Jack London, 1883

Special note: If you want to tattoo someone's name on you, we'd strongly advise you to think twice about it. The relationship may end, but he or she will be with you forever. Don't forget that Johnny Depp had "Winona Forever" tattooed on his arm while he was with Winona Ryder, but he had to change it to "Wino Forever" after they split up!

The Right Tattoo for You

Finding that perfect Tattoo Friendly™ design reference may take some time. For many, it takes months or even years to decide what kind of tattoo to get. Some things that might inspire your tattoo include hobbies and interests, stories or folklore you identify with, your religious or spiritual beliefs, special achievements, and your cultural (or subcultural) identity.

Once you decide what you want to have tattooed on you, there are many ways to find the right design. This book is one of them! The internet can also offer tons of inspiration, providing myriad photographs, drawings, and animated images that can inspire you. Just be aware that not everything you find there, or in various books or magazines, can translate into a fantastic tattoo. As we've explained, often, the images you find will need to be reworked by an artistically inclined tattooist so they translate properly onto your skin. For that reason, searching Tattoo Friendly™ collections of flash art might be preferable.

Tattoo on You: What's Your Best Location?

While cost and pain threshold are often part of people's location decisions, the most important factor in your tattoo's location should be desired visibility. Think carefully about this. Do you want it to be seen by anyone and everyone? Or do you want it to be located in an intimate spot, where only you and a very select few people can view it?

Another important consideration in location is what type of tattoo you want—and how large you want it to be. You can choose to have a tiny daisy tattooed on the top of your left shoulder, for example, but on that considerably vast landscape of skin, it may be as obvious as a freckle. But how obvious or subtle it appears is all up to you.

Typically, guys go for tattoos on their arms and shoulders, upper backs, and chests, while women tend to ink their ankles and wrists, hands and feet, lower backs, and necks. Of course, tattoo hot spots (and even the gender-based decisions on location) are changing all the time. Those lower back "tramp stamp" tattoos used to be universally "cool" . . . until some started thinking they weren't.

Really consider the big picture when choosing a location for your tattoo. For example, a vine motif could make for an elegant and incredibly feminine design, extending from a woman's fingertips, wrapping around her arm to the shoulder. A man might make a strong statement with a bold tribal symbol inked on his forearm (almost like Popeye and his anchor tattoos). Or maybe the design is deliberately married to a prominent muscle, such as a bulging bicep, helping to really hit home a message of strength and masculinity.

As we discussed earlier, you should experiment with a washable magic marker or temporary tattoos to help you figure out the best placement for your new tattoo. Finding a design that works for you is, of course, important, but that won't really matter if it's in a poorly chosen location. Some tattooists are willing to apply just the nonpermanent stencil to your skin and let you wear that for a while to "try before you buy." That way you can make sure you're happy with the design, size, and location before the tattoo becomes permanent. The bottom line is that you just want to be sure that "where" you've decided to get a tattoo works for you; it's at least as important as the "what."

Tattoo Pain: Mind over Matter?

Getting tattooed is a unique experience for every individual. Some people will tell you that it definitely hurts. Others will tell you that it kind of hurts, while still others might be more sensitive to the other sensations that the tattoo machine sparks on their skin besides pain. There might be a sense of tingling or burning. You may experience a sense of scraping or scratching. Some of the other aspects may also be uncomfortable, such as sitting in uncomfortable positions for long periods of time. Sometimes people dislike the sound of the tattoo machine or the vibrations the machine causes. Every person will react differently to the sensations.

Also, how it feels and how much it actually hurts really depend on any one person's tolerance for pain—as well as their imagination. If you go in stressed out, thinking that you're going to be in constant pain, chances are, you will be. And vice versa: If you keep a mindset that it's probably going to hurt a bit, but maintain your belief that your new tattoo will be worth it, then this could help transcend the pain, and you're likely to have a more comfortable experience. For some people, though, the pain is a "rite of passage" in getting a tattoo—the pain makes the experience of "transformation" real. So while some people would be more excited about tattoos if there were no pain involved, others might feel let down, almost like they hadn't earned it. And then, of course, there are all the mindsets in between.

People often ask, "Where on the body does it hurt the most/least to get tattooed?" Getting tattooed on bony areas, like elbows or ankles, may be more uncomfortable than tattoos inked on fleshier parts of your body, like your upper arms or backside. For more "squishy" areas, like the stomach, inner thighs, or under the arms, the vibrations might be less intense. However, there may be more instances of sharp pain happening in these spots, a sensation of being "pinched." This is because the skin in these areas does need to be stretched somewhat when the ink is applied. Some areas of the body, such as hands, have more nerve endings than other parts of the body.

Inevitably, you will find those who say that the traditionally painful areas of getting tattooed hurt much less than the traditionally less-painful areas. More than anything else, though, how much discomfort will be felt really depends most on the individual's unique threshold for pain, as well as on how they interpret that experience of pain. And the bottom line is this: Get a tattoo on your body where you really want to get it, not where someone else tells you it will hurt the least. While the pain will be temporary, the location of the tattoo will be permanent.

Selecting a Tattooist and Studio

Tattooing is a trade that is generally learned through an apprenticeship with one tattooist (the master) teaching a student the "craft." But, while the apprenticeship tradition has produced some incredible talent over the years, it can fall victim to weak links in the chain, and some apprenticeships simply don't produce good tattooists. And to compound the issue, there is nothing preventing a "disreputable" tattooist from apprenticing others and producing more poorly trained tattooists.

Did You Know?

- 61 percent of people say that the reputation of a tattoo artist and studio is the most important factor when selecting who will tattoo them and where they will get tattooed.
- 23 percent say the selection of art reference to choose from is the most important factor when selecting which tattoo studio to use.
- 8 percent say the price for tattooing is the most important factor when choosing who will tattoo them.

Original source: Flash2xs.com Polls, TattooFinder.com

There is no uniform set of standards, training, or testing on the craft of tattooing. Governmental regulations at the state, county, and local levels will vary widely—from having no regulations at all to mandatory testing and licensing—but they generally focus on safety and health concerns, with no criteria for testing actual tattooing skills. If any regulations exist in your area, they are probably also going to be difficult to find—sometimes folded into the state's cosmetology standards, and other times regulated by localized health departments. Consequently, tattooing is largely a "self-regulated" industry, meaning that tattooists themselves are the ones who decide which ethical approaches apply to their work.

Health is one concern, but outcome is equally important. Some tattooists will be more committed than others to making sure that you get the tattoo you want. When tattooists quote a price for a tattoo, they are generally estimating the TOTAL TIME it will take in working with you, quite possibly including assisting you in finding design reference and refining that reference (if required) to come up with the final design. However, you should confirm this when they quote you a price range. Some tattooists who don't charge for their "design preparation" work may try to speed this process along as quickly as possible—for them, time is money.

Tattooists Love Tattoo Friendly™ Design Reference, Too!

Cost should not be your main consideration for selecting a tattooist. Think of your tattoo as what it is: a long-term investment. Of course, you don't want to get something you can't afford; on the other hand, "bargain hunting" could potentially lead to subpar work and health consequences. Most reputable tattooists will give you a fair price for the work, generally basing their estimate on the number of hours it will take to do any design modification and to actually apply your tattoo. You can, of course, limit this time and cost by doing your homework and being prepared with a Tattoo Friendly™ reference.

Most tattooists love it when you come to them prepared with good design reference and stencils in hand because it makes the design process quick and your communication easy. Although a big part of their job is to help you prepare and develop artwork (and some tattooists love this process), most professional tattooists are in the business because they love to tattoo. In other words, they might not be particularly invested in thorough design collaboration. Providing your tattooist with Tattoo Friendly™ artwork will help you communicate your tattoo vision, and high-quality stencils will help insure that your vision is efficiently and accurately translated onto your skin.

Now you just need to make sure you have the right tattooist!

Ten Tips on Finding a Good Tattooist

1. Listen to your friends . . . and your gut.
2. Decide if the tattooist's skills and specialties match your particular needs.
3. Scrutinize portfolios.
4. Inspect the premises.
5. Make your health your primary concern.
6. Make sure you feel comfortable with this person.
7. Ask about apprenticeships and training.
8. Understand what is (and what isn't) guaranteed.
9. Make sure you and your tattooist share the same vision.
10. Communicate any special needs or considerations you may have.

1. Listen to your friends . . . and your gut.

Chances are that if one of your friends had a good experience at a particular studio or with a certain tattooist, so may you, but you still need to find someone that you feel comfortable working with. If you don't click with a particular tattooist on a gut level, don't let them tattoo you. You can get a good sense of a studio's work by looking at their portfolios (online, if they have them posted), but you can only get a sense of the artist by actually meeting them in person. For that reason, you should really consider visiting several studios, starting a dialogue with the tattooist, and looking over his or her portfolios in person. After all, depending on how complicated your tattoo is you, could be with this person for hours.

2. Decide if the tattooist's skills and specialties match your particular needs.

Any reputable tattooist should be able to skillfully apply any tattoo design to skin (keeping in mind the limitations of the craft). But some tattooists do focus their work on certain types of tattoo styles, like photo-realism or old-school styles. This type of specialization might be based on a tattooist's personal preference, so if you have a particular vision in mind, find someone who you feel is genuinely interested in doing your tattoo. Sometimes this can be determined by simply looking through their portfolio and at the type of work they most commonly do.

Also, when considering your particular needs, don't forget about your tattoo plan. Whether you prefer a personalized, custom, or couture approach will impact your decision on the tattooist you choose, particularly with regards to their artistic skills (in addition to craftsmanship). If you go with a personalized tattoo plan, you will need to find a tattooist who is simply a good craftsperson (artistic skills are not really required). If you decide on the custom approach, you may need to evaluate a tattooist's artistic capabilities in addition to their craftsmanship (depending upon how much you will rely on the tattooist for artistic assistance). To determine if a tattooist has the skills required for your tattoo plan, you will need to examine their portfolios.

Experts Know . . .

Guy Aitchison, long-time professional tattooist, explains, "The personal connection must be there. You don't want bad tattoo mojo." Feel free to ask any and all questions of your prospective tattooist and expect to have them addressed respectfully and intelligently.

3. Scrutinize portfolios.

Any reputable tattooist should have a photo album of tattoos they have created for you to review to determine their level of craftsmanship. Their previous tattoo work should be diverse and well done, with a large percentage of the examples looking healthy and healed (unhealed or just-completed tattoos will look red around the edges, swollen, and have a definite sheen). Do the black lines in the tattoos look smooth and clean or are they raggedy and uneven? Are the color fields solid or patchy? Are the transitions from shading to solid pigment smooth or awkward? Try to look at the tattooist's past work with an aesthetic eye. While you may not personally connect with all of the work displayed, you should take note of the professional touches. Also, if a particular tattoo was done from tattoo artwork in the studio, ask to see the original design on the wall. How does it compare with the actual tattoo in the photo?

If your tattoo plan requires a tattooist to be artistically skilled and not just skilled at the craft of applying ink to skin, the standard tattoo photo portfolio review will *not* be enough. You should also request to see a portfolio (or other examples) of this tattooist's original artwork, such as a sketchbook or tattoo flash sheets that he or she created that are hanging on the walls in the studio. And, of course, artists have different styles, so you will need to make sure this tattooist's artistic style matches your vision for your final tattoo. You definitely want to avoid working with a tattooist to create or further a design concept, only to find that what he or she is creating isn't at all what you had been picturing for your next tattoo. Generally, this results in wasted time for both you and your tattooist (and perhaps wasted money). Even worse, there are those who might cave to the pressure in the moment of "settling" on a design they don't particularly like and having that design permanently inked on their body! Again, one of the benefits of providing your tattooist with Tattoo Friendly™ design reference is less reliance on the artistic capabilities (and style preferences) of the tattooist.

4. Inspect the premises.

When you're considering a tattoo studio, look around. No, not just at the pretty pictures on the walls! Check out the premises, too. Is it clean? Use the bathroom. No, we're not kidding! Is it sanitary and presentable? The outward appearance of a tattoo shop can often reflect a tattooist's dedication to cleanliness and sterilization practices in general. The shop should feel clean and hospitable. Your tattooist, too, should look clean and kempt, regardless of their personal fashion tastes.

5. Make your health your primary concern.

Reputable tattoo studios should have a policy regarding "Universal Precautions"—the Centers for Disease Control and Prevention (CDC) guidelines recommended to prevent transmission of HIV and other blood-borne diseases. According to the CDC, hands must be washed routinely, gloves should always be worn, and all tattooing tools and equipment must have some barrier (paper towel, plastic, etc.) between them and the usual work surface. The sterilizer used in the shop ("the autoclave") should undergo monthly spore testing to make sure the equipment is working properly, and your shop of choice must practice a "single-use-needle" policy. As a matter of fact, all needles and tubes should be taken from their sterilized packaging before each individual use, and you can note a color indicator that turns brown once they're properly sterilized. You have every right to ask your tattooist to set up in front of you, show you their spore-testing records, and make available their applicable health and inspection documentation, as well as any certification required by the local authorities. If a tattooist refuses any of these requests or if you're uncomfortable with what you see, don't hesitate to leave and seek out a studio that stands behind their professional practices.

6. Make sure you feel comfortable with this person.

Needles alone can be unsettling, so being tattooed by someone that you're not comfortable with is only additional stress. You may be artistically collaborating with this person, spending several hours together during the tattooing process, and, quite possibly, showing them parts of your body you wouldn't generally let others see. Part of your tattoo experience is your memory of actually getting your artwork tattooed and your time spent in the chair. Your shop of choice should provide you with top-rate customer service.

7. Ask about apprenticeships and training.

Generally, a reputable tattooist has gone through some type of apprenticeship (often lasting several years), during which they would have learned the many skills required of the craft. More recently, there has been an influx of "tattoo schools," but there is definite resistance to this from within the industry. Since these programs are generally short term (sometimes six months or less) and don't often include any actual tattoo studio experience, it's hard to balance the education of a "schooled" tattooist with someone who has gone through an apprenticeship. Talk to your tattooist about their training experience, including education on health precautions and practices.

8. Understand what is (and isn't) guaranteed.

Some shops guarantee their work for life, while others will only guarantee your tattoo for a certain period of time, maybe six months or a year. Some shops abide by a "one pass, first class" policy, which means that, if there is a problem with the tattoo, they believe it's the fault of the client and ultimately due to incorrect healing and aftercare. If your studio has this policy in place, you should expect to be charged for any subsequent touch-ups. Ask questions and educate yourself before you're tattooed—you should be aware of and comfortable with whatever shop policies are in place.

9. Make sure you and your tattooist share the same vision.

Both you and your tattooist should have the same design goals of what your tattoo will look like before the needles hit your skin. Again, your tattoo plan is part of this. Whether your plan is personalized, custom, or couture, you should both be on the same page and be in agreement about how to proceed.

The best way to ensure that the vision of what you want will be reflected in the tattoo you get is to provide your tattooist with a Tattoo Friendly™ design reference. If your tattooist isn't committed to making sure you get exactly what you want, you may need to find someone else to tattoo you. Avoid tattooists who are less focused on your vision and more on their own and don't let your excitement in getting new ink distract you from really evaluating them and choosing a tattooist who shares your vision. Compromising on this point may leave you with a tattoo that the tattooist wanted to create, but not one that you want to wear forever.

"My body is my journal, and my tattoos are my story."

—Johnny Depp

Experts Know . . .

According to a TattooFinder.com poll, 41 percent of those considering a tattoo would pay up to 50 percent more for a tattoo artist known to have a good reputation and who is certified by their local health department.

10. Communicate any special needs or considerations you may have.

If you want to cover a scar, have a dark skin complexion, or if you have any conditions that might affect healing or how well the ink takes to the skin, you need to include these factors when communicating with a tattooist. Also, if you have any conditions that may factor in here, like hemophilia or other blood diseases, or if you have a condition that may be contagious or dangerous to the tattooist, you must make that known.

Make sure you are working with a tattooist who has experience in dealing with your particular needs or circumstances and don't be afraid to ask for evidence through photos, stories, or both.

Dollars and Sense

With any important purchase, you never look solely at the cost, particularly if you're going to make an investment in something. Investment is about more than just cost. It's about value, which means getting the best-quality product at the best price. You're not going to buy the cheapest car because it's the cheapest. You're going to buy the one that you feel best meets your needs at the price you are willing to pay. The same goes for a dishwasher, or even a pair of boots. You save the "cheapest" option for things that are disposable. Like toilet paper.

"Cheapest" should not be on the table when deciding what tattoo you want and who will tattoo you. After all, your tattoo is hardly disposable. It's an important investment and will be with you forever, and for that reason, you should consider what it costs over time to determine the value. One hundred or two hundred dollars for something that will be with you for thirty, fifty, maybe even seventy years suddenly doesn't sound so expensive; however, if it's a terrible, amateurish job that you'll be stuck looking at for the next thirty, fifty, or seventy years (and may even pay more to "fix" later), well, it doesn't really matter how good a "deal" you got, does it?

Just because cost is a consideration in getting a tattoo doesn't mean you have to blow your life savings on one or pay a higher price for the sake of paying it. What does a tattoo typically cost? In 2012, it could be as inexpensive as $50 and as high as several hundred dollars. Some larger and more elaborate tattoos, such as full back or chest pieces, can even range into the thousands of dollars. However, keep in mind: the cost will most likely never fall below $40, as this is a common minimum fee generally charged to cover time and materials.

Cost and Size

Overall, cost really depends on what you want—the detail and complexity of the tattoo you want to create and the time it will take to create it. Surprisingly, size doesn't always matter. Just because a tattoo is big doesn't mean it will automatically be more expensive than a smaller tattoo—especially if that smaller tattoo has considerably more detail. *The biggest factor in the price of a tattoo is the time it takes the tattooist to get the final product onto your skin*—from consultation to drafting and redrafting, to the actual work with ink and needle. A tattooist will estimate the time that it will take to complete your tattoo, and they'll quote you a price range based on that time. Asking what a tattooist charges by the hour isn't particularly useful to the consumer, since each tattooist works at a different speed. It's best to get a price range quote for the completed work.

Cost and Location

Where on the body a tattoo will go can also potentially play a role in the cost—some body parts are simply easier to ink and take less time to tattoo than other parts. Tattoos going on more "sensitive" areas of the body often cause people to need more breaks, thus taking longer to apply. Tattoos applied to more "squishy" areas of the skin require more stretching of the skin, which can also take longer to tattoo.

Regardless of size and location considerations, having a design in mind—and, better, in hand—will generally save time for you and the tattooist. If he or she doesn't have to plan from scratch what your tattoo will look like because you came prepared with a Tattoo-Friendly™, stencil-ready art reference, that's time saved. And time saved is generally, of course, money saved.

To Tip or Not to Tip?

It is customary to tip your tattooist if you are satisfied with his or her work. Estimate between 15 and 25 percent, depending on the quality of the service and your satisfaction with the end product. Let's face it, if you're willing to tip your waiter or waitress 20 percent to bring your lunch to the table, don't you think it's worth giving a little extra to someone who has given you something that you love and will have for the rest of your life?

How do you keep tattoo costs down?

1. Just be aware that the size and complexity of the tattoo design will affect the price, so the larger and more complex a design is, the more it will probably cost.
2. If you decide to go with a larger and/or more complex tattoo, many tattooists will allow you to break up the work into several sessions (and payments). Consider starting with just getting the line work tattooed. You could always go back later to get (and pay for) the completed tattoo.
3. Understand that the location you choose for your tattoo might impact the price. More sensitive areas generally take more time to tattoo, and this could mean a higher cost for you.
4. Provide your tattooist with a Tattoo Friendly™ reference. Not only because it means you'll have a better chance of being happy with your tattoo, but also because the process is generally less expensive, keeping design and consultation services to a minimum.
5. Ask around. Some tattooists may be as good as others, even if they are not evenly priced. Just as you would shop around to find the best deal on any big-ticket item, you can shop around for the best value in getting your tattoo.

Now You Know . . .

- Tattoo Friendly™ reference, including stencils, is the best way to ensure the tattoo you want is the tattoo you ultimately get.

- Getting a tattoo is an investment—of both time and money. If you're not willing or able to spend both of these right now, it might not be the best time for you to get a tattoo.

- Pain is a fact of life when it comes to tattooing, but how much pain one experiences, and whether the sensation is deemed uncomfortable or empowering, is pretty much an individual response. Cost definitely shouldn't be the only factor when choosing a tattooist. Get recommendations from trusted friends, inspect the studios, and, most of all, and make sure you feel comfortable with the person you ultimately choose.

Butterflies & Insects

Happy Summer Day
Medium

Longeftily
Large

Tarianna
Medium

Jungle Lace Butterfly
Large

Kissing the Vine
Medium

Monarch on Hibiscus Flower
Large

Purrty Butterfly Profile
Small

Blue Pink Repeat
Extra Large

Pastel Butterfly
Large

Flirting Butterflies
Medium

Zaxirid Butterfly
Medium

Bug Eyed Heart Butterfly
Medium

Tribal Lace Butterfly
Medium

Goldiefly
Medium

Cool Fade
Medium

Circle of Flowers and Butterflies
Medium

Bubblefly Rising
Extra Large

Cobalt Wings
Large

Stabby Butterfly
Large

Billowing Butterfly
Small

Deco Butterfly
Medium

Khokhloma Silent Butterfly
Large

Buttertribe Effect
Medium

Black Green Butterfly Wings
Medium

Purple Butterfly
with Blue & Pink
Medium

Majestic Blend
Extra Large

Butterfly in Garden
Extra Large

Startennae
Medium

Dangle Tribal Butterfly
Medium

Red Black Striped Butterfly
Medium

Silhouette Butterfly
Medium

Blossoming Butterfly
Medium

Cupped
Medium
Candy Dragonfly
Small
Hottrib Butterfly
Medium
Bluetterfly
Medium
Greenspeed
Small

Wide Aperture Butterfly
Large

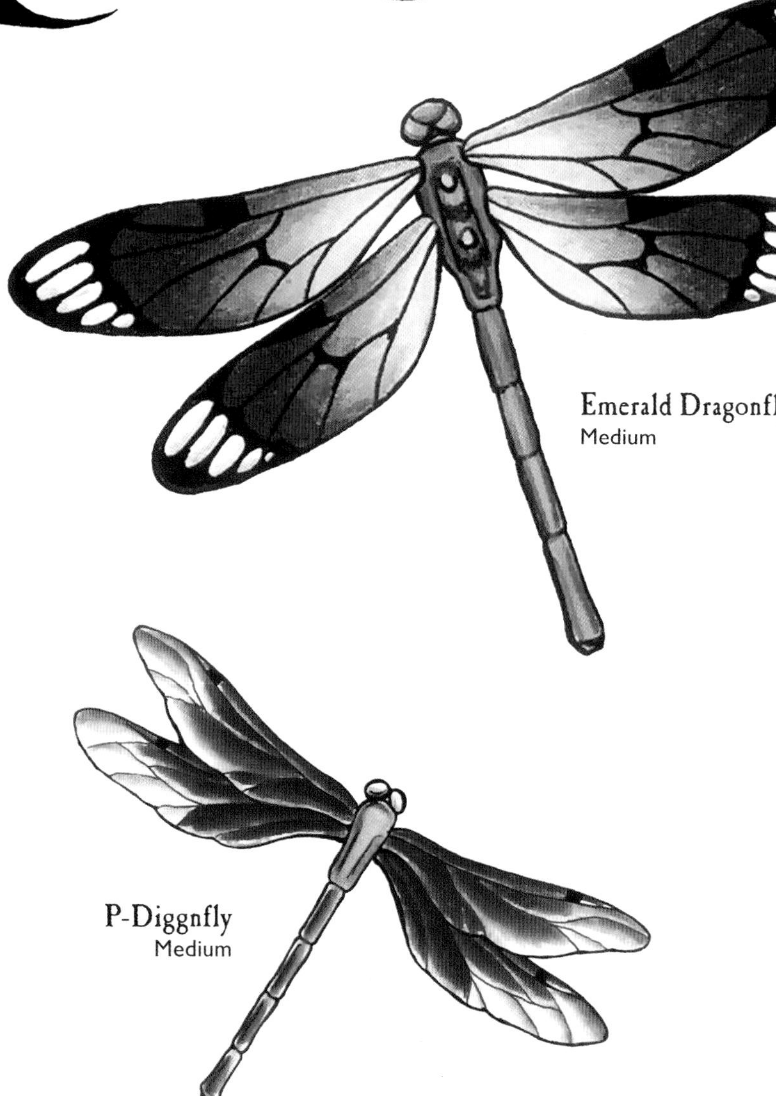

Emerald Dragonfly
Medium

P-Diggnfly
Medium

Dragonfly with Blue Wings & Foliage Tail
Medium

Lergapoke
Small

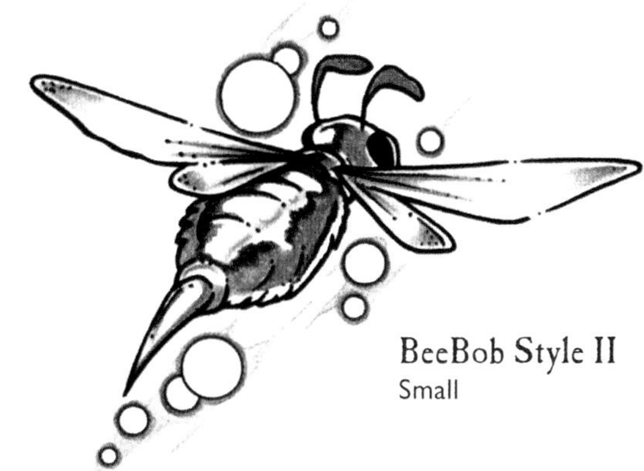

BeeBob Style II
Small

Purple House Fly
Medium

Pain
Medium

Praying Mantis
Large

Skeeter
Medium

Toadstool Sit
Small

Black Widow Mushroom
Medium

Metal Wasp
Medium

Colorful Butterfly and Stars
Medium

Triple Bee
Medium

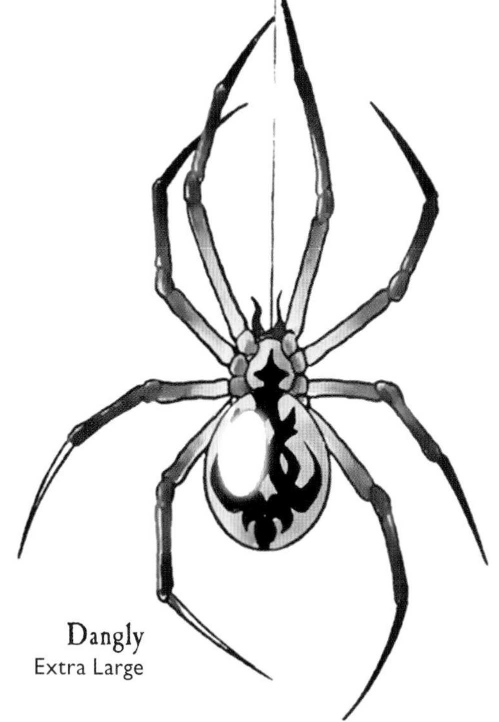

Dangly
Extra Large

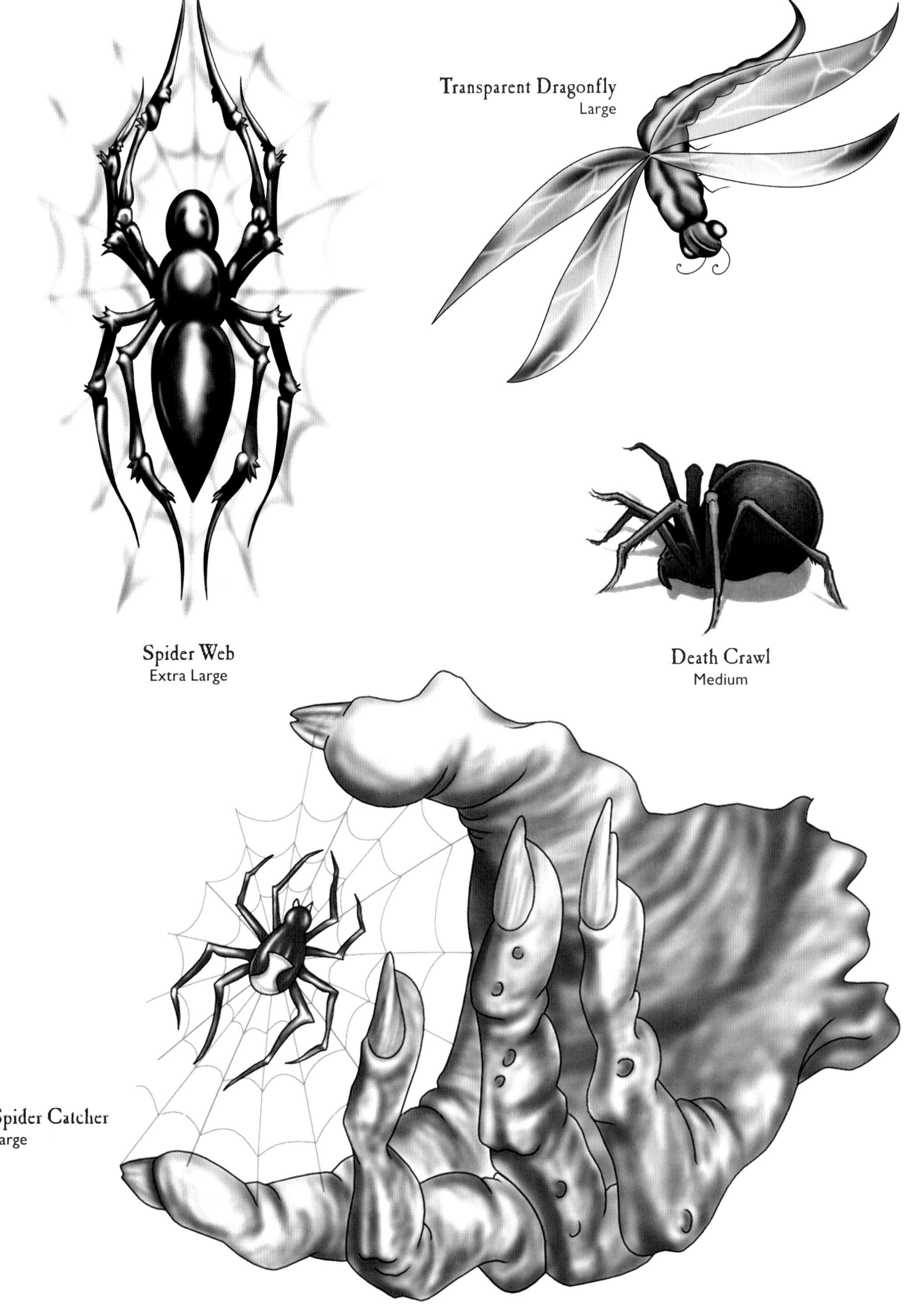

Transparent Dragonfly
Large

Spider Web
Extra Large

Death Crawl
Medium

Spider Catcher
Large

Heart Vendor Butterfly
Medium

Many Insect Tribal
Medium

Trails of Tribal Butterfly
Large

Butterfly Vortex
Extra Large

A Work in Progress
Large

BT Ibally
Medium

Deadly Face Butterfly
Medium

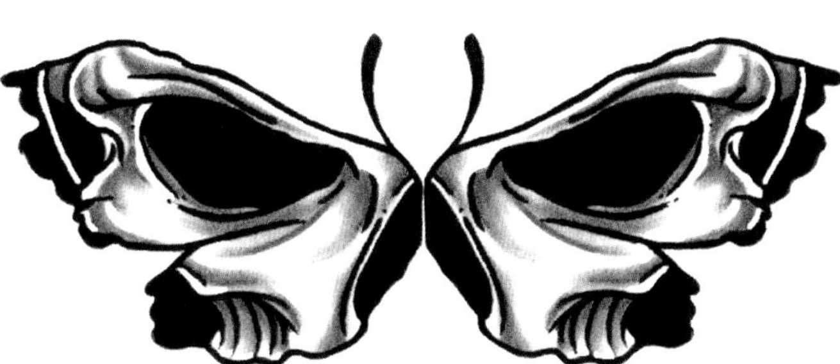

Inner Skull Butterfly II
Medium

Purple Praying Mantis
Medium

Four Curl Butterfly
Medium

Butterfly Design Wings
Medium

Web Spread
Medium

Rainbow Colored Butterfly
Medium

Killer Caterpillar
Extra Large

Green Grasshopper
Medium

Fat Bee
Medium

Monarch Falls
Medium

Moonset Butterfly
Medium

Ribbontail Butterfly
Enwater
Medium

Butterflies Vines
Large

Butterfly Love Lift
Medium

Tribal Backed Bubblefly
Medium

Flirting with a Flower
Medium

Britenue
Medium

Ladybug
Medium

Lello
Large

Black Widow
Large

Little Lightning
Large

DensksFly
Medium

Calligraphy

Believe

Small Believe
Medium

Dad

Small Dad
Medium

Mom

Small Mom
Medium

Peace

Small Peace
Medium

In Loving Memory

Large In Loving Memory
Large

Medium Strength
Medium

Medium Forever
Medium

Medium Trust
Medium

Medium Respect
Medium

Small Honor
Medium

RHS
Medium

Jesus Lettering
Medium

Jesus Lettering
Small

Revolution
Extra Large

Wild at Heart
Medium

Bad at Heart
Medium

Rebel
Medium

Vampy
Small

"Chaos"
Small

Red Rose Love
Medium

Sinner Script
Medium

Familia
Medium

"Dragon" (Kanji, Tibetan)
Medium

"Love" (Kanji, Tibetan)
Medium

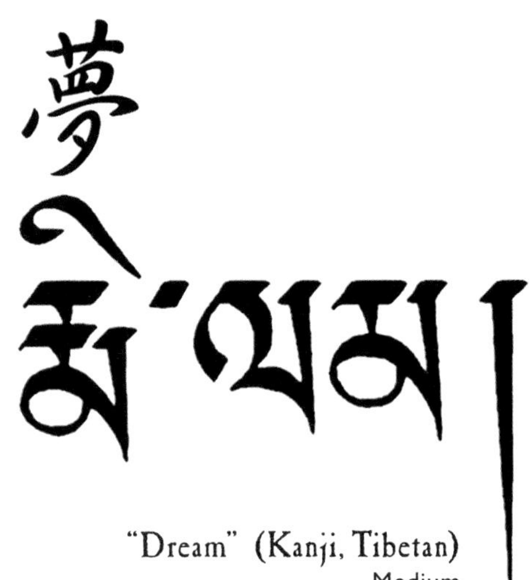

"Dream" (Kanji, Tibetan)
Medium

"Destiny" (Kanji, Tibetan)
Medium

"Eternal" (Kanji, Tibetan)
Medium

"God" (Kanji, Tibetan)
Medium

福

བསོད་ནམས།

"Good Fortune" (Kanji, Tibetan)
Medium

"Strength"
Medium

友情

གྲོགས་པོའི་བརྩེ་སེམས།

"Friendship" (Kanji, Tibetan)
Large

"Justice" (Kanji, Tibetan)
Medium

"Hate" (Kanji, Tibetan)
Medium

天使

"Angel"
(Chinese)
Medium

Blooming Branch
("Cherry Blossoms")
Medium

英雄

"Hero" (Chinese)
Medium

Twoskull Kanji Means "Evil"
Medium

"Peace" (Chinese)
Medium

"Truth"
Large

"Faith" (Chinese)
Small

Spoiled Rotten
Medium

Insatiable
Large

Loser Lettering
Medium

Sick
Large

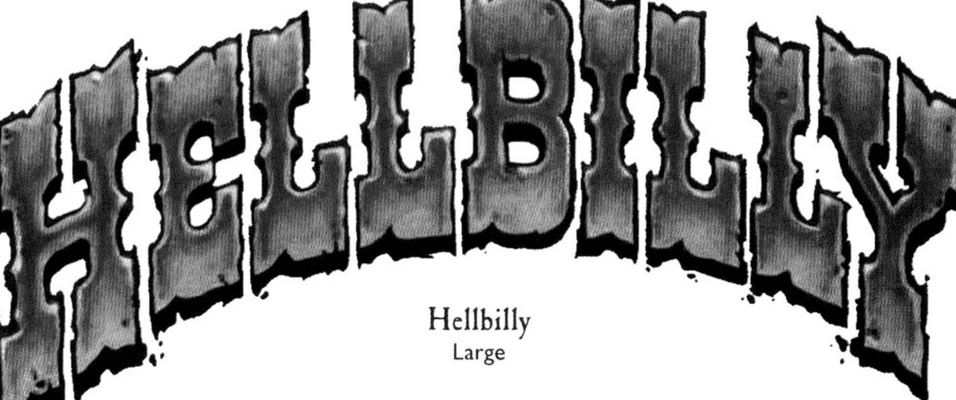

Hellbilly
Large

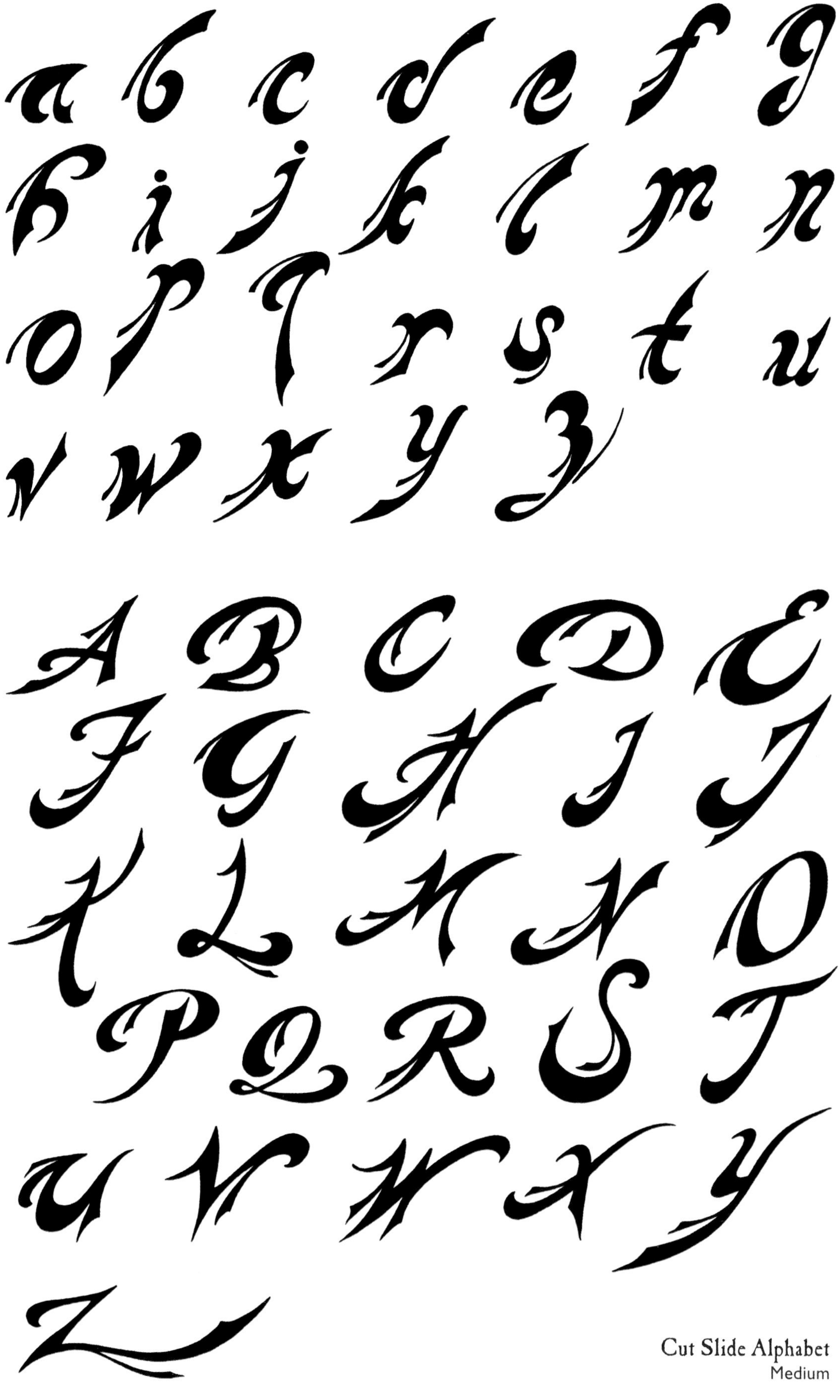

a b c d e f g
h i j k l m n
o p q r s t u
v w x y z

A B C D E
F G H I J
K L M N O
P Q R S T
U V W X Y
Z

Cut Slide Alphabet
Medium

A · B · C · D · E · F
G · H · I · J · K · L · M
N · O · P · Q · R · S · T
U · V · W · X · Y · Z

Celtic Alphabet
Medium

ABCDEFGHI
JKLMNOPQR
STUVWXYZ

Black Tribal Letters
Medium

AaBbCcDd
EeFfGgHh
IiJjKkLl
MmNnOoPp
QqRrSsTt
UuVvWwXx
YyZz0011
22334455
66778899

Cursive
Medium

Greek Alphabet
(Reflecting American
Alphabet)
Medium

Arabic "Always"
Medium

Arabic "Peace"
Medium

Arabic "Strength"
Medium

Arabic "Respect/Honor"
Medium

Arabic "Happiness"
Medium

Arabic "Sister"
Medium

Cartoons & Clowns

Romantic Little Fox
Medium

Love Now Cry Later Duo
Medium

Red Heart Rabbit
Medium

Proper Kitty II
Medium

Pink Bunny Rabbit
Medium

Claws out Brown Cat
Large

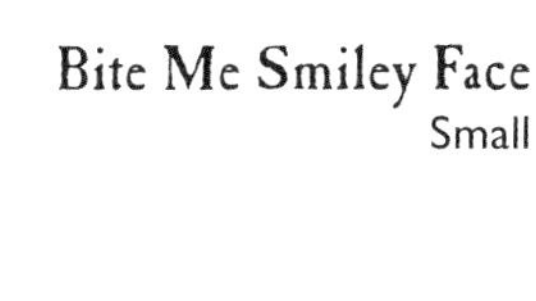

Bite Me Smiley Face
Small

Kitten With a Yarn to Tell
Medium

Turtle Takes the Checkered Flag
Medium

Mouse Surprise
Medium

Golden Bulldog
Medium

Clown Fangs
Medium

Clowns Are Evil
Extra Large

No Joke Here
Extra Large

End of the Rope
Extra Large

You Scared
Medium

Laugh and Cry Clowns
Extra Large

Party Starter
Large

Big Bad Pencil
Large

Bucktoothed Mockery
Large

Jokergrin
Medium

Monkey Business
Extra Large

EL Clown 1
Extra Large

Clawing Clown
Extra Large

Crazy Clown Eats Carrots
Extra Large

Heart Belly Relax Teddy
Small

Happy Hallucinogen
Medium

Fuzzy Wuzzy
Small

Turquoise Jester
Medium

Relaxing Shroom Bear
Small

Joker's Surprise
Large

Design & Background Fill

Delicate Star Script
Large

Vine of a Tribal Mess
Large

Black Design Circle
Pink Flowers
Medium

Symbol of Swirls
Medium

Green Splets
Small

Large Flower Piece Shaded
Extra Large

Curly Flowers
Large

Blue Vines
Medium

Ornamental Tulip
Medium

Purple Green Ribbon
Large

Trail of Stars
Large

Design Black Medium
Medium

Circle Swirl Design
Medium

Jensband
Extra Large

Thorivino
Extra Large

Pastel Butterfly Band
Large

Tri Raised Stars
Medium

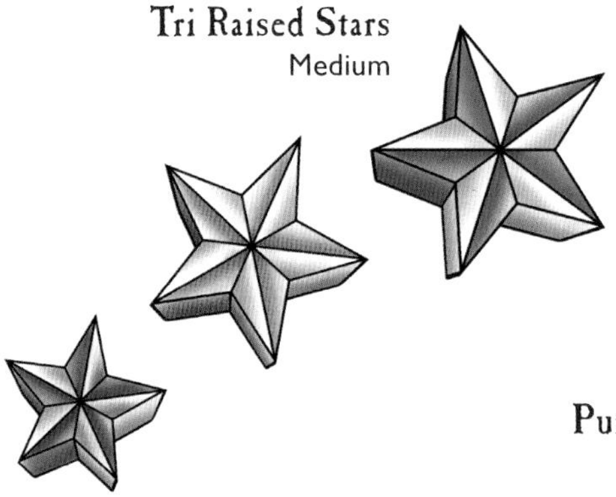

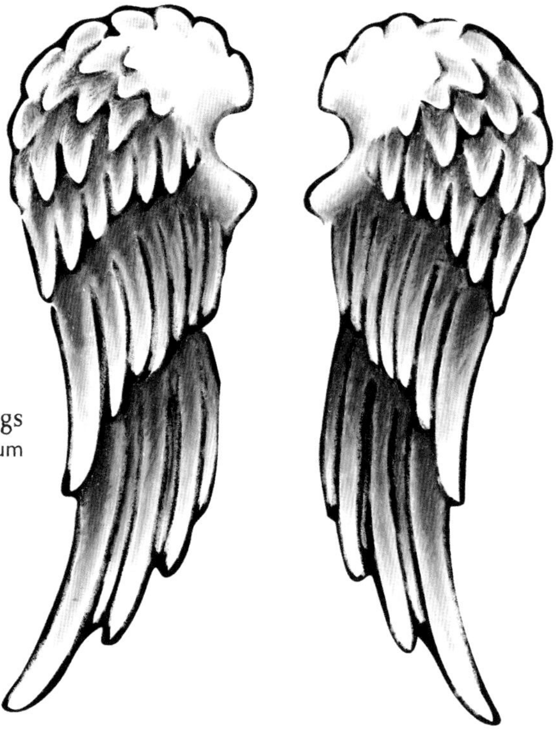

Purple Angel Wings
Medium

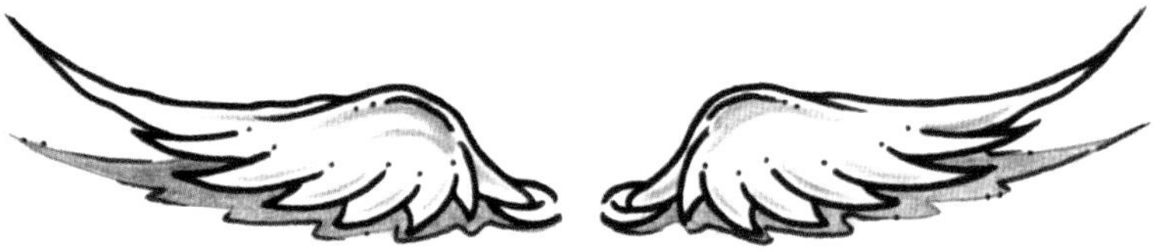

Get Your Wings
Medium

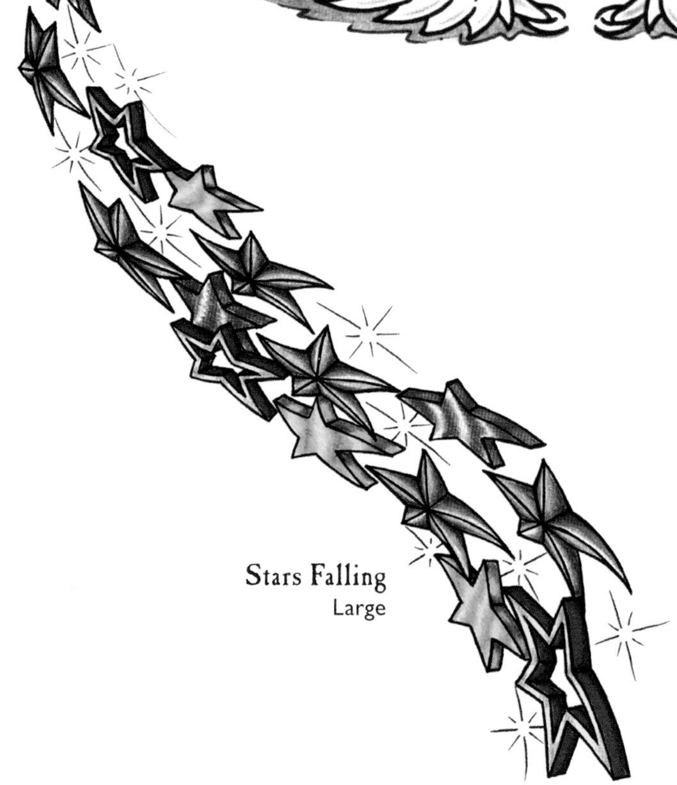

Stars Falling
Large

Raised Wings of Gold
Large

Within the Water
Large

Swirling Cherry Blossoms
Large

Droppin Blossoms
Large

In the Curve
Large

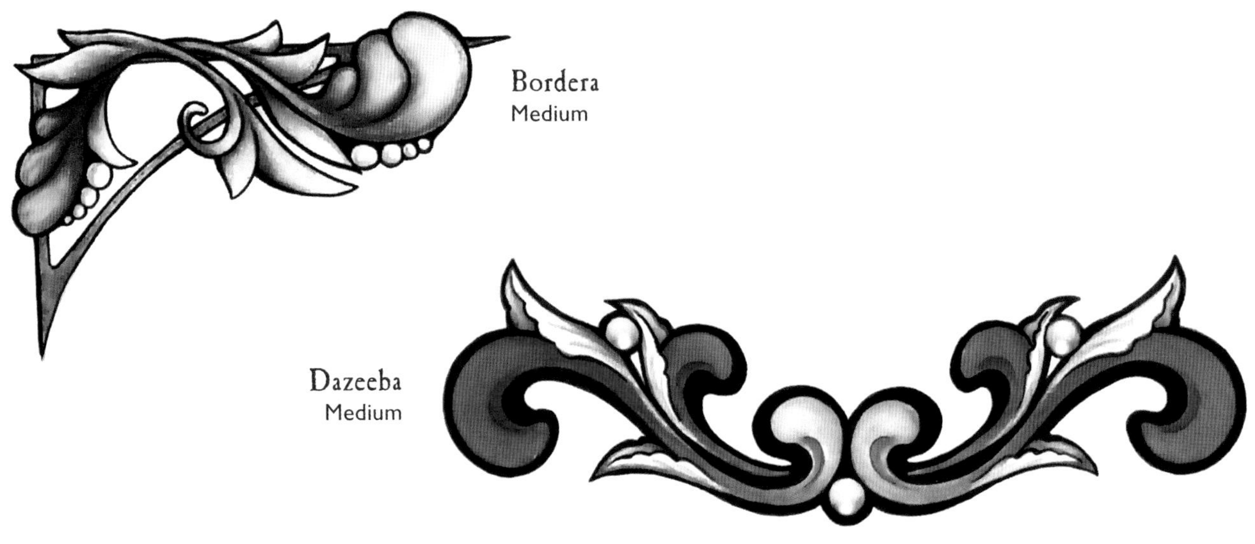

Bordera
Medium

Dazeeba
Medium

Sharp Thorns
Medium

Bow
Small

Spikivine
Large

Custom Scribble
Large

Smokey Blue Winge
Large

Fado Cuping
Large

Golden Winged
Extra Large

Fitinway
Extra Large

FIRE!
Extra Large

One Twig
Medium

Swirly Freeform Tribal Shaded
Medium

Folijig
Medium

Ribboning
Medium

Longvine Lowerback Flower
Extra Large

Borderb
Medium

English Ivy
Extra Large

Rainbow Ivy
Large

Furmavines I
Large

Dry Scaly Skin
Large

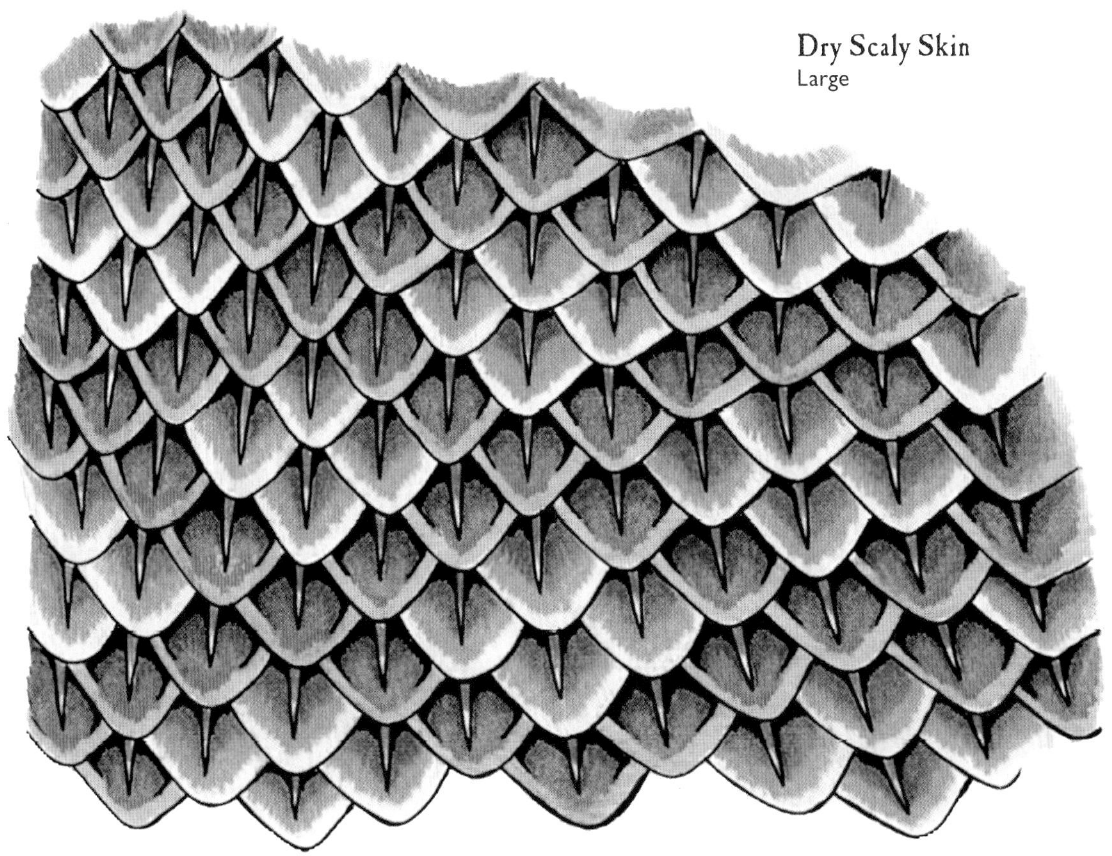

IMARO Tiger
Large

Devils & Demons

Jewel Devil
Extra Large

Evil Roping
Medium

Moon Sillhouette
Medium

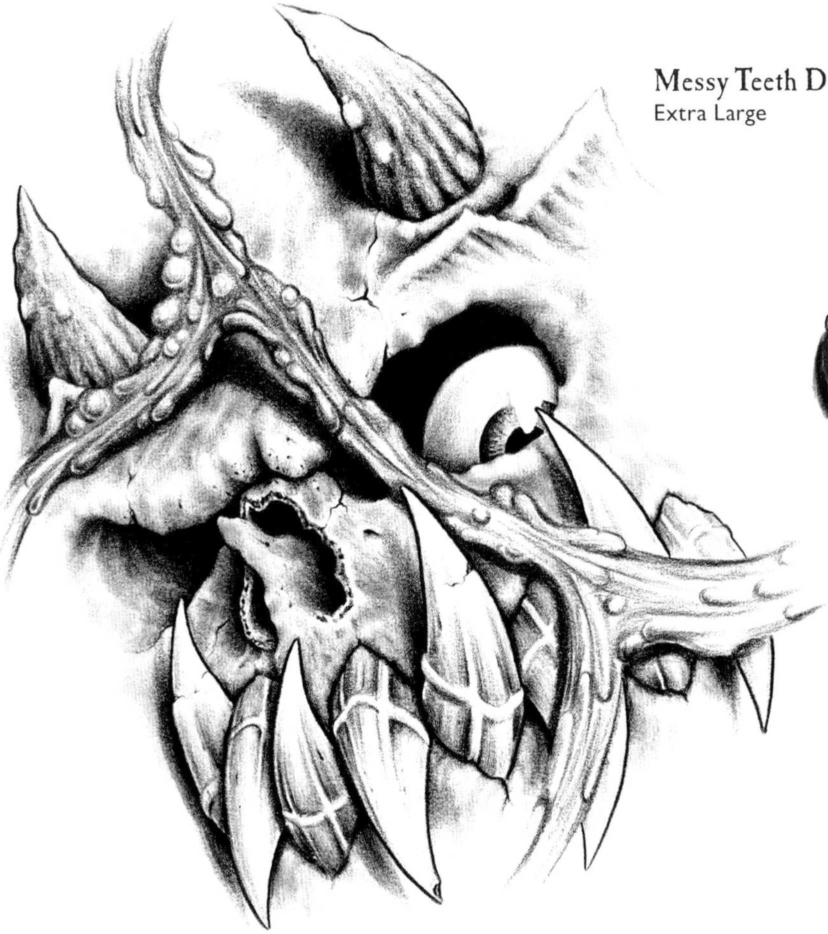

Messy Teeth Demon
Extra Large

Screaming Dripping Demon
Large

Laughing Horned Demon Tribal Design
Large

Saczet
Large

Double Bladenskull
Extra Large

Pointed Curve of the Demon
Large

Demonic Tribal
Extra Large

Digging Through the Dirt
Large

Down in Georgia
Extra Large

Facemelt Torment
Large

Laugh Tribal
Extra Large

Cupid Arrow
Extra Large

Tilted Gaze
Extra Large

Built Demon
Extra Large

Dr. Greenhorn
Extra Large

Devil Man
Medium

Swing'n on the Trident Devil Stripper
Extra Large

Devil Woman II
Extra Large

Flip You
Medium

Last Cigarette
Medium

Forheavy
Medium

Goted
Large

Hmph
Medium

Smilencry Devils
Medium

Surly to Be Up
Extra Large

The Devil Wears Tribal
Extra Large

Chuud
Large

Pumping Through
Extra Large

Dragons

Perched Green Dragon
Extra Large

Eastern Black out Dragon Piece
Extra Large

St. George's Dragon
Extra Large

Evil Eye Dragon
Large

Eslent Dragon
Medium

Dragon Wrapping Skull
Extra Large

Majago
Medium

Steely Dragon
Extra Large

Skull Squatter
Extra Large

Quick Flight Change
Extra Large

Dragon Eye II
Medium

Scowling Avenger
Extra Large

Dragon Armor
Extra Large

Dragon Bust
Medium

Celtic Spiral Dragon
Medium

Dual Dragon Tribal
Extra Large

Little Wing
Extra Large

Snake Dragon
Large

Dragon Claw Tear
Medium

Dragotrib
Extra Large

Dragona
Extra Large

Burnished Dragon
Extra Large

Twist Tight Dragon
Large

Kanji Dragon Splash
Large

Shaded Dragon Piece
Extra Large

Wteca Dragon
Extra Large

Honor Tribal Dragon
Medium

Serpantmania
Large

Against the Flame
Extra Large

Arkaball Dragon
Extra Large

Neck 2 Neck
Extra Large

Inyan Dragon
Extra Large

陰陽

Dragon
Biomechanical
Large

Asian Dragon Water
Large

Spinik
Extra Large

Balanced Dragons
Medium

Clicre
Extra Large

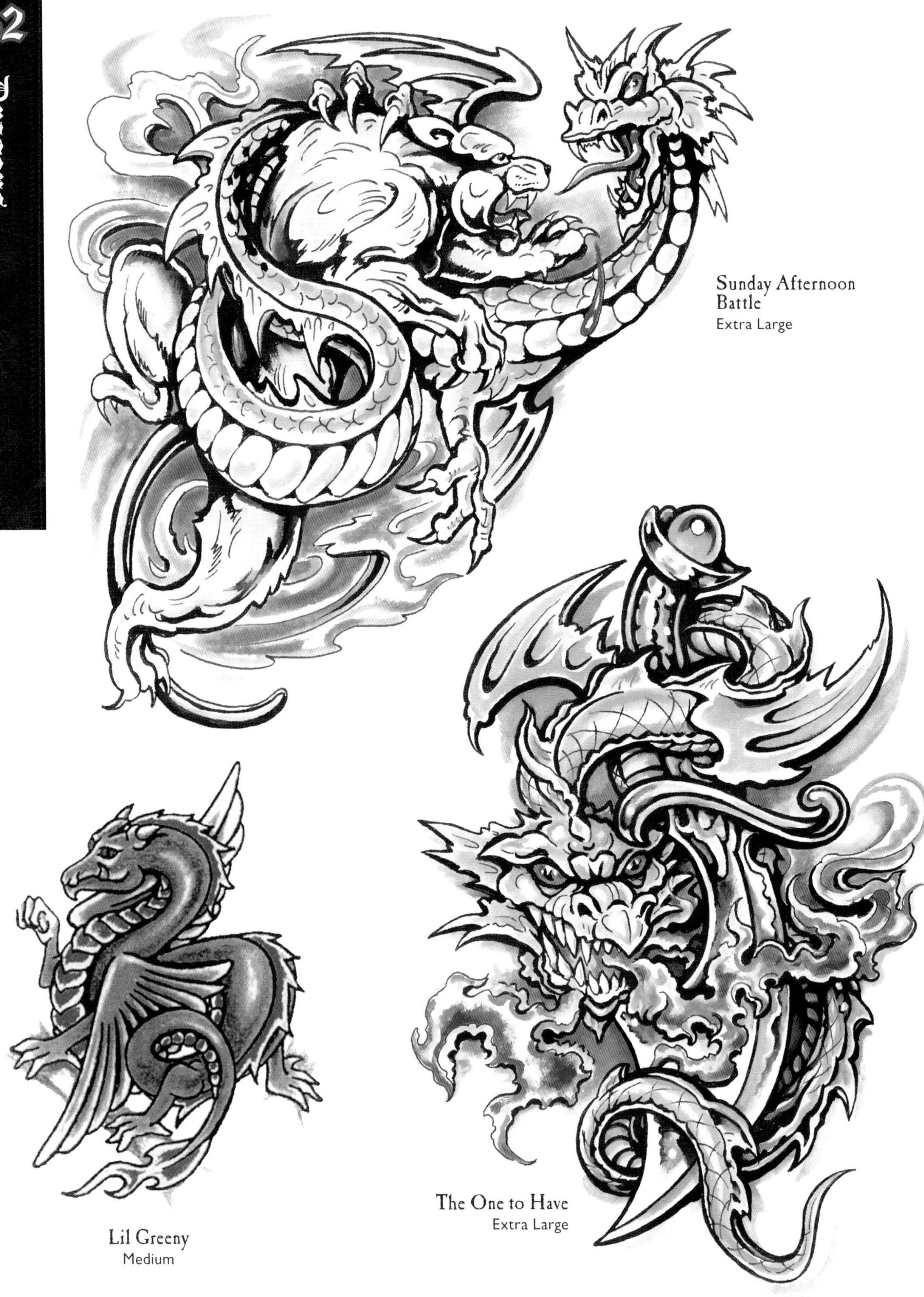

Sunday Afternoon Battle
Extra Large

Lil Greeny
Medium

The One to Have
Extra Large

Draceyetrib
Large

Hungry Dragon Flower
Extra Large

Magic Dragon
Extra Large

Over Head
Extra Large

Dragon Triballow
Extra Large

Gray and Purple Dragon
Extra Large

Upright Dragons Brigade
Large

Winged Rainbow Dragon
Extra Large

Dragon Tongues
Extra Large

Fire Dragon
Large

Earth & Sky

Catalog Cover 06
Extra Large

Fireball
Large

Feel Radiant
Large

Sun Spikes Burning
Medium

Smiling Khokhloma Sun
Large

Mathematical Sun
Medium

Sunendar
Medium

Way too Hot
Large

Solar Flare
Extra Large
Flicker Dance
Extra Large
Shield Sun
Medium
Tribal Leaf Star
Medium

Twisted Snake Sun
Medium

Hot Summer Sun
Large

Tribal Sunrise
Small

Ocean Sunset
Medium

Twisted Pinky Life Tree
Medium

Sharp Tree
Extra Large

Tribal Mushroom in the Sun
Medium

Juicy Apple Khokhloma
Large

ThpThpThp
Large

Opposing Elements
Large

Irritated Skull Sun
Medium

Quartered Firey Sun
Medium

Three Burning Stones
Extra Large

Nautical Sun
Medium

New Sun
Extra Large

Sunentribfront
Large

SPF 3
Large

Snowflake Tribal
Extra Large

Blueflakes
Medium

Wave Curl
Medium

Blue Tribal to the Sun
Extra Large

Flakers
Medium

Water Eternity
Medium

Waterball
Large

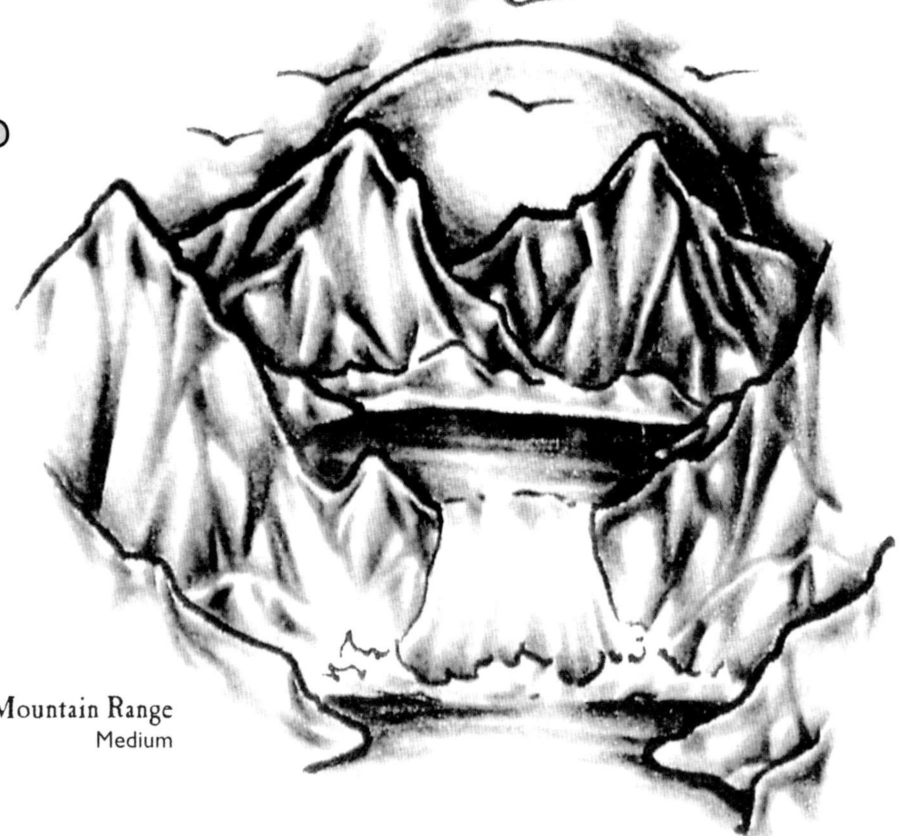

Mountain Range
Medium

Skitstar
Medium
White Hole Sun
Small
Suniswirl
Medium
Sun Design Piece
Large
Hollow Stars
Large

Snugglesun
Small

Shaded Sun
Medium

Sunter Knot
Medium

Moonensun Frilly
Extra Large

The Star and the Moon
Medium

Classic Sun
Medium

Happy Moon,
Happy Sun
Medium

Moonenviney
Large

Stars Moon Sun
Medium

Angry Orange Moon
Small

Stern Moon
Medium

Partly Cloudy Forecast
Large

Getting Comfortable
Medium

Ol Swirly
Medium
Curled Sun Moon and Stars
Large
Sun Warmth
Medium
Cripplesun
Large

Solar Eclipse II
Medium

Moon Ray God
Medium

Vibrasun and Moon
Large

Paradise Found
Medium

Orange and Turquoise Shooting Stars
Large

Eternal Star
Medium

Purple Falling Stars
Medium

Purple Shooting Star
Medium

Shooting Tribal Star
Small

Star Wave
Medium

Blue Yellow Star
Medium

Plastel Stardust
Medium

Star with Swirl
Medium

Black Design Star
Large

Earth
Small

Black out Swirly Tree
Extra Large

Twisted Tree
Large

Windy Moon Tree
Extra Large

Fairies & Fantasy

Sunset Pegasus
Medium

Pretty Pegasus
Extra Large

Promising Pegasus
Large

Pegasus Flight
Medium

Pegasus Overlay
Extra Large

Pegasus Moon
Large

The Old Ways
Medium

Pink Wizard
Large

Spiral Wizard
Large

Tribal Piece Unicorn
Medium

Spirit Troll
Medium

Cloud Opening
Extra Large

The Return
Large

Submersed Mermaid
Large

Mermaid Transport
Extra Large

Champagne Mermaid
Extra Large

Dark Mermaid
Extra Large

Powherful
Large

She's Got the Look
Extra Large

To the Surface
Extra Large

High Depth
Extra Large

One Eyed Wizard with Baby Dragon
Medium

Heroic
Extra Large

Fairy Sitting on Mario Mushroom
Medium

Green Fairy in the Pink Dress
Large

Sparkle Rising
Large

Cherry Fairy
Medium

Daisy Holding Fairy
Large

Lucky Little Fairy
Medium

Hottie
Large

Thimbleina
Medium

Plain Bored Pixie
Medium

Fantasies Modesty
Medium

Inked Fairy
Extra Large

Purple Demaid
Extra Large

Kneeling Fairy
Large

Naughty but Nice Fairy
Large

Fairy Petals
Medium

Beehive Fairy
Extra Large

Ballet Steppin Fairy
Medium

Dancing with Dragonfly
Extra Large

Uncomfortable Fairyensnake
Extra Large

Flittercub
Medium

You Can Call Me Ginger
Medium

Crypt Faerie
Large

To Shroom or Not to Shroom
Large

Humble Fairy
Medium

Fantasy Butterfly
Extra Large

Fight the Girl
Extra Large

Animated Warrior Princess
Extra Large

Doublefall
Medium

Who Me?
Medium

Fairy Queen
Extra Large

Water Moccasan Mermaid
Large

Wild Wizard
Medium

The Answer
Medium

Celestial Unicorn
Medium

One Does Not Simply Ride Bunnies into Mordor
Medium

Winged Night Stallion
Medium

Fragility
Large

Together
Large

Unicorn Overlay
Medium

Releasing the Drop
Medium

Lily Fairy
Medium

What
Medium

Hairless Fairy Sad
Medium

On the Breeze
Medium

Fairy Bear
Medium

Merlin Moon
Medium

Shroom Gnome
Large

Shroom over
Shoulder Fairy
Extra Large

Breaking Free
Large

Paraflower Fairy
Large

Princess Fairy Flower
Large

Surrounded by Friends
Medium

Sweet Pea
Medium

A Leaf a Part
Medium

Fairies Flower Swing
Large

Quick Rest
Medium

Breezy Dreams
Medium

Gambling & Vices

Die of 7 Fire
Medium

Lady Luck
Extra Large

Starry Dice
Medium

Lucky Rose Piece
Medium

Nothing but Luck
Medium

Texas Holdem
Extra Large

13 Dice
Large

13 Spade
Small

Smilin Spader
Medium

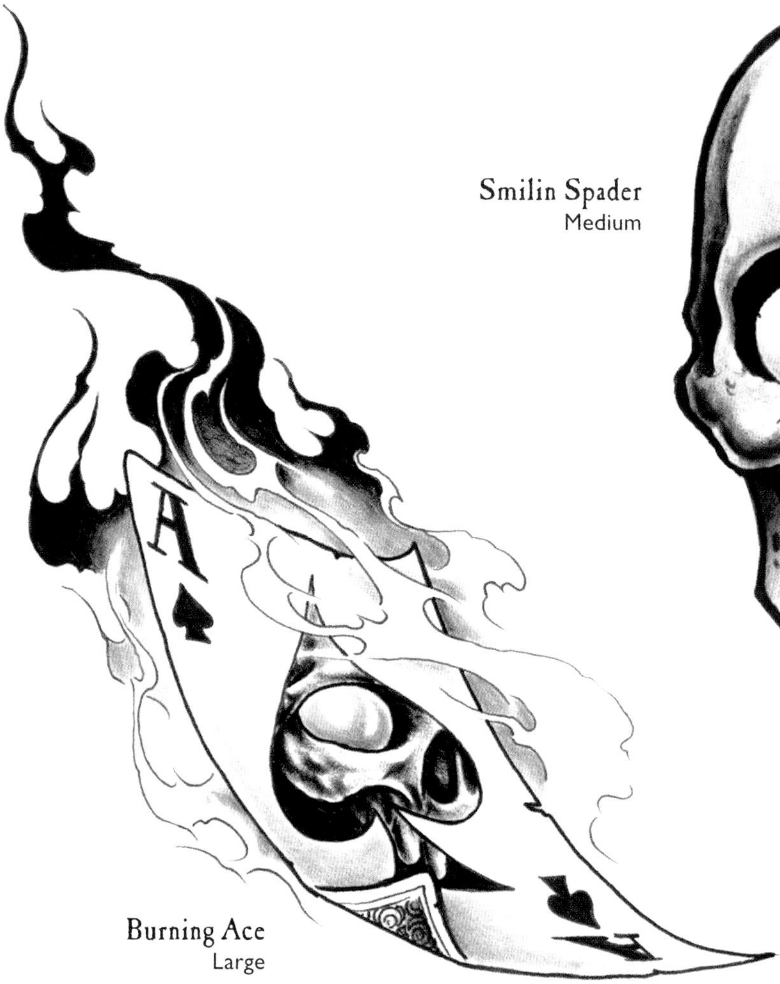

Burning Ace
Large

Blue Martini
Medium

Thorn 8 Ball Bomb with Cards & Dice
Medium

Ace of Roses
Medium

Make a Bet?
Extra Large

Full o'Luck
Medium

More the Merrier
Large

Aces High Man's Ruin
Extra Large

Two Cherries
Medium

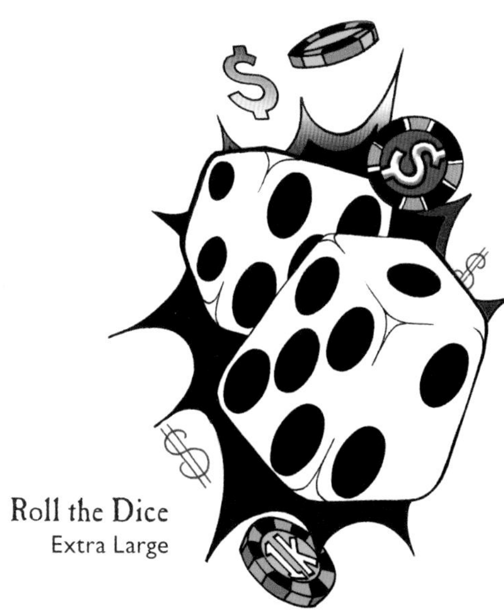

Roll the Dice
Extra Large

Cash Rose
Medium

Cherry Chest
Lady Luck
Large

Life's a Gamble
Large

Blue Drape Pinup
Small

Ultimate Hustla
Extra Large

Beauty in a Bathing Suit
Large

Life Aint Nothin' but...
Extra Large

Risky Bizness
Large

Golden Dollar Sign
Medium

Purdy Pinup
Large

Geek

Keys in Limbo
Extra Large

You Missed a Spot
Medium

Live Long and Prosper
Medium

Evil Forbidden Fruit
Medium

Mobius
Large

Section 3:

Art in Action:

What to Expect When You Get Tattooed . . . Now and Later

"You may lose your most valuable property through misfortune in various ways. You may lose your house, your wife, and other treasures. But of your moko, you cannot be deprived except by death. It will be your ornament and companion until your last day."

—Netana Whakaari of Waimana, a chief of the Ngai-Tama and Tuhoe tribe in the 1800s

Preparing for the Big Event

You wouldn't just step into the race on the day of a marathon without any training. Nor would you have any kind of medical procedure without taking proper precautions and making the necessary preparations. As with any significant event, getting tattooed is something you need to get ready for—both physically and emotionally. Here's what you need to do before your time in the chair.

Make Sure You're Healthy.

First and foremost, make sure you're healthy. Getting a tattoo is an invasive procedure—like surgery, though less extreme, of course. No matter how well you think you'll react to the tattoo machine, it can still be a physically exhausting experience for your body, and, for that reason, you should be free of any colds or illnesses. If you're under the weather, put it off. For women, menstruation could negatively affect the experience, as your body may be feeling more sensitive. If you are pregnant, now is not the time to get a tattoo, which your obstetrician will also tell you—while the risks are not great, they are still not worth taking at this time.

Make Sure the Area to Be Tattooed Is Pristine—no Rashes or Sunburn.

Not only should your physical health be in top shape, so should your skin. To get the best results, your skin should be in its natural state—that means no sunburn, rash, or other skin irregularities. Also, the area being tattooed should be unshaven, as well as free of lotion, glitter, or any cosmetic product. If there are any other healing wounds (including piercings) in that area, please wait for them to heal before getting your tattoo.

Make Sure You've Taken a Shower or Bath Beforehand.

This might sound funny when you first read it, but once you get a tattoo, bathing gets complicated. In fact, it's generally recommended that you not take a bath or go swimming for two weeks after you get your tattoo. You will be able to shower, but you will need to be extremely mindful of the newly tattooed area. It's also important to be clean so that your tattooist (who may have his or her face close to your body while tattooing) won't have to put up with unnecessary body odors from you.

Dress the Part—Wear Loose Clothes You're not Afraid to Get Stained.

The tattooing process can sometimes be messy, involving water, rubbing alcohol, or other sanitation liquids, plus ink, ointments, and blood. Don't dress to impress or wear anything you'll be sorry to stain, and don't wear clothing that will rub against your tattoo or tattooed area. Doing so may affect the healing of your tattoo right from the start, and tight clothing may be fairly uncomfortable to wear. If you're getting tattooed on your feet or ankles, wear the most comfortable shoes you have.

Avoid Alcohol and Aspirin, which Thin the Blood.

It's not a good idea to get a tattoo during or after a night of heavy drinking, no matter what you've seen in the movies. Both alcohol and common headache-remedy aspirin thin the blood, which means you will bleed more when getting tattooed—which means your tattooist will have a more difficult time actually seeing what he or she is doing. Not to mention that all the excessive wiping of blood could compromise the stencil or further irritate the area being tattooed. Other drugs could affect you in various ways, so speak to your physician about any medication you are on before getting a tattoo. Illegal drugs will also affect you, so it's best to avoid these as well.

Purchase Any Healing Equipment Required (Ointment, Fresh Bandages) Before You Go to the Tattooist.

You should always be prepared: Get what you need for healing before you even step into the tattoo studio, including ointments and bandages. Talk to your tattooist beforehand to see what brands he or she recommends for the healing process. Also, never share ointments or bandages, as it is possible to transmit diseases or infections in this way.

Eat Well Before You Go.

To optimize the tattoo experience, you will want to be as comfortable as possible, and that includes being well fed. It's not comfortable to sit in a chair for an extended period of time if you're hungry, and if you take a break to get a bite to eat, that time could be on the clock if your tattooist charges by the hour. There is also a greater chance of nausea if you get tattooed on an empty stomach.

Make Sure You're Properly Hydrated.

Make sure you're hydrated for the procedure, but not overly hydrated—bathroom breaks every fifteen minutes will only slow down the tattoo process. In addition, you might want to bring along some cookies and juice for after the procedure—this is the same nourishment you'd be given after donating blood.

Make Sure You've Confirmed the Cost and Payment Method, and Have Payment Ready and Available.

Find out beforehand what you will need to pay, including any extra fees before you have the work done. Even if you decide to pay with a credit card (if that's an option), it's best to tip your tattooist in cash, if possible.

If You Go with a Friend, Make Sure that Friend is a Patient One.

It's a great idea to bring someone along with you when you get a tattoo—a person to lend some moral support, a set of eyes to watch the action if you're getting tattooed on a body part you can't see without a mirror, or maybe even someone to photograph or video the action (you'll need the tattooist's permission for this, though). Just be sure you choose the friend wisely. Anyone who gets bored easily is not the right choice, and children are definitely not ideal companions in this situation. Make sure it's someone you feel comfortable with, and who's as excited about your tattoo as you are, and that will make all the difference.

The 5-Step Tattoo Process

There are typically five steps to the tattoo procedure: Stencil application, body positioning, line work, shading and coloring, and bandaging.

1. Stencil Application

After you've checked in with your tattooist, you should take some final moments to look over and confirm your tattoo artwork. Make sure that it's exactly what you want, and, if you have words appearing in your tattoo, now is the last time to double-check the spelling.

After your tattooist has put on rubber gloves and professionally prepared the skin to be tattooed (generally by cleaning and shaving), they'll apply your design stencil. Generally made using a thermo fax machine and carbon copy paper, the stencil (when applied to skin) leaves temporary lines as a "blueprint" for the artwork.

You may be impatient for the real ink, but it's *very* important that you inspect the stencil mark now while it's still temporary. Make sure that it's perfectly positioned on your body and don't be afraid to ask your tattooist to reapply the stencil if it's not exactly where you want it. Most reputable artists will be just as concerned with placement as you are, and they'll wash it off and reapply it until you're both pleased with it.

2. Body Positioning

Once you've determined that you are happy with the stencil placement, you'll need to find as comfortable a position as possible for both you and your tattooist to stay in during the actual tattooing process. Depending on your design, the process may last anywhere from a few minutes to several hours, so positioning is a surprisingly important part of the procedure. Longer sessions will likely include breaks (you'll want and need them), but having to shift positions too often will inconvenience both you and your tattooist.

You need to be comfortable, but so does your tattooist. The studio will most likely have a variety of chairs (similar to those in salons or barber shops), stools, and fold-out and cushioned tables, as well as a host of other props that can be positioned to suit both of you. You may also need to remove or pull aside some of your clothing to keep it out of the way. Your tattooist might put paper surgery towels around the area and either tape or tuck them into surrounding clothing to keep them in place and make an effort to keep your clothes clean in the process.

3. Line Work

The first part of your tattoo process is referred to as "line work." This is generally a black outline of the tattoo design, which includes any solid lines that will exist in the finished tattoo. As your tattooist creates these lines by tracing the stencil, the tattoo machine will vibrate and buzz as they operate it with a foot pedal, and they'll stop intermittently to refill the needles with ink. As they work through your design, you'll see that they are constantly wiping the needle and your skin to remove excess ink and fluids. Your design stencil will be wiped away in this process as well.

Some people describe line work as feeling like you're being cut or scratched, and the needles of the tattoo machine may seem like they're moving fairly slowly over your skin. The area being tattooed could also begin to feel hot or numb, and, as your body processes the trauma it's receiving, you might also feel overheated or cold. It's important to keep your breathing slow and consistent and to tell your tattooist if you begin feeling either sick or faint.

4. Shading and Coloring

After the line work is completed, shading and coloring will begin. Similar to line work, in this stage the tattooist will continue to replenish their ink and wipe off any excess fluids as they work.

Shading can feel significantly different from line work, with your tattooist moving the tattoo needles in little circles or other small movements, unlike the slow, more constant strokes associated with the tattoo outline. Moving in a concentrated area in this way may feel abrasive, like a steel-wool pad scrubbing a spot off a dish. As before, you should always focus on steadying your breath and trying to relax.

5. Bandaging

Once the tattoo is completed—and everyone breathes a sigh of relief—your tattooist will wipe down your tattoo with a light solution to remove excess ink and fluids. After you both examine the work, the tattooist will often apply a bandage to protect the tattoo and help prevent infection. Your tattoo is technically an open wound, and it's very important to carefully follow any healing instructions given by your tattooist, keeping it bandaged, cleaned, and treated as he or she instructs.

Caring for Your New Tattoo

Just as your doctor would give you aftercare instructions when you have a medical procedure, so will your tattooist after you get your new tattoo. While you might be excited in the moment after getting your ink, these aftercare instructions are extremely important, as they help you avoid some of the complications that can sometimes occur.

Your tattoo artist will probably have specific directions that you should definitely follow. They may tell you verbally, but they should also hand you a list of preprinted instructions. Below are the main measures you can take in caring for your new tattoo.

1. Keep Your Tattoo Covered.

Each tattooist has slightly different aftercare instructions. While some don't cover newly inked tattoos with a bandage, most will. Tattooists vary on their advice as to how long you should keep the tattoo covered. You've presumably chosen a tattooist because you trust their skill and judgment, so just make sure you listen carefully to his or her instructions for aftercare. You should always, however, keep your tattoo out of direct sunlight (particularly while it's still healing).

2. Remove the Bandage in Water.

You absolutely do not want to take a bath or otherwise submerge your new tattoo, but we do recommend taking off the bandage under a warm shower stream. This will facilitate removal of dead skin and ointment and also ensure that you'll be in a clean place when your tattoo gets exposed to the world! However, you don't want to take a "hot" shower or use a washcloth on the tattooed area. Clean your tattoo lightly and thoroughly with your fingertips and gentle soap, such as glycerin soap. Work up a good lather to remove all debris. You may have to wash several times to ensure all the ointment comes off.

3. Lightly Pat or Air-Dry.

Don't rub your tattoo dry. You need to either let it air-dry on its own or gently pat it dry with a clean towel or, better yet, clean paper towels. You don't want to expose your tattoo to any unnecessary friction (which will likely feel uncomfortable anyway), and that includes not wearing clothing that will constrict the area for several days.

4. Don't Let it Dry out.

With clean hands, be sure to apply moisturizing lotion to your tattoo frequently—at least three to five times per day for at least the first ten days. Many tattooists recommend a mild and sensitive moisturizer, but you should check in with your tattooist to see what brand he or she recommends. *Do not* use petroleum jelly. *Do not* use rubbing alcohol or peroxide. *Do not* use lotion that has aloe vera or vitamin E in it. *Do not* let any moisturizer "pool" on the tattooed area—all lotion applied should be absorbed.

5. Let Skin Shed Naturally.

As your tattoo heals, it will likely become itchy, even if you moisturize it regularly. In the first two to seven days, it will behave in a similar way to a sunburn. The tattoo will peel or shed a layer of skin on its own—and should not have any help from you. So whatever you do, don't rub, scratch, or pick at your tattoo. Let the skin fall off naturally, including in the shower. No need to do extra scrubbing of your tattooed area when the shower softens your skin. Just like you did immediately after getting your tattoo, clean the inked area with a very light touch.

6. Take Extra Precautions for at Least Two Weeks.

You need to treat your tattooed area with special care for at least two weeks after the procedure. This means taking extra care in the shower, being selective about the clothes you wear, not scratching or picking at it, and applying lotion regularly. Also, you should *not* do anything that will soak the tattoo—no swimming, baths, hot tubs, or saunas for at least two weeks.

You also should *not* expose your tattoo to direct sunlight during this time frame. If you have to be out in the sun, keep your tattoo covered. This is good practice anyway, because sunlight can cause the ink to fade over time. You should regularly keep the tattoo out of direct sunlight or apply sunblock to it any time it will be exposed.

If you have any questions or concerns, be sure to contact your tattooist, who can make recommendations for you. If your tattoo becomes inflamed or infected, consult your doctor immediately.

Did You Know?

- 17 percent of those who have a tattoo have considered having it removed.
- 5 percent of those with a tattoo have had it covered with a different tattoo design.

Source: TattooFinder.com Poll, June 2004

Falling out of Love . . . with Your Tattoo

Just as a romance can fade, so too can passion for your tattoo. Sometimes, even after putting an immense amount of thought and research into the process of getting your tattoo, the magic you once felt goes away.

While this doesn't happen with everyone, if it happens to you, don't worry. There are things you can do to make your tattoo less visible—and even invisible. When your tattoo overstays its welcome on your body, you can rescue the original design, cover it up with another tattoo, or have it removed altogether. And we'll tell you how to do all three correctly.

Rescue it

Many tattooists strongly advocate "tattoo rescue" (rework and refresher jobs) instead of a complete cover-up. They see a fun challenge in beautifying and reworking a piece that was done haphazardly. Situations exist in which people might like the tattoo they have if it had been done correctly. Some tattooists specialize in these rescue efforts. They can clean up an existing tattoo so you can be thrilled about your ink instead of grimacing at it.

Before defaulting to tattoo removal, first consult a number of tattooists who specialize in cover-ups and rescue. Some people believe that their only option is to have the tattoo removed because a tattooist who did not specialize in this area told them it was impossible to do anything else with it. It never hurts to get a second professional opinion.

Cover it

One of the biggest trends in tattoo fixes is the cover-up. If your ex's name on your bicep is a painful reminder or if you simply aren't happy with your original ink, the cover-up might be an option for you.

If done properly, a cover-up should look like a brand-new tattoo. Essentially, it works with the lines of your original tattoo to create a whole new design. However, people who have very dark tattoos and/or scarring on their original work might have a little more difficulty in achieving a successful cover-up. Dark tattoos frequently "bleed through," and new ink won't remove raised scar tissue. So if you're not working with a talented tattooist who is experienced with this specialized skill, your beautiful new cover-up could end up looking more like a big mess-up.

If you've decided to go ahead with investing money and time in camouflaging your ink, go back to the beginning of the process and ask yourself the same questions (see pages 14–19). Except this time, ask the questions about *covering* your ink. And ask yourself these very important questions as well: Are you unhappy with your tattoo just for now—or forever? Can you visualize a time in your life, sometime in the future, when you might possibly fall back in love with your ink? Because even if there's a remote chance of you mourning that tattoo once it's gone, it's gone for good.

It's also important to understand that you will be limited in your design choices when looking for new artwork to cover your old tattoo. We'll provide you with more guidance on this shortly.

1. Cost

Don't plan on your tattoo cover-up costing the same amount as your original tattoo, even if you end up using the same tattooist. There is generally a lot more time and effort spent in deciding what the new cover-up tattoo will be, since you will be limited as to what kind of designs will work to truly camouflage the original. Then there is the actual time it takes to ink the new design. Don't forget, the time your tattooist spends with you on both of these factor heavily into the cost of your cover-up. And since the cover-up is generally larger than your original, and your tattooist will be working within the constraints of your old tattoo, that's most likely more time in the chair. Finally, creating great cover-ups requires specialized skills from a tattooist, and therefore the rates charged overall will probably be higher. When all is said and done, a cover-up tattoo could end up being more expensive than the original.

2. Time

The time spent covering up a tattoo isn't just time spent in the actual inking process. Frequently, it's the process of determining what will work as the new and tattoo that will be just as labor intensive (or even more so). When you got the original tattoo, your tattooist was working with a clean slate, so whatever you wanted was possible (within the constraints of the craft). For a cover-up, the goal is to seamlessly "blend" a new design with the old, and figuring out just how that will work takes time.

3. Size

If the reason you want to cover your tattoo is that it makes you feel self-conscious when others see it, or if you're tired of looking at it, make sure you really want to increase the area of inked skin. As we mentioned earlier, a tattoo created to cover your existing tattoo will probably be bigger than the original. This means it will most likely be more obvious and more conspicuous than your existing tattoo. On the other hand, if you love the end result of your new cover-up, perhaps bigger is okay after all.

4. Blending

Tattooists without much cover-up experience might insist that very dark colors, particularly black, are the only ways to cover up your original tattoo. This is why you frequently see tribal designs used in cover-ups (because black is believed to cover up all other colors). This is not always true, however. The term "cover-up" can actually be misleading, because the process actually involves "blending" new ink into the old ink. The key is that if you try to blend a light color to "cover" an existing darker color, the darker color will eventually come through. One key to a good cover-up is, as much as possible, to match the black line work of the new design with the black line work of the old design. If this can be achieved, then the darkest color black will only need to blend with more black. Additionally, if there is scarring (raised skin surfaces) in the line work of your old tattoo, at least it will match up with the line work in your new tattoo.

5. Special Skill

Covering one tattoo with another is a specialized skill, so it's important you find a tattooist with a lot of experience in this kind of work. You will want to interview tattooists, and you definitely want to see examples of their work in this area. Additionally, friends may be able to offer recommendations, but still make sure that you meet with the tattooist prior to any work carried out.

What Will Work?

Chances are, your dream tattoo won't be possible with a cover-up. More likely, you'll have to go for a compromise and choose something you can live with—but hopefully this will also be something you genuinely like. The most frequent question people have when considering a cover-up is: "What design will work to cover this tattoo?"

The answer depends, in large part, on your current tattoo, as well as the skills of your tattooist. Many tattooists will suggest that you find five designs that you like as a starting place. You then find five designs, bring them to your tattooist, and most likely he or she will tell you why those won't work, and then you go out and find five more (and so on).

But from what you have read here, you should now understand *why* some types of designs work better for cover-ups than others. A portrait tattoo, for example, will generally not work as a cover-up, because portraits have too few hard black lines, which are essential to "match up" the lines in your existing tattoo. Any designs that are soft in nature, with large areas of fill or open skin areas (no ink), will not work well for cover-ups. Designs that are "nonorganic" also will not work well (think anything linear and rigid).

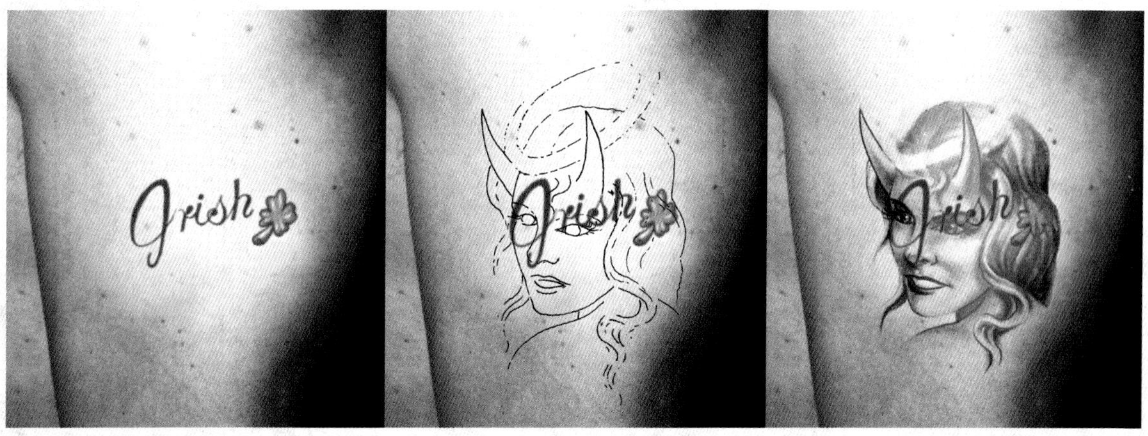

An example of an unsuccessful cover-up: this portrait tattoo has too few hard black lines to match up with the original tattoo.

Generally designs that *do* work well for cover-ups are "organic" in nature. Foliage, for example, can often work well. In nature, vines, flowers, trees, leaves, etc. all twist and wind and bend, thus being flexible enough to match the new line work with the old. Fire and water are also very organic in nature (they can be bent and molded naturally to match the existing line work). Other types of tattoo designs commonly used in cover-ups are those with lots of visual texture, such as dragons (scales texture), birds (feather texture), and tigers (stripes texture). Scales, feathers, and jaggedy tiger stripes can all be adjusted to match line work in an existing tattoo.

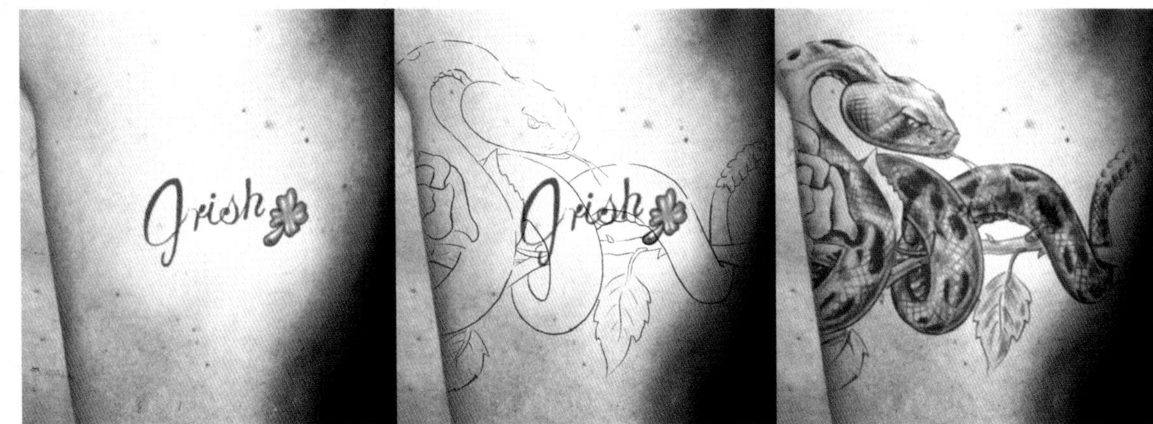

An example of a successful cover-up: The hard black lines and texture of the snake match up with the original tattoo

Tribal designs are often used in cover-ups, because you are covering everything with black. But, as noted on page 308, especially if the original tattoo was done poorly and there is some scarring/raised skin, the texture of the original tattoo will still come through. And if you simply cover an old tattoo with wide swaths of tribal, you generally end up with a thick and heavy overall design. However, tribal can be used well. Perhaps for those few stray lines in the old design that stick out here and there, tribal accents can be used and incorporated into the design.

So now when your tattooist suggests for your cover-up that you go out and find five tattoo designs you like, you have some ideas about *what* to look for and *why* you are looking for it!

Remove it

If covering your tattoo is not an option, and you definitely don't want your ink to be a part of your life anymore, you may want to look into having the tattoo removed altogether. However, tattoo removal is not an easy process, especially considering the art of tattooing is supposed to be permanent. Once tattoos get under your skin, they're pretty stubborn about wanting to stay there. For that reason, tattoo removal can be painful, time-consuming, costly, and potentially ineffective. In other words, there is no guarantee that the mark will disappear 100 percent, no matter which removal process you use.

In the next section, we'll examine the most common and effective tattoo-removal methods. If you are serious about having your tattoo removed, please read this section carefully. You might discover after reading this information that removal isn't worth the expense (including financial, emotional, and time).

Because tattoos fade over time, older tattoos are sometimes easier to remove than sparkly new ones. The size of a tattoo may also factor in to how easily it can be removed. A tattoo does not get removed with the same painstaking detail in which it was applied. So the smaller the tattoo, generally the easier it is to remove, as there's less area to cover. It's also crucial to consider the skill level of the tattooist who did the ink. A more experienced, skilled tattooist can get the ink into only one layer of the skin, while a less-skilled practitioner will get it into several. When the ink is all in the same place, it's easier to remove.

Methods of Removal

Note: The information provided in this section is for general information only. It is not intended in any way to replace medical advice, be interpreted or used as a medical treatment program, or be used to diagnose or cure any disease or medical condition. If you're considering getting a tattoo removed, we recommend that you first discuss this process with your doctor.

There are several common ways that professionals can remove a tattoo: Laser removal, dermabrasion and excision, cryosurgery, Variot tattoo removal, trichloroacetic acid (TCA), and tattoo-removal creams.

Laser Removal

Laser removal is popular because it is thought of as the most effective method—about 95 percent effective, in fact. The only drawback? Laser removal can be very pricey. Imagine that a standard treatment costs around $400 and that it takes about eight to ten sessions to remove a tattoo, and you can see how it expensive it can be—upward of $3,000!

How does it work? Different lasers are used to remove different colors of ink, though some can remove more than one color. This means that, depending on the design of your tattoo, your laser surgeon may need to use three different types of lasers. Make sure you confirm with your doctor that he or she has *all* of the lasers needed to remove your particular tattoo.

Before treatment, your doctor may recommend acetaminophen for minor aches and pains—not aspirin, which thins the blood and could promote bleeding. Ibuprofen or other anti-inflammatories aren't recommended, either, as they could promote bruising.

Tattoos are permanent because the ink particles are too big for the body to remove. During laser tattoo removal, light is aimed at tattooed areas, which heats up the ink and breaks up the pigment. The broken-down ink is absorbed by the body and eventually flushed out.

The laser procedure is not instantaneous. It will take place over a period of time: approximately eight to ten sessions with three-week intervals between sessions. Estimate that it's going to take a good six months before you're tattoo-free.

Laser tattoo removal can have drawbacks, including severe pain if there's no anesthesia involved, as well as scarring. It's best to have a surgeon with lots of experience do the work. Look for practices that specialize in laser tattoo removal, and for doctors who perform the service themselves. Side effects may include hyperpigmentation (in which the skin becomes darker) or hypopigmentation (in which the skin becomes lighter), infection, or permanent scarring.

Dermabrasion and Excision

Dermabrasion is just what it sounds like: "derm" being skin, and "abrasion" meaning, literally, a sanding of the top layers of skin with an abrasive tool. Excision, on the other hand, is tattoo removal, which involves removing the affected area of skin, literally cutting it away from the body. As you can imagine, neither one of these options is incredibly popular, but they used to be the main "go-to" methods before laser technology came along.

Like laser, these processes can be expensive. There's also a high effectiveness rate of 95 percent, and they can be very painful without numbing the area. There's also a chance of extreme scarring, with residual ink still left behind in the dermabrasion process. For excision, however, there's no chance any part of the tattoo will be left behind, as it gets cut out with the skin.

Cryosurgery

Typically used to remove warts, moles, skin tags, skin cancers, and other skin afflictions, cryosurgery uses the destructive force of freezing temperatures to remove tattoos as well. When cells are frozen, ice crystals will form that tear them apart. So when tattooed skin is frozen in this way, the ink particles break apart. Freezing agents include liquid nitrogen, carbon dioxide, argon, and even propane. While cryosurgery is effective for many tattoos and generally more affordable than laser treatments, laser still has a higher success rate.

Variot Tattoo Removal

With an effectiveness rate of approximately 90 percent, Variot tattoo removal, named after the French physician who invented the process in the 1800s, is also not as painful as some of the other treatments and is usually less expensive. Generally performed with a topical numbing cream, Variot is essentially a process where you coat an existing tattoo with a solution of tannic acid, glycerin, and distilled water. This solution under the skin produces a thick scab that, when it heals and falls off, will take the tattoo (or at least most of the tattoo) with it.

This was a popular method of tattoo removal for years, despite the considerable amount of scarring as a result. The procedure was tweaked and improved over the years, and the *Journal of the American Medical Association* considered it the best way to remove tattoos in the 1920s. With the advent of laser technology, and when tannic acid was found to be a carcinogen decades later, this procedure was nearly forgotten. Then, in 2004, it was reintroduced to doctors by the *British Journal of Dermatology*, as the "Chemical Extraction Technique." The solution was improved, removing the tannic acid, and a new machine was created. Despite the improvements, however, Variot is still not as popular as other options, even though, when done properly, it can be cheaper and (potentially) gentler on the skin than laser removal.

Trichloroacetic Acid (TCA)

Acid in the face seems a drastic price to pay for beauty, yet many cosmetic procedures actually involve applying acid to the skin for removing fine lines, wrinkles, and acne scars—essentially a facial peel. On the body, this method is used to remove fine stretch marks, brown spots, warts, and calluses on the hands or feet. Essentially how this works is that the acid burns the skin, and new skin is grown. In the process, the ink naturally breaks apart and migrates to the surface with the new skin growth. Applied to thc skin with a cotton swab, TCA is less painful and less expensive than other methods of tattoo removal, with a purported effectiveness rate of about 85 percent.

Tattoo-Removal Creams

Tattoo-removal creams seem like a good idea in theory, but there isn't any quantifiable evidence to prove that they actually work. In fact, they may actually do more harm than good. Some contain an ingredient called hydroquinone, an ingredient occasionally used in skin-bleaching creams, which have been banned in several countries, including the U.K., as it has been linked to causing cancer and Exogenous Ochronosis, a hyperpigmentation of the skin. Legislation is holding back a similar ban in the U.S.A., proposed by the FDA in 2006. If you're thinking of using a tattoo-removal cream, be sure hydroquinone isn't in it.

Be Warned!

There is no such thing as perfect, pain-free tattoo removal. Most tattoos are never 100 percent removed, and there is usually some skin discoloration. Patience and persistence are usually the most important ingredients in any tattoo-removal strategy. That being said, it is possible to get most of the tattoo removed to the point that it's no longer recognizable as a tattoo, and it may easily be covered with a little foundation—or a new tattoo.

Hearts & Flowers

Broken Ribbon Heart
Medium

Heart Mace
Medium

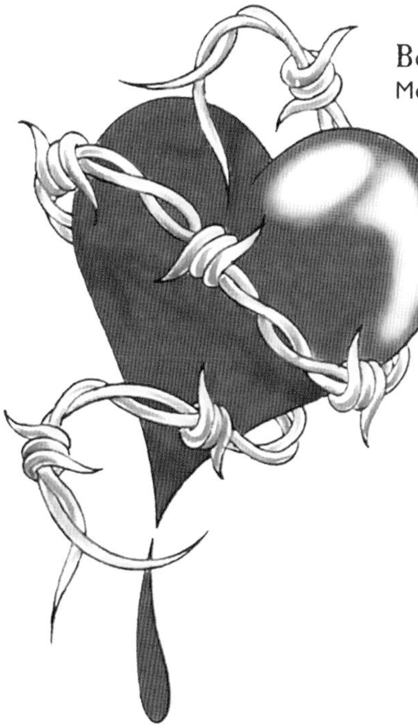

Bound by Love 02
Medium

Asteroid Heart
Medium

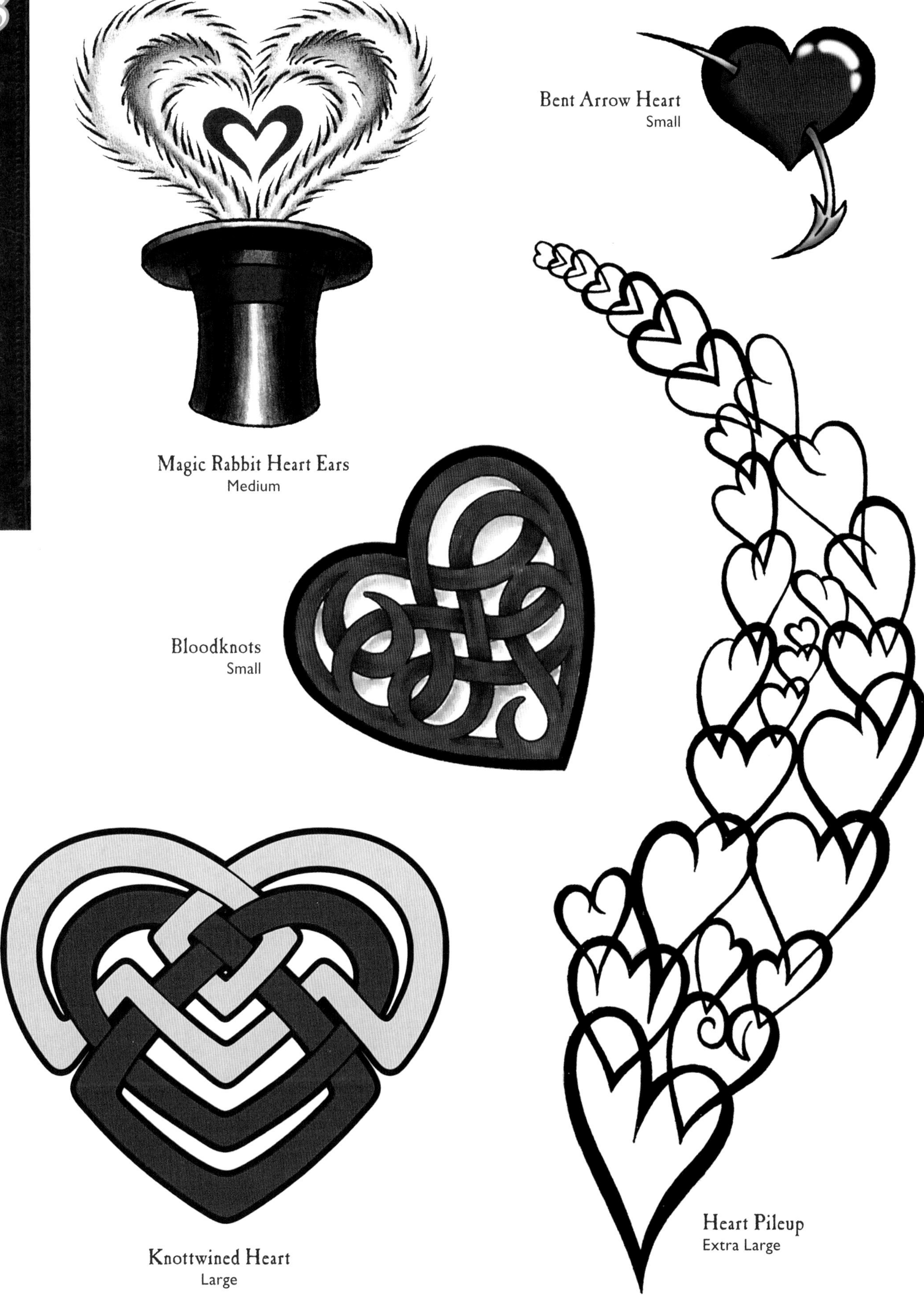

Bent Arrow Heart
Small

Magic Rabbit Heart Ears
Medium

Bloodknots
Small

Knottwined Heart
Large

Heart Pileup
Extra Large

Love Bubbles
Medium

Heart of Sun Fire
Medium

Sawblade Heart II
Medium

Heart Razing
Medium

Hearts Grow
on Vines
Medium

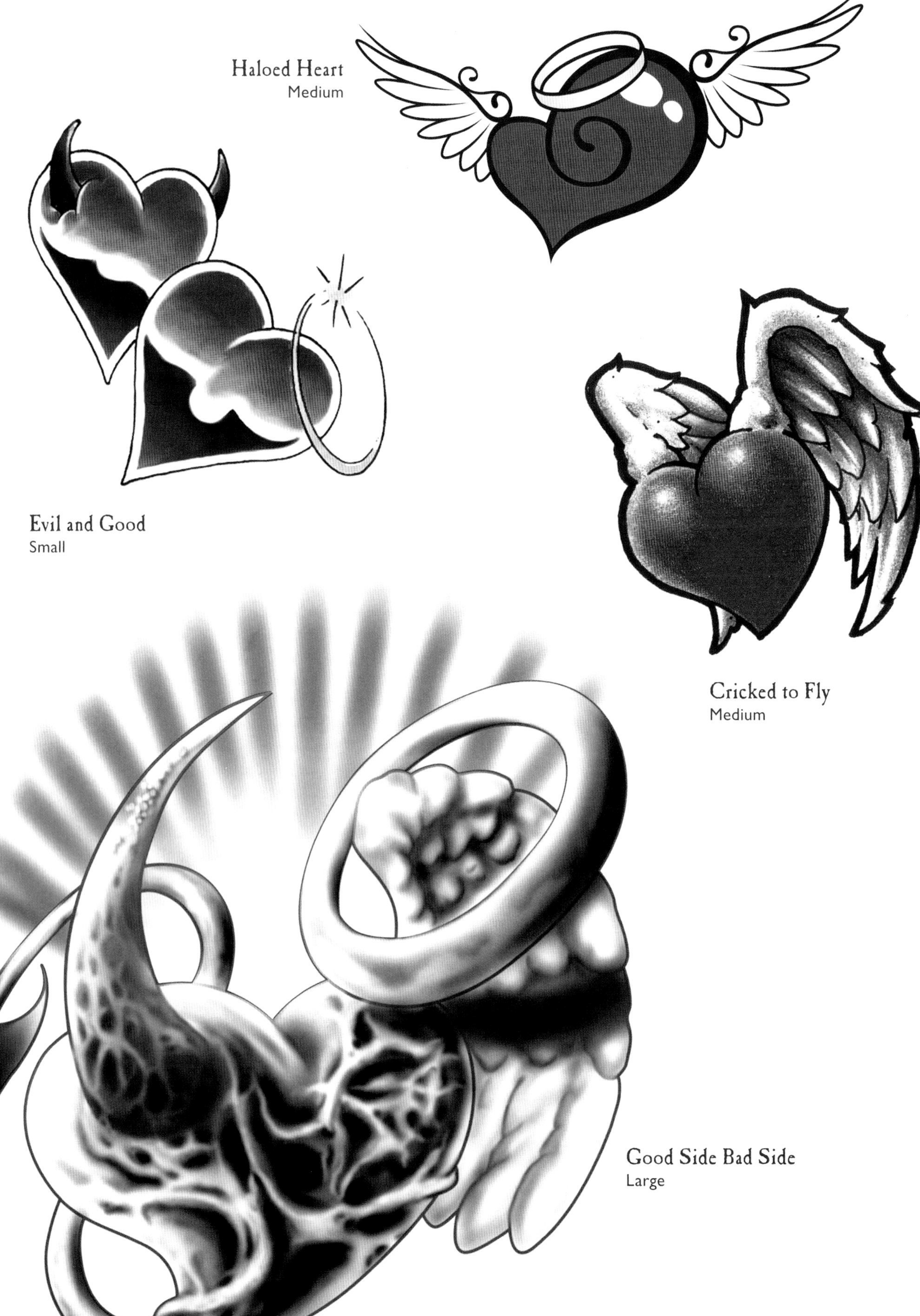

Haloed Heart
Medium

Evil and Good
Small

Cricked to Fly
Medium

Good Side Bad Side
Large

Pin Heart
Extra Large

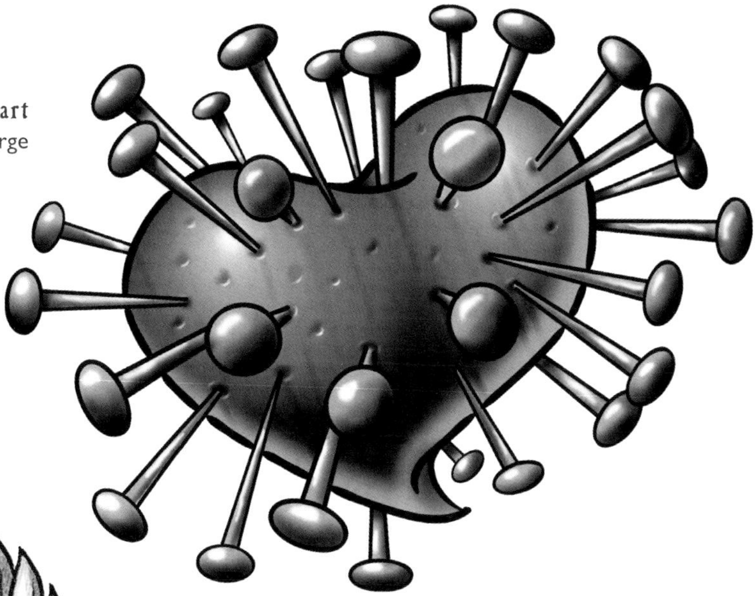

Cesar Heart
Medium

Pitchfork Stabbity
Medium

Swollen Heart of Tribal
Medium

Fancy Red Hearts with Black
Medium

Winged & Poked
Medium

Bleed Sacred Heart
Medium

Break These Chains of Love
Large

Odd Heart
Medium

Unique Orange
Tribal Heart
Extra Large

Black Brown Design
Heart
Medium

Golden Winged
Sacred Heart
Medium

Heart and Crosskeys
Medium

Five Hearts Stacked Vertically
Medium

Lavish Heart King with Rose
Extra Large

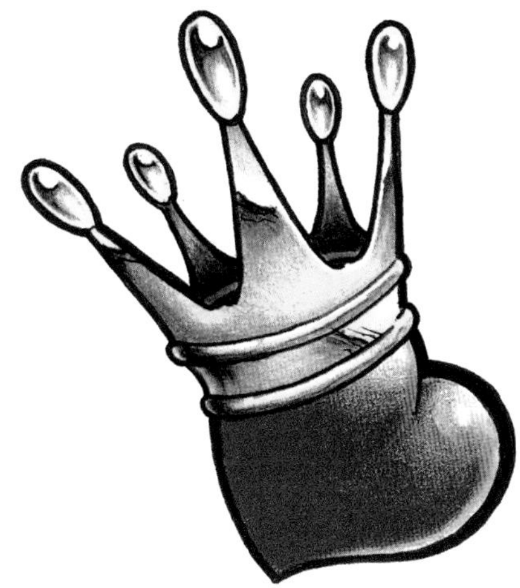

Dead King Heart
Medium

Crowned Heart
Medium

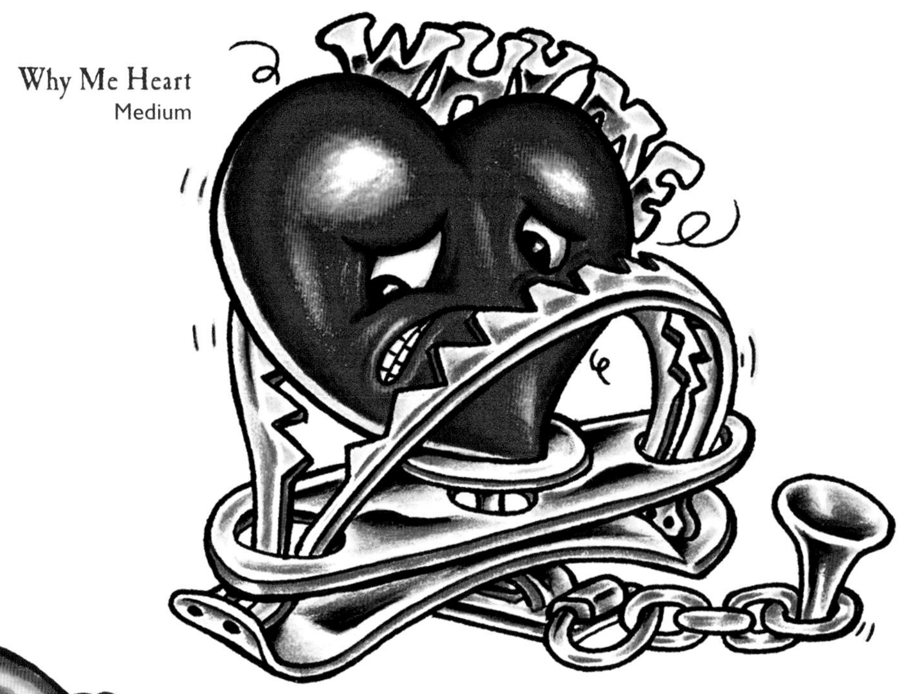

Why Me Heart
Medium

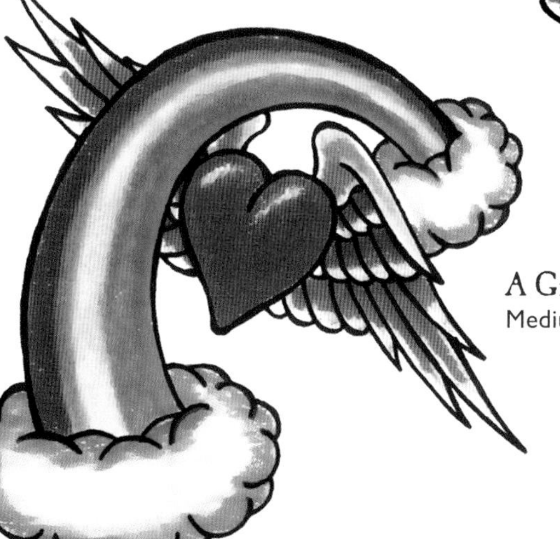

A Great Day
Medium

Heart Framed Rainbow
Small

Story Heart
Large

Leopard Heart
Medium

Tick Tock Heart
Medium

Rotted Heart with Knife and Rose
Large

Heart Curls Heart
Large

Hidden Heart Stack Tribal
Extra Large

Sacred Locked Heart
Large

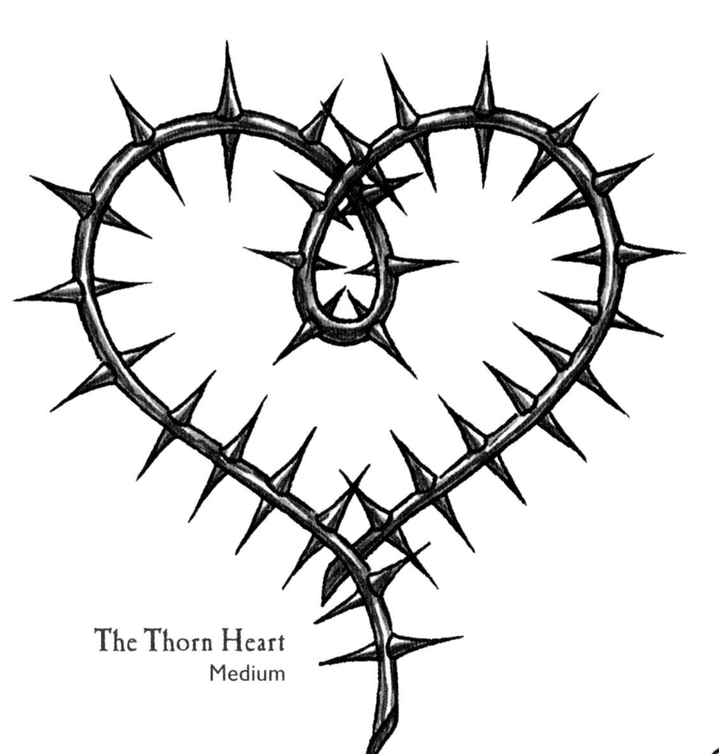

The Thorn Heart
Medium

Plump Heart Cherry
Medium

Red Heart
Black Design
Medium

Gunnin Heart
Medium

Grenadeheart
Medium

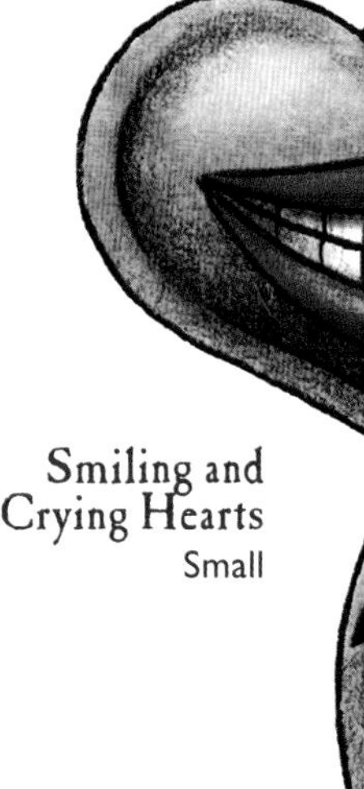

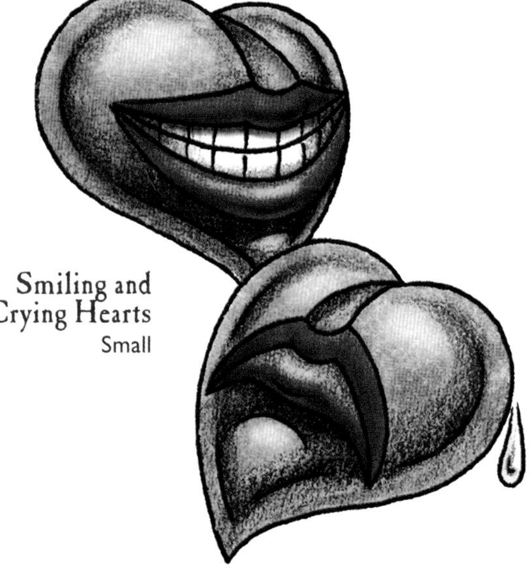

Smiling and Crying Hearts
Small

Heartcuffs
Medium

Heart Shrooms
Medium

Sacred Heart Faith
Large

Heart on a Ribbon
Large

Heart for Rent
Small

Heartbreaker Rose Explosion
Medium

XXX Sparrow Key Heart Lock
Large

Smiling Hidden Devil Heart
Extra Large

Phoenixfire Heart
Large

Key to Your Heart
Large

Heartenwing
Flowerpatch
Medium

Heartenwave
Sunset
Medium

Two Butterflies Purpleheart
Medium

Dusky Rose
Medium

Flying Thorny Heart
Medium

Thorned Around
Medium

Double Pink Rose Heart
Medium

Cast Rose
Medium

Rose of Death
Extra Large

Cursive Rose
Large

Black Stone Rose
Medium

Sharp Pleasantness
Extra Large

Webbed Rose
Medium

Three Sisters
Medium

Faded Rose
Extra Large

Lil Yellow Sunflower
Small

Purple Tentacle Flower
Medium

Sunflower Face
Medium

Real Dahlia
Extra Large

Sunflower String
Large

Garden on
Large

Asian Floating Flowers
Extra Large

Open Blue Lily
Large

Colorful Pollenation
Extra Large

Vivid Red Petals
Medium

Purple Drowning Flower
Medium

Multi Colored Chrysanthemums
Extra Large

Flower and Snake
Large

Gallawanna
Large

Loletori
Medium

Tawila
Medium

Doublefleur
Large

Fleure
Large

Night Flowers
Extra Large

Multivine
Extra Large

Eater Lilly
Medium

Swirling Ivy
Large

Dangling Buds
Extra Large

Redenpurple Flowers
Large

Pedalblue
Extra Small

Pink Heartleaf
Medium

Arrowhead Vine
Extra Large

Alien Cup
Medium

Spiral Petals
Medium

Hot Bud
Medium

Bublinpink
Medium

Bright Lotus
Large

Fly on Heart
Medium

Purple Orchid Flower
Medium

Iris with Black Leaves
Medium

Squating Golden Flower
Medium

Center Star Flower Khokhloma
Large

Three Flora with Vines
Extra Large

Twoand Nubuds
Large

Yellow Rose & Heart
Medium

Friendship Roses Two
Medium

Bleeding Black Rose
Medium

Roses are Red & Blue
Large

Double Blue
Medium

Wearing the Heart on the Vine
Medium

Simply Tribal Rose
Small

Three Open
Extra Large

Bee Enflowers
Extra Large

Oranilla Trio
Large

Rose Dew
Large

Irish &
Celtic

Iriclov02
Medium

Irish Lettering II
Medium

Wild Irish Rose
Banner
Medium

Claddagh Luck
Medium

Green Four Leaf
Clover Black Design
Medium

Chaste Charm
Large

Blue Horseshoe
Medium

Eire Banners
Medium

Bloody Irish
Large

Celtic Knot Pot Leaf
Medium

Green Celtic Knot in a Knot
Medium

Green Tribal Celtic
Medium

Pipe Leprachaun
Medium

Irish Collage
Medium

Tribal Clover in Tribal Heart
Medium

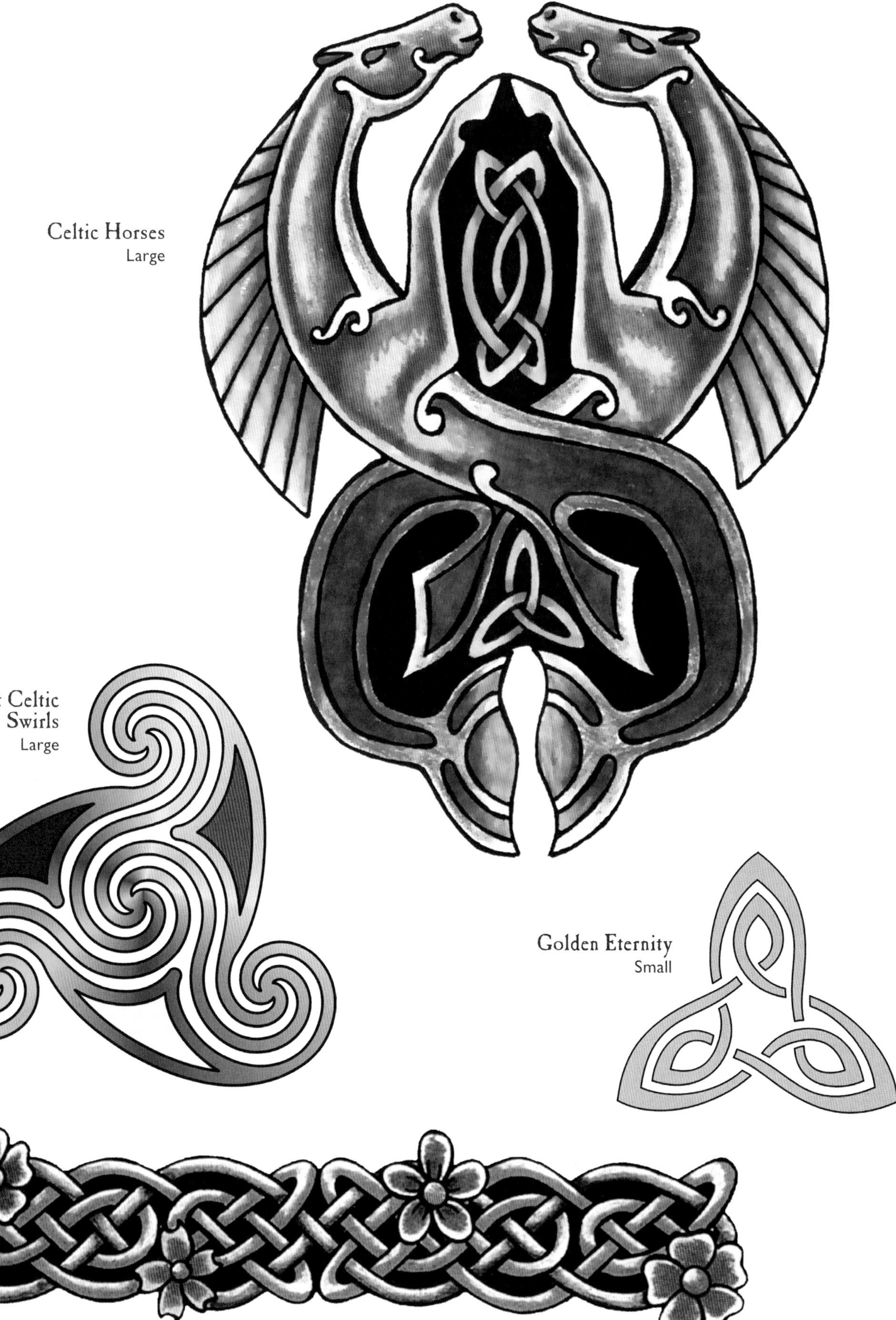

Celtic Horses
Large

Tight Celtic Swirls
Large

Golden Eternity
Small

Floral Green
Large

Celtic Clover II
Medium

Dark Celtic Shamrock
Small

Green and Purple
Celtic Swirl
Large

Celtic Eternity
Medium

Red Celtic Horse
Large

Silver Celtic Cross
Extra Large

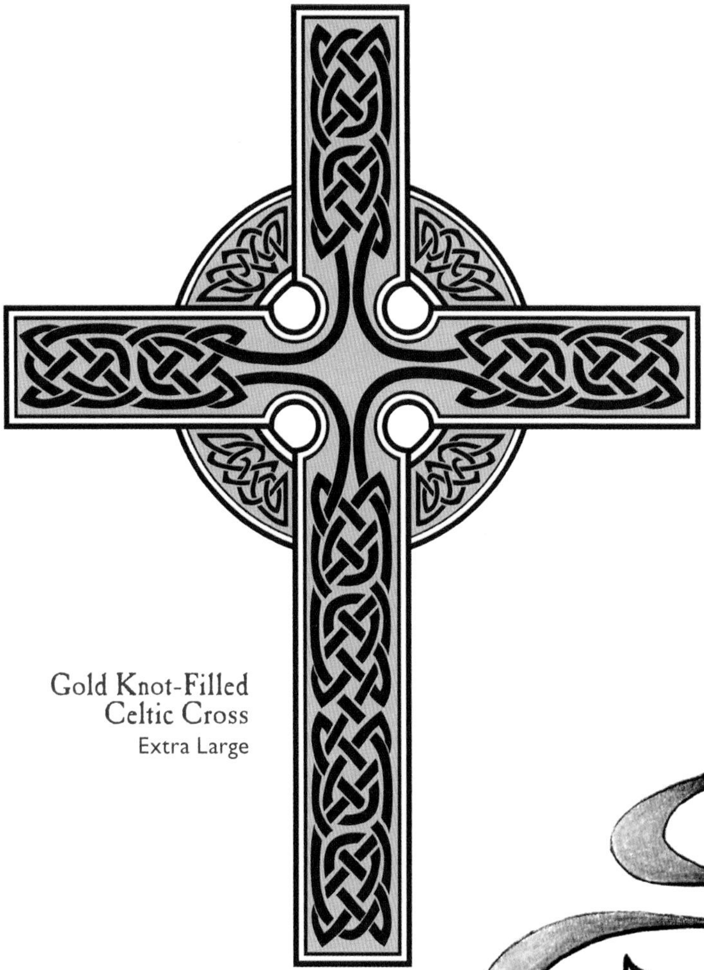

Gold Knot-Filled Celtic Cross
Extra Large

The Guard
Extra Large

Long Celtic Armband
Extra Large

Inlaid Gold Irish Cross
Medium

Celtic Cross Dragon
Extra Large

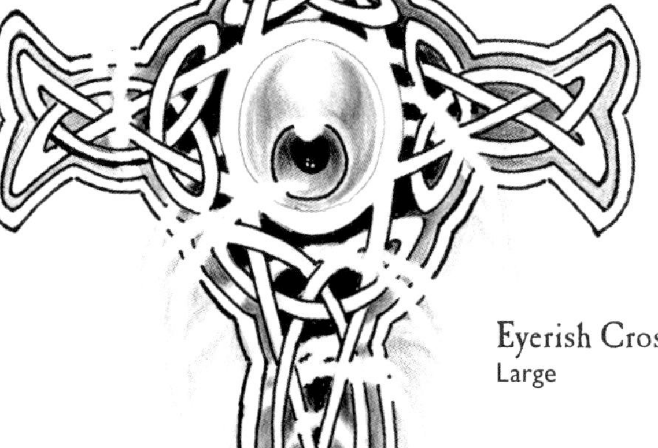

Eyerish Cross
Large

Celtic Snowflake
Medium

Celtic Crossendragons
Large

Celtic Star Armband
Extra Large

Point and Swirl Gold Celtic Band
Large

Professions

Courage and Honor
American Fireman
Extra Large

Fireman Cutting
Through Skin
Large

Honor Fireman
Large

Hacking Though the Fire that Will Never Forget
Extra Large

Fire Dog Piece
Medium

God Help Me Save 'Em All
Medium

Medical Fire Fighter Emblem
Large

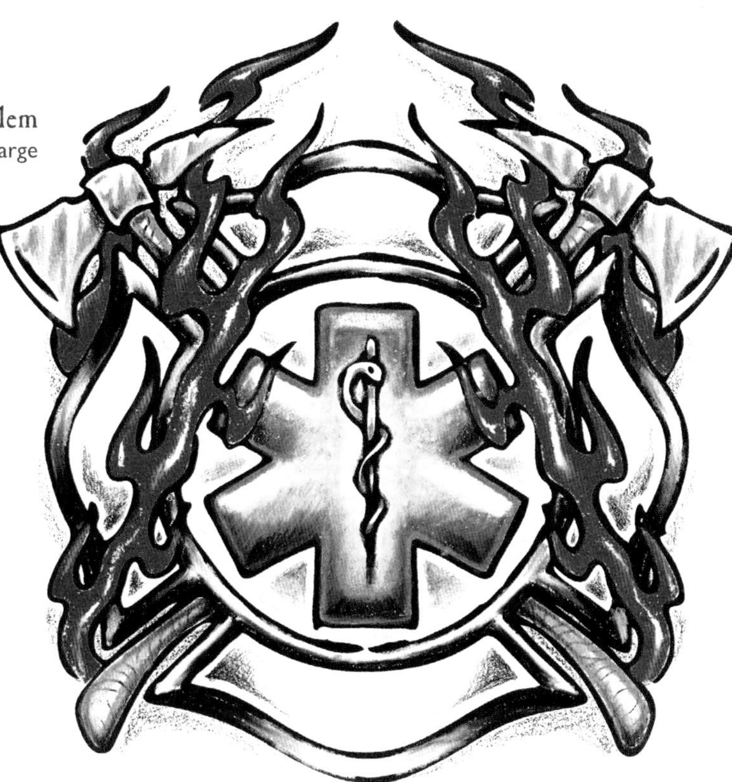

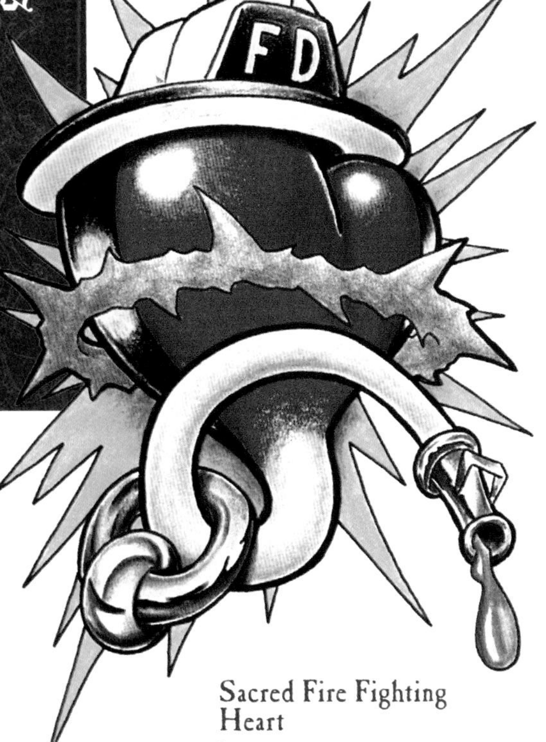

Sacred Fire Fighting Heart
Large

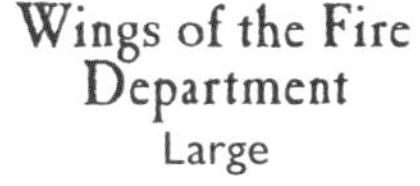

Wings of the Fire Department
Large

Fire Fighting Emblem with Axes
Medium

My Brother's Keeper
Extra Large

Fireman Steam
Medium

To Serve and Protect
Medium

Sedated Syringe
Medium

Bright Eyed Nurse
Medium

Daily Vitamins
Extra Large

Dentist's Dream
Medium

Vertical USMC
Medium

Skull and Bones Sailor
Medium

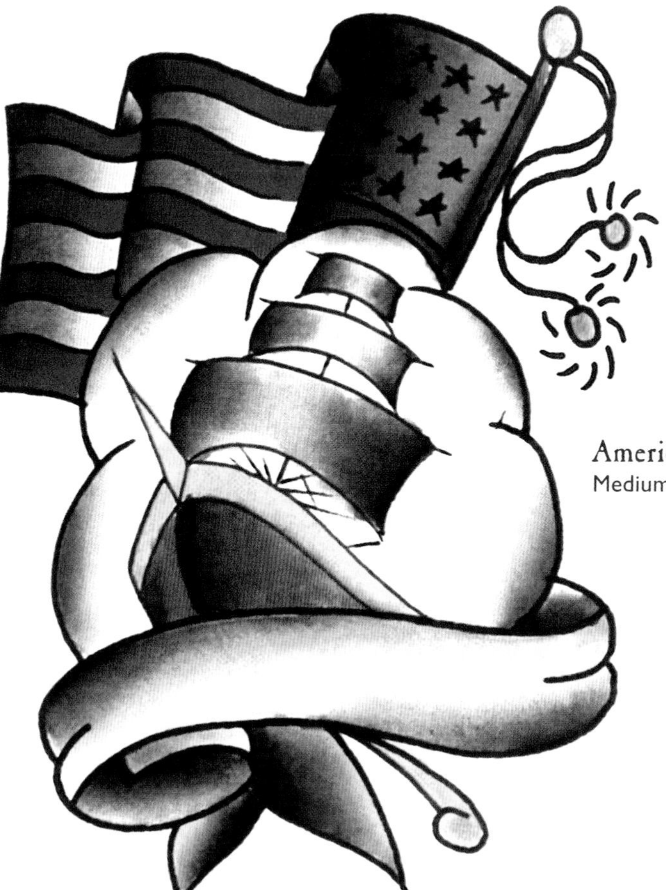

American Sailor
Medium

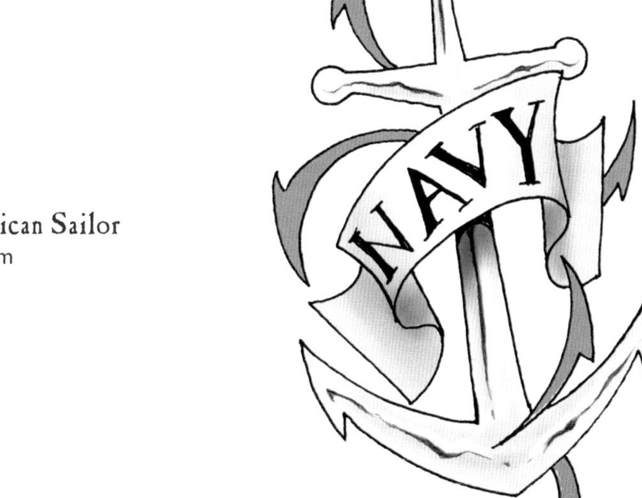

Navy Anchor
Medium

U.S.M.C. Armband
Extra Large

Cracked Egg
Medium

Skull and Chef Bones
Medium

High on the Hog
Large

Iron Works
Medium

Maniacal Grease Monkey
Extra Large

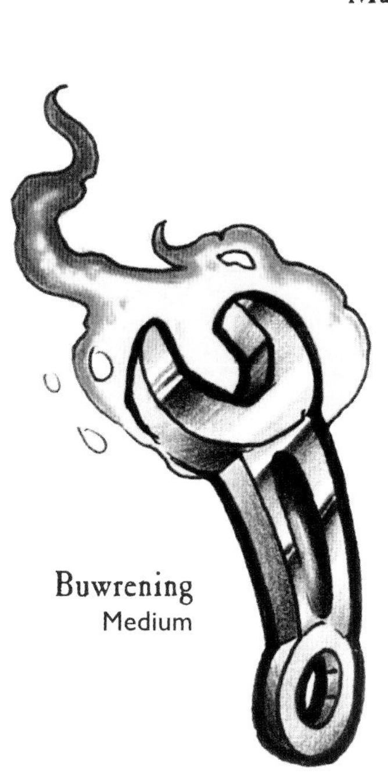

Buwrening
Medium

Honest Days Work
Medium

Flaming Guitar
Medium

Religious

Floral Jesus
Extra Large

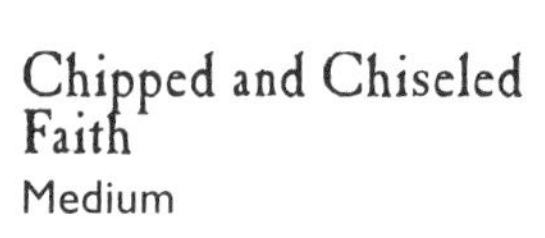

Chipped and Chiseled Faith
Medium

Vine Wrapped INRI Cross
Medium

Star and Crescent of Islam
Medium

Cross of Leaves
Medium

Only God Can Judge Me II
Extra Large

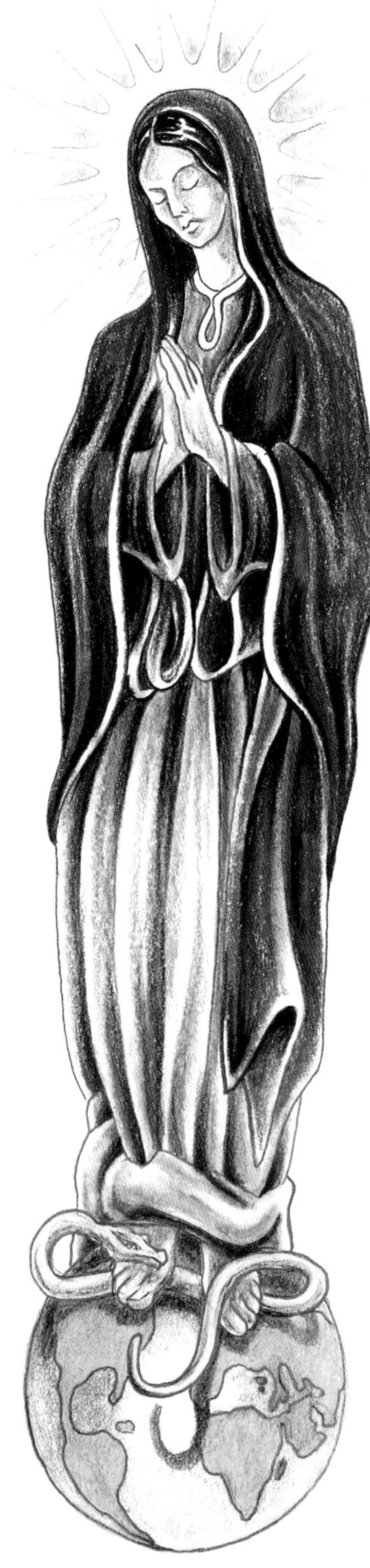

Worldlabovely
Extra Large

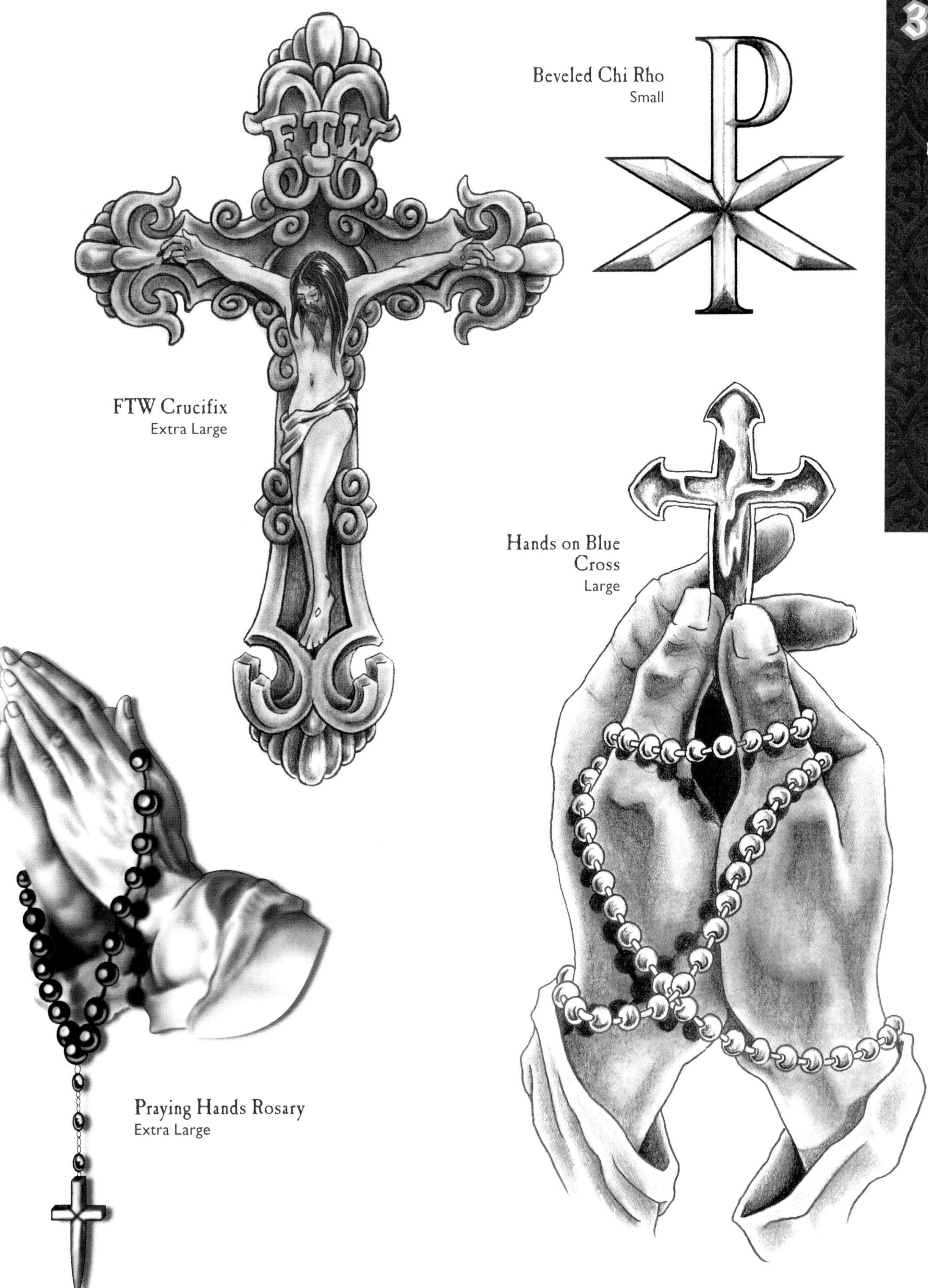

Beveled Chi Rho
Small

FTW Crucifix
Extra Large

Hands on Blue Cross
Large

Praying Hands Rosary
Extra Large

Full of Grace
Extra Large

Rose Filled Cross
Medium

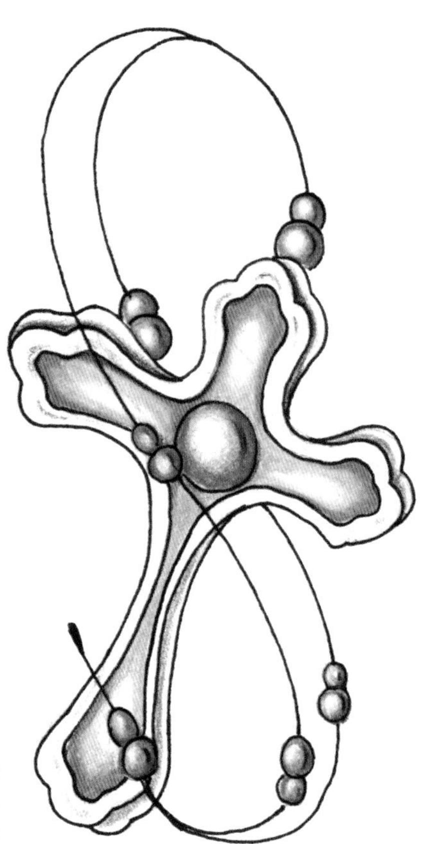

Emerald Cross Necklace
Medium

Misted Crucifix
"John 316"
Extra Large

Yellow Cross Knot
Extra Large

For God and Country
Medium

Ribbon Wrapped
Cross with Wings
Large

Simple Iron Cross
Extra Small

Endless Burning Cross
Medium

Jesus Tribal
Large

Phoenix Cross
Large

JESUS
Medium

JESUS

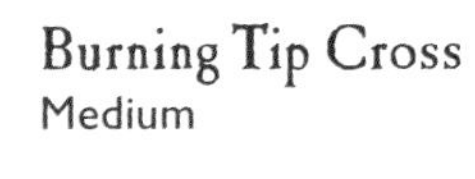

Burning Tip Cross
Medium

Cross of Thorns
Extra Large

Modern Cross Design
Medium

Mother and Child in Stone
Extra Large

Wasted Crucifix
Extra Large

Mary in the Sun
Extra Large

Cross with Wings
Small

Blood Fish
Medium

Boned Cross
Extra Large

IXOYE Fish
Large

Lost Lamb
Extra Large

Weeping Cross
Medium

Handmade Cross II
Medium

Gothica
Large

Contrast Jesus
Medium

Hot Celtic Cross
Extra Large

Crown of Thorns
Medium

Golden Fish Symbol
Medium

Cross of Suns
Medium

Swirling in Wind
Medium

Awesome Wonder Cross with Wings
Extra Large

Flying to Heaven
Medium

Jesus Praying
Medium

Looked upon
Extra Large

Two Nails in Cross Shape
Medium

Beads with Jesus Cross
Large

Wrought Details Cross
Extra Large

Rose and Wings Cross
Extra Large

Jesus in the Clouds
Medium

Gothic Cross in the Sun
Medium

Holy Glow
Large

Long Beaded Rosary
Extra Large

Hot Cross Burns
Medium

Jesus Nazarenus
Extra Large

Sacred Heart Seraph
Large

Love Faith
Sacred Heart
Medium

Flower Inri
Extra Large

Ondes
Medium

INRI Twist Cross
Medium

Purple Jesus Cross
Extra Large

Arabic "Allah/God"
Emblem
Large

Pentastar
Medium

Arabic "Allah/God"
Lowerback
Medium

Fiponul
Small

Interweaving Star of David
Small

Fuel for Life
Large

David's Rose
Large

Knotted Star of David
Medium

Buddhist Icon
Medium

Hot in Prayer
Extra Large

Content
Extra Large

Big Buddha
Medium

Fiery Om
Large

Hindu Ganesh Eternity
Medium

Tibetan Om Lotus
Medium

Crossings
Medium

Aoten
Large

Simplified Angel
Medium

Red Haired Angel with Blue Sash
Extra Large

Mid Flight Angel
Medium

Skulls & Death

Loveskull 2
Medium

Skull Wrench Flames
Extra Large

Sweet Grimmy
Extra Large

Triple Skullenfire
Extra Large

Hollow
Medium

Grim Reaper Puppet
Medium

Skuzzle
Medium

Never Laugh, Never Cry
Large

Missing
Tooth Skull
Extra Large

Black Rose Top Hat
Extra Large

"Time Waits for No One"
Medium

Robe of Death
Large

Parted by Death
Extra Large

Skull Death Kanji
Large

Skelejoker
Large

Skull Consumed
Extra Large

Karounds
Small

Lottafango
Large

All Fired up
Medium

Neon Skullimplosion
Large

Skully Ring
Medium

Tsunami of Death
Medium

Showered with Roses
Large

Overbite
Medium

Fire Sun Skull
Extra Large

Golden Winged Skull
Large

Skull Sense
Extra Large

Dos Dia de los Muertos
Extra Large

Angry Adorned Skull
Medium

Guitar Rocker Skull
Extra Large

Death Orb
Medium

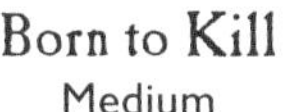

Born to Kill
Medium

Skulls and Roses
Large

Debt Collector
Large

Golden Skull
and Crossbones
Medium

Death Before
Dishonor Banner
Large

The Forsaken
Are Metal
Medium

Tribaljaw Skull
Large

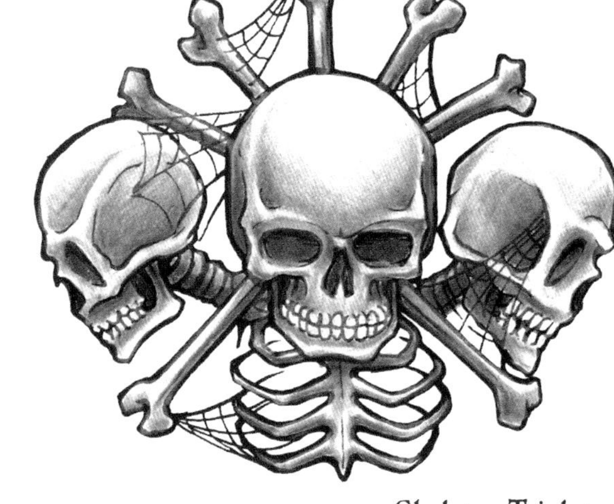

Skeleton Triplets
Medium

Touched Cross from within
Large

Ripped
Medium

Death Messenger
Large

Bow Tie Top Hat Skeleton
Large

Skullenwire Tribal
Extra Large

Winged Skull & Crossbones with Spider Webs
Large

Chaos Bullets
Extra Large

This Skull Has Worms
Medium

Mr. Skunkhead
Extra Large

Unavoidable Truth
Large

Hidden Red Eyes Tribal
Medium

Make Way for the Reaper
Extra Large

Burning Shield Reaper
Extra Large

Swashbuckler
Extra Large

Skull Samurai
Large

Blue Feathered Skull
Large

Back for More
Large

Reaped Again
Extra Large

Blue Devil Skull Wings
Medium

Nothin to the Right
Medium

Savage Skull
Large

Headbang
Medium

A Look
Large

Celtic Laughingskull
Extra Large

In the Balance
Extra Large

Ready for Death
Extra Large

From Skull Comes Life
Extra Large

Tallhorn
Skullycircle
Large

Blaming Hell
Large

Death Is a Lonely Business
Large

Fate Sealer
Large

Skull Girl 001
Medium

Smokin' Reaper with a Gun
Large

Skulltribalfire
Medium

Skull Money
Medium

Reaper on Reaper
Large

Grim Says Your Time Is up
Large

Pissed Reaper
Medium

Grim on the Wind
Extra Large

Grim Reaper's Laugh
Medium

Skull Combo Skull
Extra Large

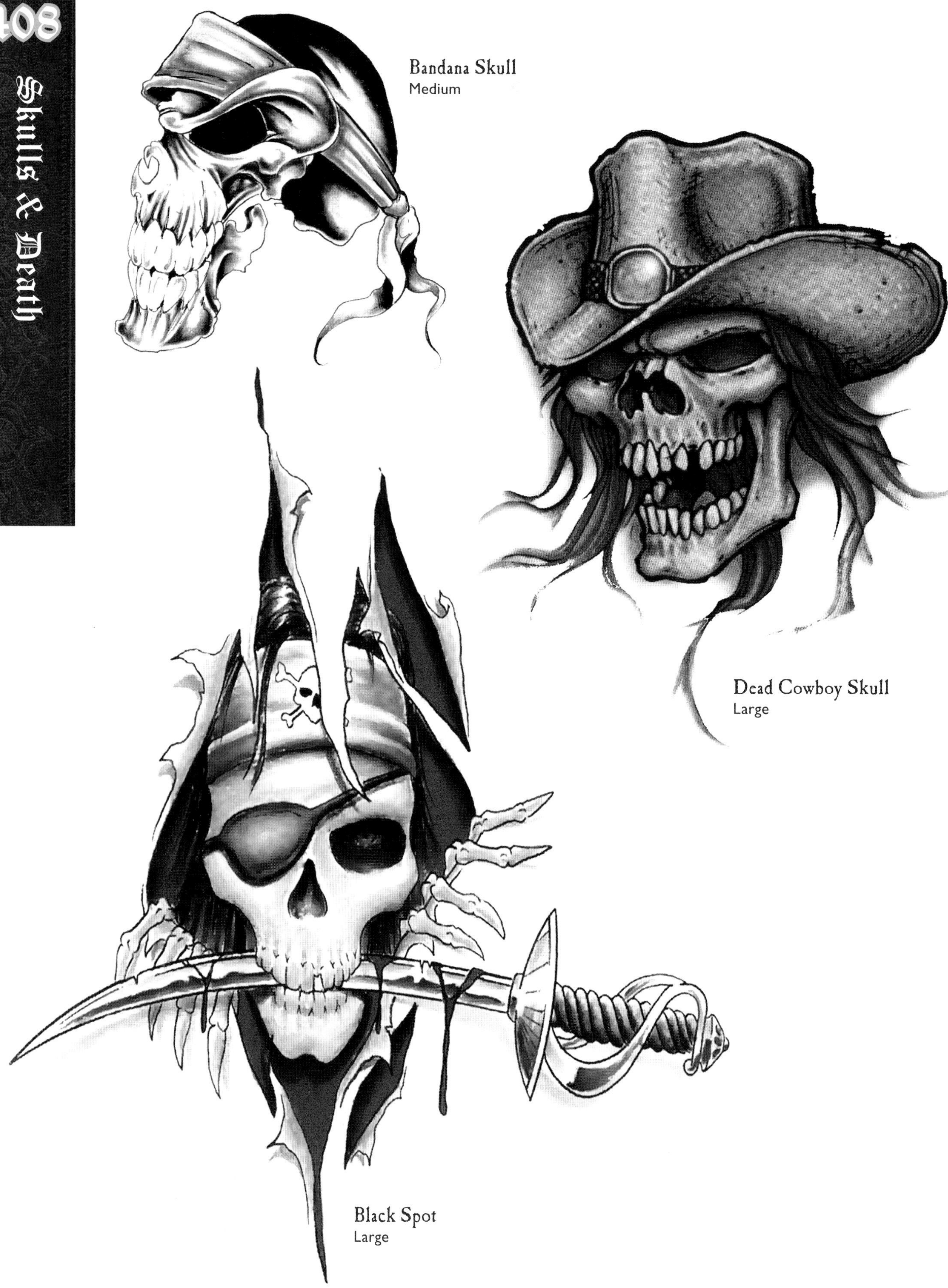

Bandana Skull
Medium

Dead Cowboy Skull
Large

Black Spot
Large

Small Skeleton Keyhole
Medium

Practically Presley
Medium

Spinal Weave
Extra Large

Pirate S&C
Medium

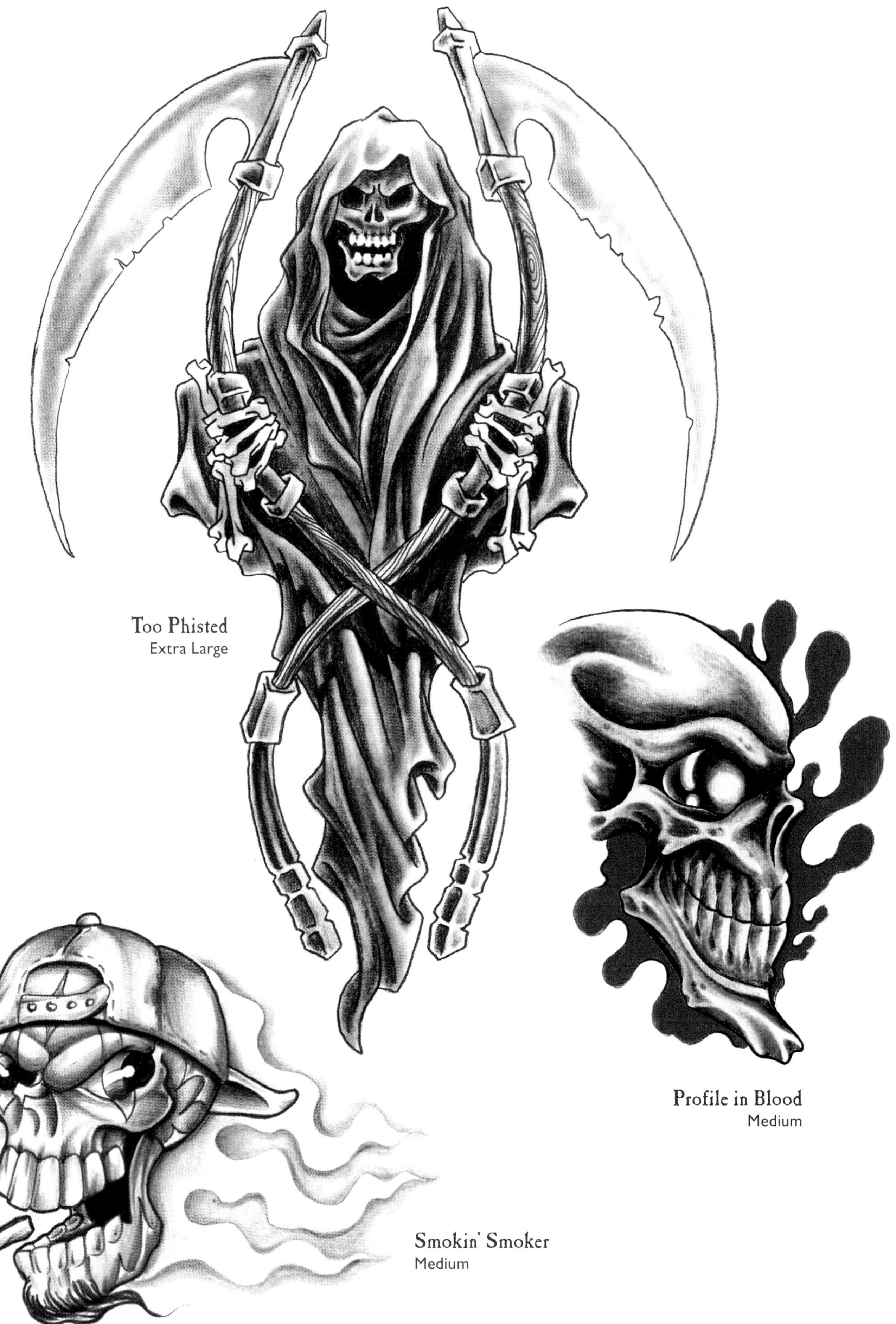

Too Phisted
Extra Large

Profile in Blood
Medium

Smokin' Smoker
Medium

Fearless Skull and Cross Axe
Medium

The Tattoo
Large

Symbols

Peace & Love
Small

Peaceful Existence
Large

Happy Peace
Medium

Flowery Peace
Medium

Balanced Peace
Medium

Stars and Peace Rainbow
Medium

PurpleYY
Medium

Twoyy
Medium

Yin Yang Foliage
Medium

Equals Steam
Medium

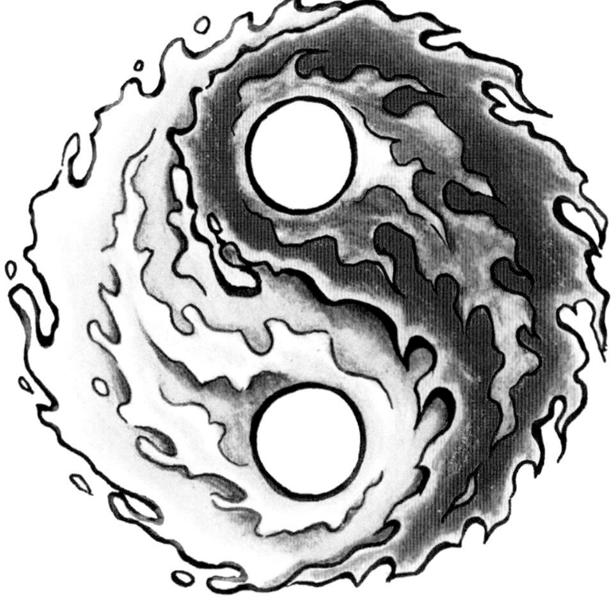

Fire and Water Yin Yang
Medium

Yin Yang Splosion
Medium

Yin Yang in Feather Tribal Piece
Large

Yinsta Yangsu
Medium

Brushed
Small

Fire & Water
Medium

Gay Memory
Small

Gay Brotherhood
Medium

Rainbow Unity Butterfly
Medium

Gay Pride Triangle
Medium

Gayband
Large

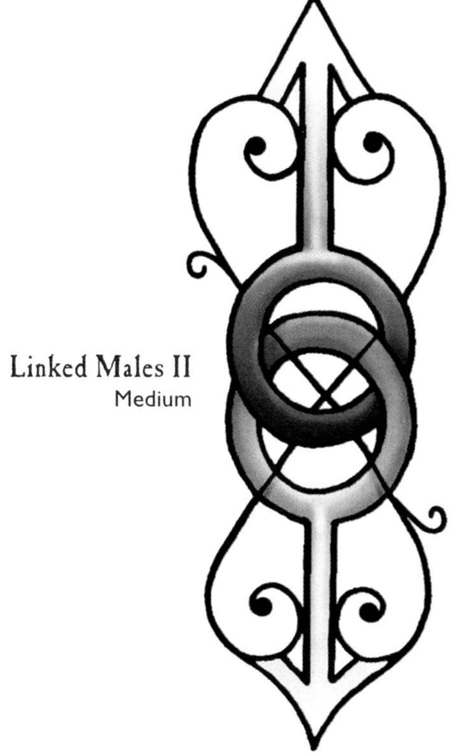

Linked Males II
Medium

Rose with Lady Love
Large

Lesbian Butterflies
Medium

Pink Triangle in Design Heart
Small

Female with Rainbow Stars
Medium

Lesbian Cherries
Large

Femme Gay Marriage
Medium

Girls Rainbow Flag
Medium

Fleur de Heart
Small

Forever

Forever Wedding Rings
Medium

Ribbon Lock
Medium

Dangle Ring
Small

Life and Death Rings
Medium

Never Get Lost
Large

Captains Wheel
Medium

Dark Anchor
Large

Blue Rose USN Anchor
Medium

Four Way Sight
Large

The Little Comma who Could
Small

Symbol in Water
Medium

Tri-Shroom Winged Eye
Medium

Five Pointed Star in Anchor of Waves
Extra Large

Om Heart
Extra Large

Glassy Firey Om
Medium

Om Rose
Medium

Abstract Dragon with Eye
Medium

Eye of All Seeing Abstraction
Medium

Not Quite Six
Medium

Time Flies
Medium

Flying Scales
Extra Large

Snakes Triangle Ankh
Medium

Ankh Moon Sun
Large

Ankh 5
Medium

Emerald Ankh
Medium

Burning Celtic Ankh
Extra Large

Blue Eye Ra
Medium

Raye
Medium

Angled Sun Eye
Large

Ankh Sees All
Medium

Mandala4
Extra Large

Orange Spiral Pattern
Extra Large

Mandala Life Bee
Extra Large

Kaleidoscope Spiral
Extra Large

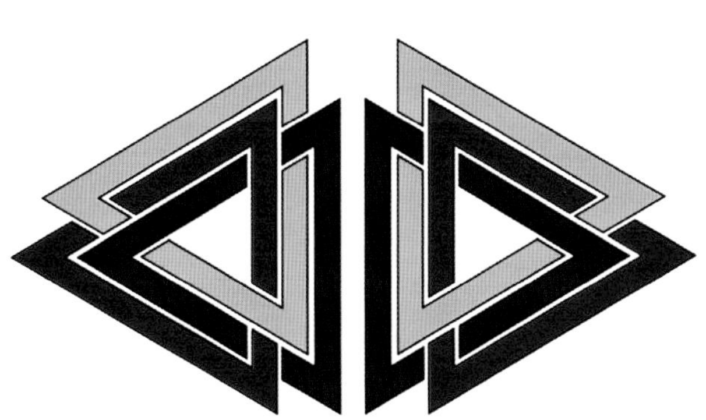

Unity on Unity
Medium

The Celwer
Extra Large

Plured
Medium

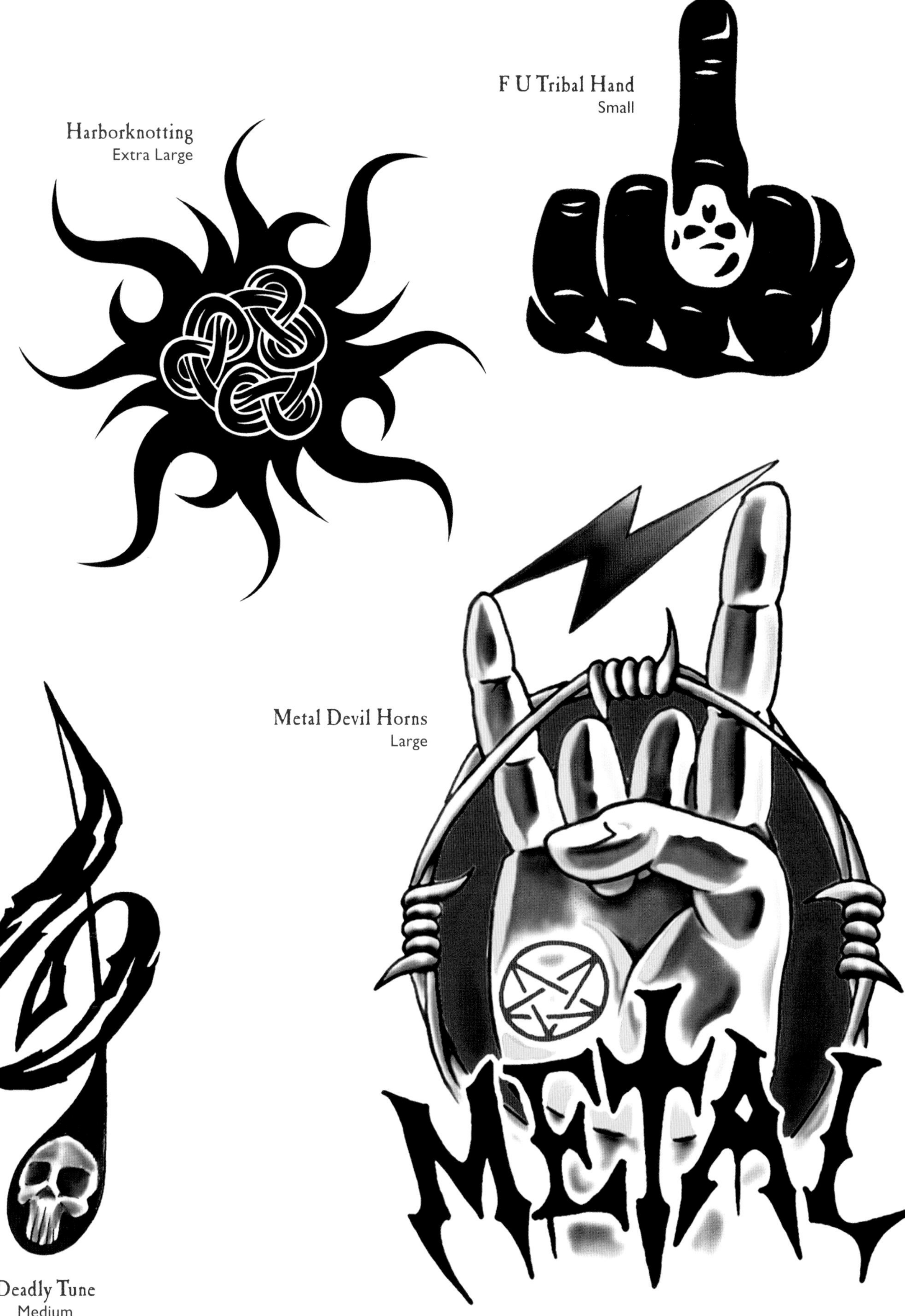

Harborknotting
Extra Large

F U Tribal Hand
Small

Metal Devil Horns
Large

Deadly Tune
Medium

A Song of Love
Large

Treble Measures
Medium

Classical Composition
Extra Large

Underlying Treble Clef
Medium

Tough Anarchy
Medium

Deadhead Anarchy
Medium

Tribal Biohazard
Large

Fire II
Small

Blue Flame Pentagram
Medium

Hazard Knot
Medium

Black Biohazard Tribal
Medium

Bioxic
Medium

P-Wheel
Large

Red Cross Flag
Large

Purpletricelta
Medium

Chaos Cross
Medium

Plain Infinity
Large

Triquetra
Large

African Adinkra
Small

Stylized 13
Medium

Luck
Small

Chaosa
Medium

Cursive Dollar
Small

Liberty Star
Medium

Triple Triquetra
Medium

Tribal

Thorny Tribal
Medium

Paivespun
Medium

Dagger Dance
Medium

Dragon Brow Tribal
Medium

Negative Sharp Points Tribal
Extra Large

Manifest
Medium

Arittene
Small

Pretty Tribal Snowflake
Medium

Tribal Wingies
Large

Indecision
Medium

Purple Victorian Tribal
Medium

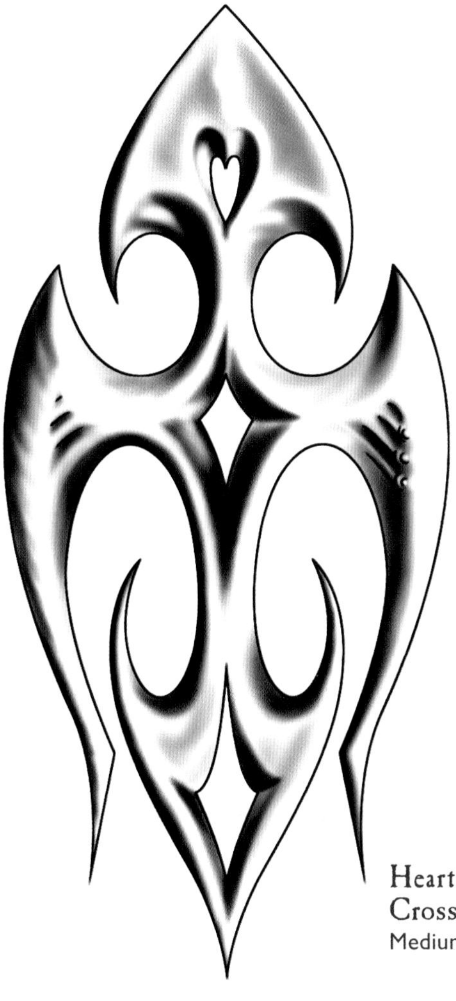

Heart Hole Tribal Cross
Medium

Bird of Prey
Medium

Ealblastal
Medium

HMRTG
Large

Touture Ring of Tribal
Small

Shroomfarm Tribal
Extra Large

Blue and Black Shaded Tribal
Large

Blue Millitribal
Large

Sharp in Flight
Extra Large

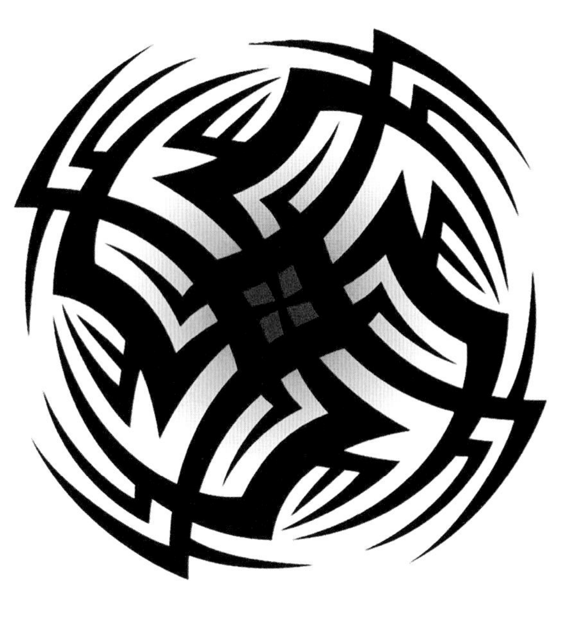

Slasher
Medium

Toucal
Large

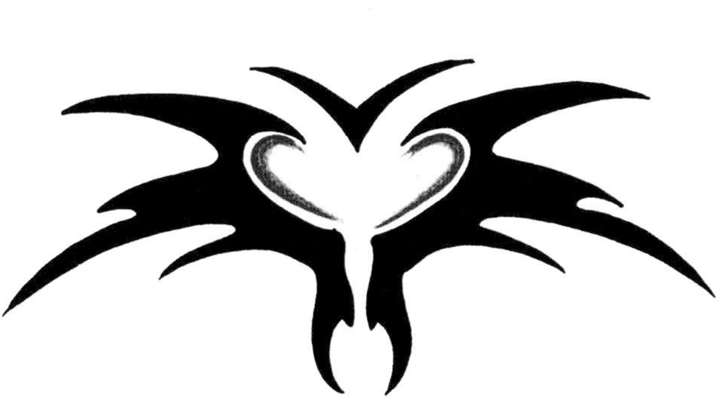

Splattered Heart
Medium

Sharb
Medium

Hard Tide
Large

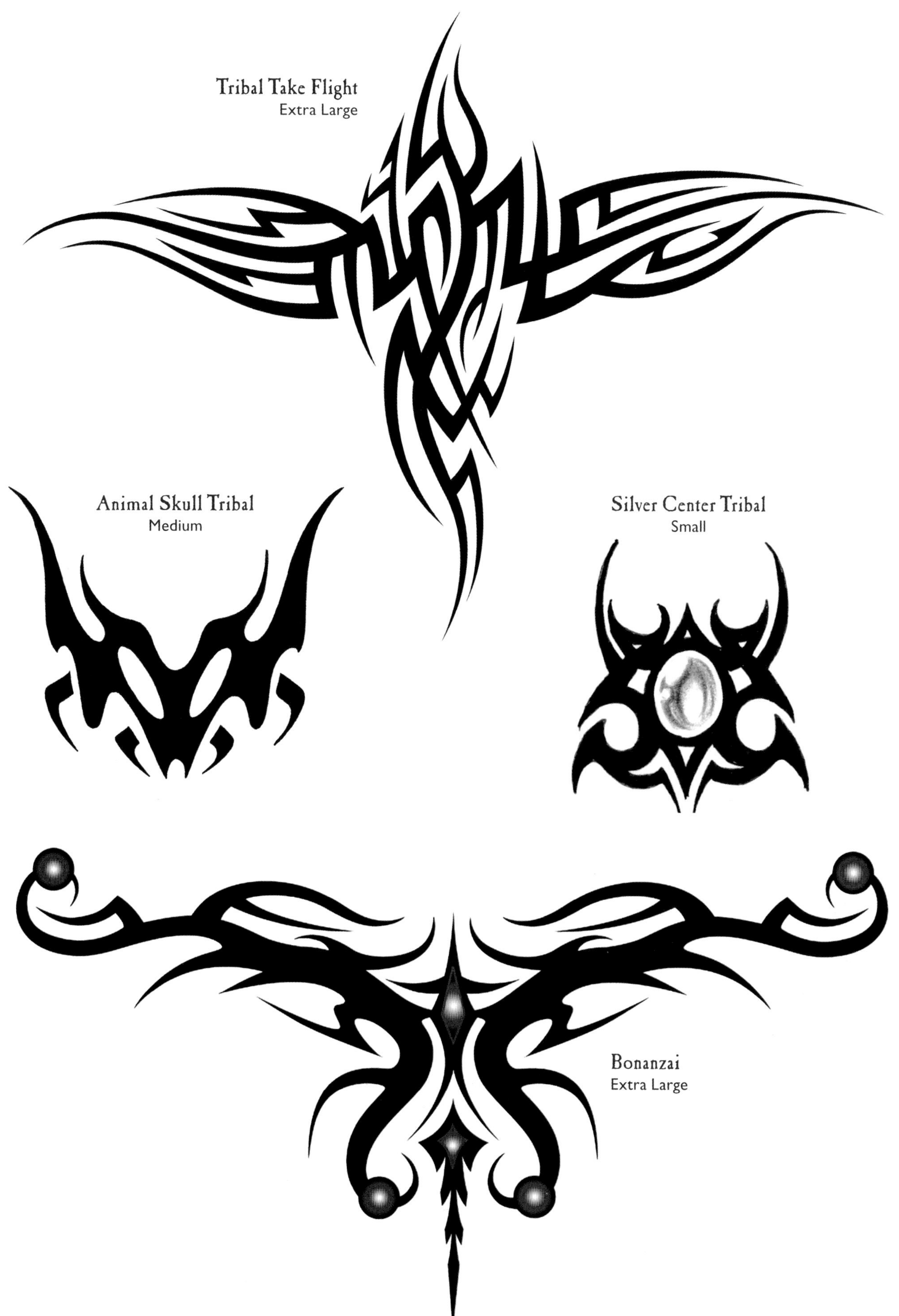

Tribal Take Flight
Extra Large

Animal Skull Tribal
Medium

Silver Center Tribal
Small

Bonanzai
Extra Large

Unglor
Medium

Clawing Lizard
Extra Large

Twizted Tribal
Extra Large

Squaredance
Extra Large

Arms out Tribal
Medium

Leopard Tribal
Large

Pink Blue Scales Tribal
Medium

Leopard Print
Extra Large

Creep up Tribal
Medium

Gelusen
Medium

Out of Control
Tribal Spiral
Medium

Chromed Tribal Piece
with Yellow Halo
Medium

One Tribal Two
Extra Large

Undulup
Extra Large

Estaiche
Large

Flame Tribal Duo II
Medium

Tribal Yarn
Small

Shaded Tribal Swirl
Medium

Bino Tribal
Medium

Tribal Sweep
Medium

Feelin' Blue Tribal
Medium

Black and Pink Tribal
Medium

Tribal Purple Red Jewel
Large

Twisted Pick
Medium

Tribal Tooth Skull
Large

Fallen into
Extra Large

Tribal Tears
Small

Celtic Wing Tribal
Large

Maori Sleeve Piece
Large

Eternal Tribal
Medium

Intricate Maori Sun
Extra Large

Maori Dolphins
Extra Large

Mask Swirl Face
Extra Large

Maori Tribal Spiral
Medium

Maori Flow
Extra Large

Zodiac

Aries Headbutt
Medium

3D Aries
Small

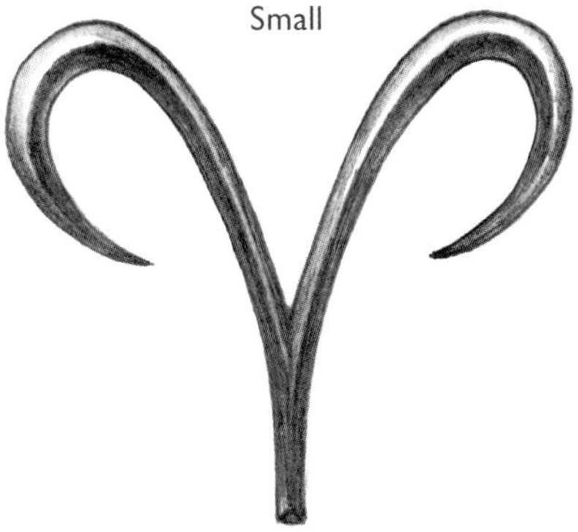

Aries
Extra Large

Aries Star Trail
Medium

ལུག་གི་ཁྱིམ།

Aries (Kanji, Tibetan)
Medium

Stern Aries
Medium

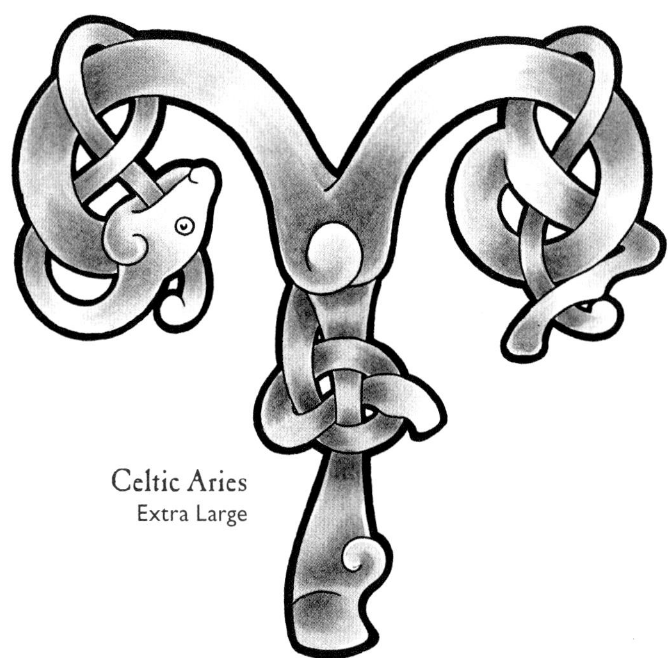

Celtic Aries
Extra Large

Aries Moon Backpiece
Large

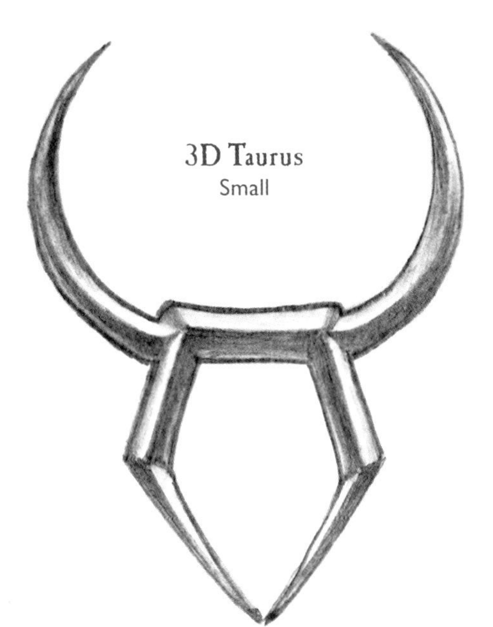

3D Taurus
Small

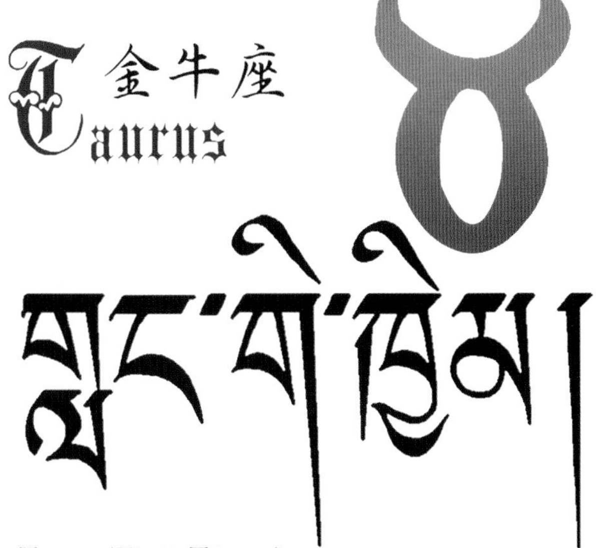

Taurus (Kanji, Tibetan)
Medium

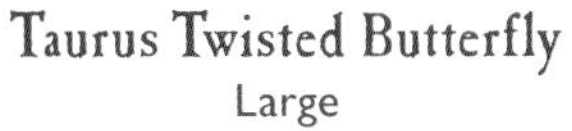

Taurus Twisted Butterfly
Large

Celtic Taurus
Large

Taurus Moon Backpiece
Large

雙子座
Gemini

འཁྲིག་པའི་ཁྱིམ།

Gemini (Kanji, Tibetan)
Medium

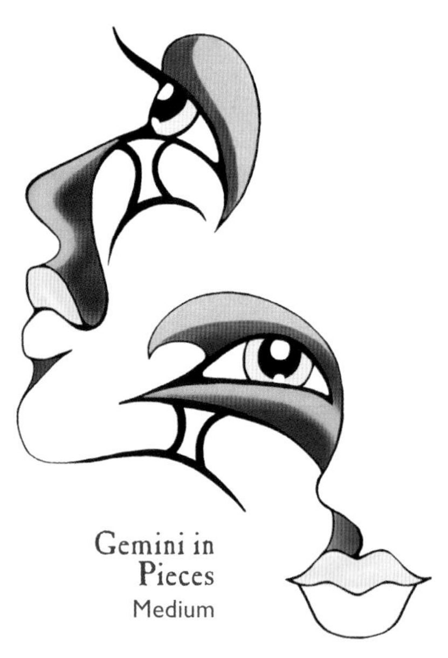

Gemini in Pieces
Medium

Gemini Power
Medium

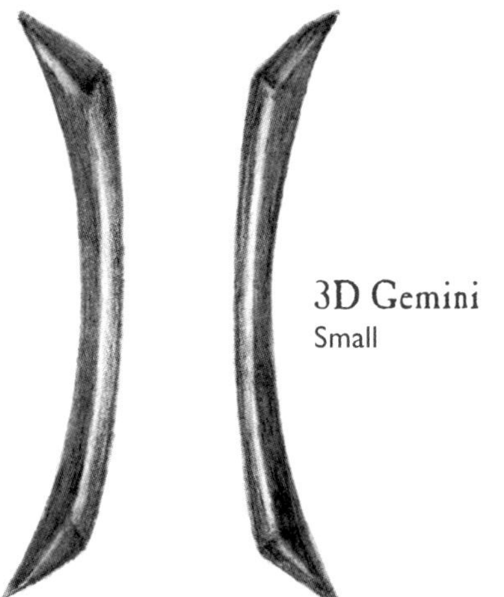

3D Gemini
Small

Gemini Moon Backpiece
Large

Cancer (Kanji, Tibetan)
Medium

Tribal Cancer Crab
Medium

Cancer Crabby
Medium

Cancer Moon Backpiece
Large

Cancer Crab Overlay
Large

3D Cancer
Small

Celtic Cancer
Large

Cancer Starburst
Medium

Sunset Warmth Leo
Small

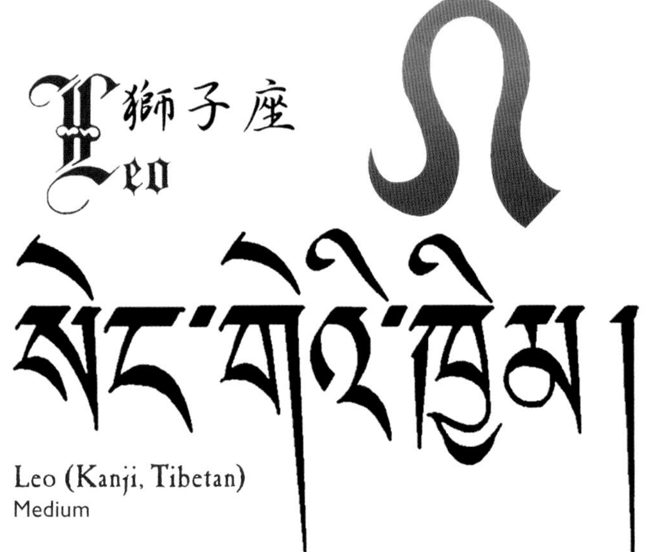

Leo (Kanji, Tibetan)
Medium

Leo Trail
Medium

Celtic Leo
Large

Leo Moon Backpiece
Large

Virgo (Kanji, Tibetan)
Medium

Celtic Virgo
Large

Virgo
Large

Virgo Moon Backpiece
Large

Libra (Kanji, Tibetan)
Medium

སྲང་གི་ཁྱིམ།

Water Libra
Medium

Shadow Libra
Scales
Medium

3D Libra
Small

Libra Moon Backpiece
Large

Scorpio 天蠍座

Scorpio (Kanji, Tibetan)
Medium

Long Black Stencil Scorpion
Large

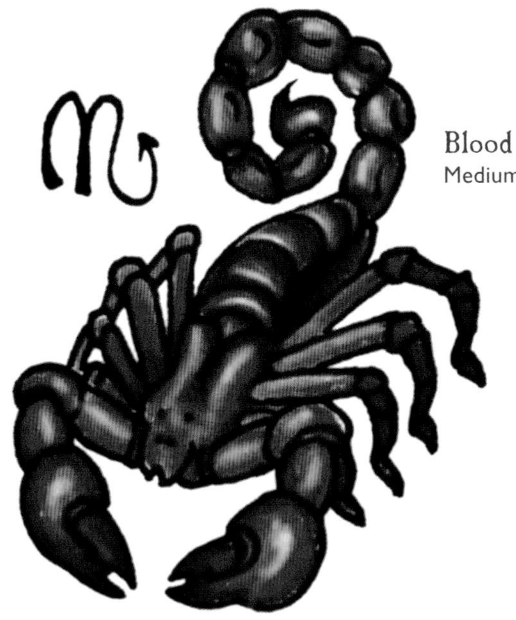

Blood Red Scorpio
Medium

MP Scorpio
Medium

Scorpio Moon Backpiece
Large

Scorpio
Large

3D Scorpio
Small

Vibrant Scorpion
Medium

Lowerback Scorpio
Extra Large

Sagittarius (Kanji, Tibetan)
Medium

射手座
Sagittarius

གཞུའི་ཁྱིམ།

Sagittarius Flarrows Butterfly
Medium

Sagittarius Sparkle
Medium

Kicking Sagittarius
Medium

Sagittarius Moon Backpiece
Large

Capricorn (Kanji, Tibetan)
Medium

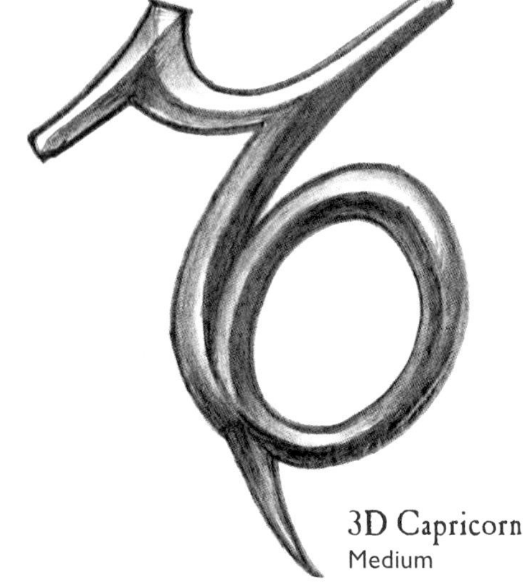
3D Capricorn
Medium

Celtic Capricorn
Large

Capricorn
Medium

Capricorn Moon Backpiece
Large

水瓶座
Aquarius

བུམ་པའི་ཁྱིམ།

Aquarius (Kanji, Tibetan)
Medium

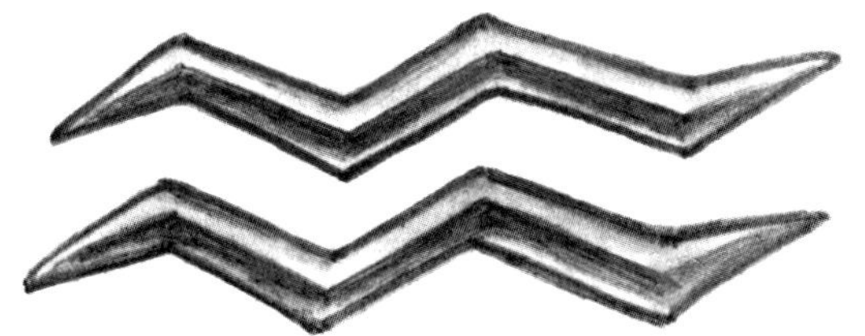

3D Aquarius
Small

Aquarius
Large

Aquarius Moon Backpiece
Large

Pisces (Kanji, Tibetan)
Medium

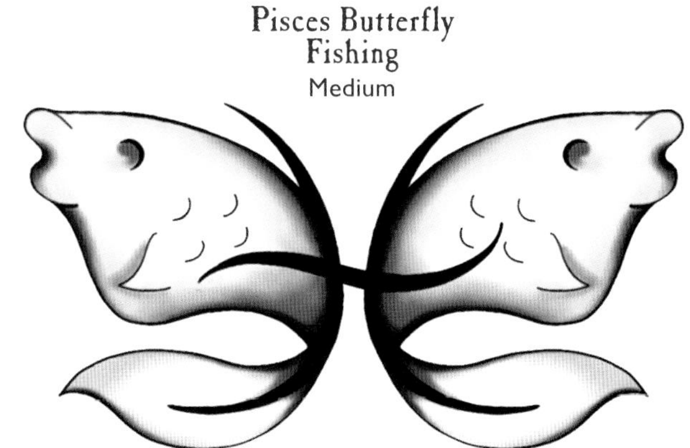

Pisces Butterfly Fishing
Medium

Celtic Pisces
Large

Pisces
Large

Pisces Moon Backpiece
Large

Flame Wrapped Pisces
Large

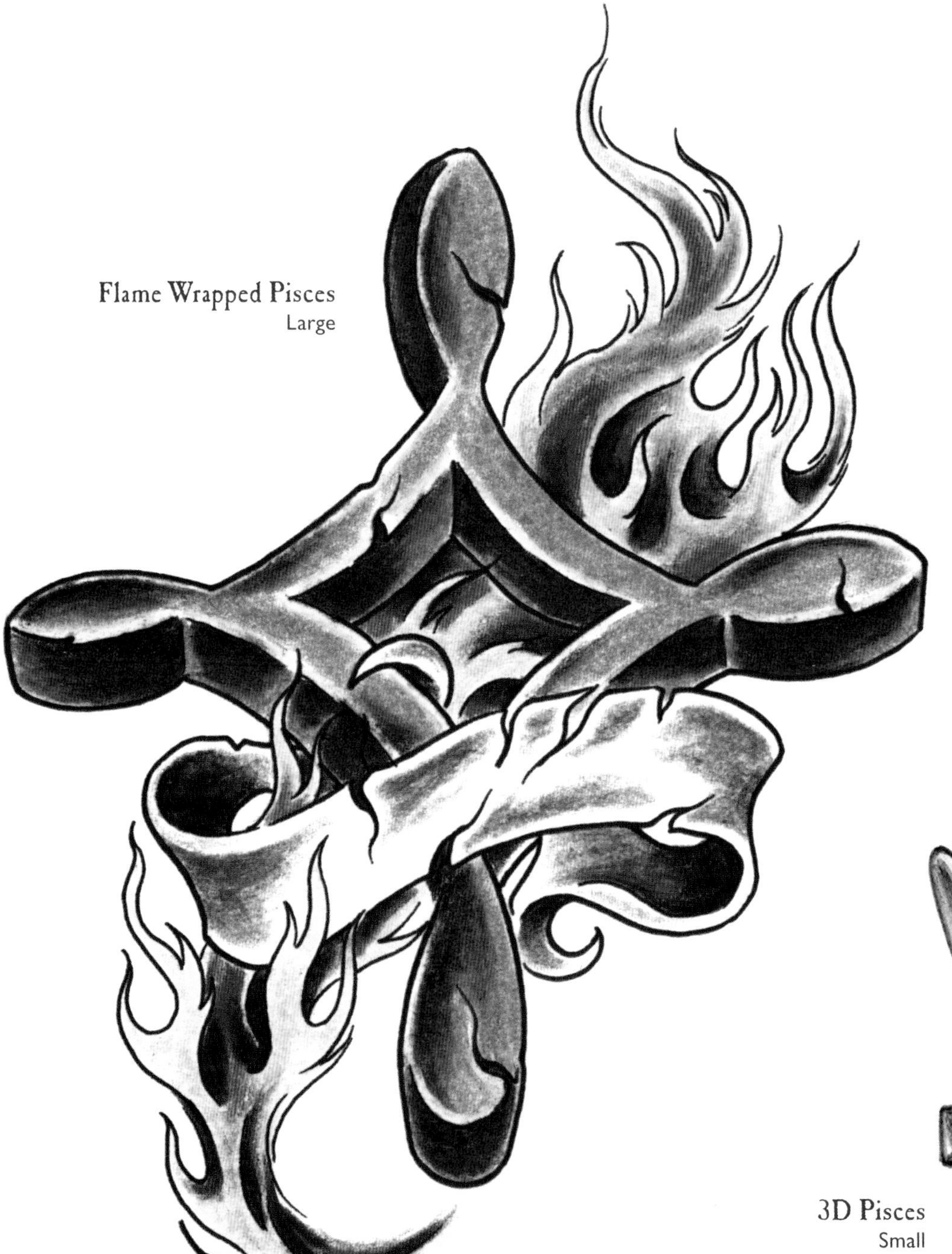

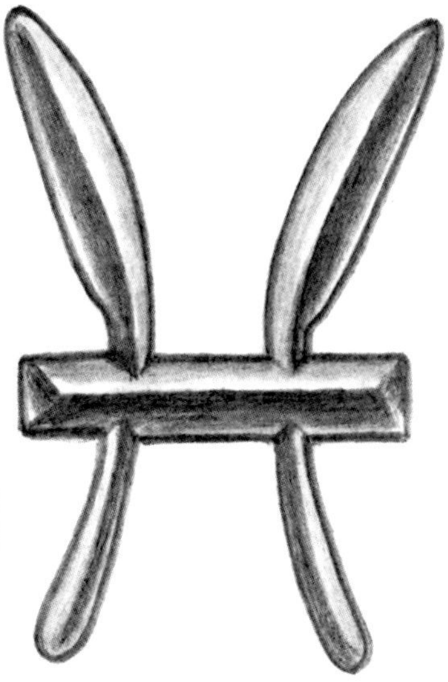

3D Pisces
Small

Goldfish Pisces
Medium

Cancer Lowerback
Extra Large

Lowerback Tribal Libra Piece
Large

Spirit Sagittarius Tribal Lowerback Piece
Extra Large

Capricorn Tribal Lowerback Piece
Extra Large

Edge Mouse/Rat (Chinese)
Extra Small

Edge Ox (Chinese)
Extra Small

Edge Tiger (Chinese)
Extra Small

Edge Rabbit (Chinese)
Extra Small

Edge Dragon (Chinese)
Extra Small

Edge Snake (Chinese)
Extra Small

Edge Horse (Chinese)
Extra Small

Edge Sheep (Chinese)
Extra Small

Edge Monkey (Chinese)
Extra Small

Edge Rooster (Chinese)
Extra Small

Edge Dog (Chinese)
Extra Small

Edge Pig (Chinese)
Extra Small

Zombies & Monsters

Monster Skull Through Skin
Large

Frankie's Head Case
Large

Sewn Mouth Monster
Medium

B&C Giver
Extra Large

Vampire Smile
Small

Burning Forehead
Medium

Flytrap Attack
Extra Large

Zombie the Kid
Large

Proper Procedure
Large

Crazy Smeagol Face
Medium

Coming Battle
Extra Large

Zombie Flames
Extra Large

Ol Frank
Extra Large

You're Fired
Medium

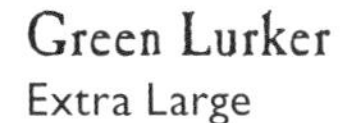

Green Lurker
Extra Large

Hook Mouth
Zombie Head
Large

Thriving Terror Zombie
Extra Large

Decaylien
Large

Angry No Armed Tripple Horned Demon Dude
Medium

Zombie Gem
Medium

Cartoon Frankinstein
Medium

Green Demon Caterpillar
Medium

It's Electric!
Medium

Monster Fighter
Extra Large

Rock and Roll Zombie
Large

Flippin' off Fiend
Medium

Wolf of Insanity
Medium

Bobo the Lobotomized Monkey
Medium

Wicked Zombie Clown
Extra Large

Mince Meat Maker
Extra Large

Artist Profiles

AntiBry
—Colorado, United States

The visual arts have been an up and down roller coaster of progression for me through the years. Occasionally I hit waves of motivation in which I can't think of anything other than slumping over a drawing table all night, and then other times I find myself terrified of a blank sheet of paper. When I'm going through creative droughts, I find it necessary to flip through every page of every art book I own—from one side of the shelf to the other—and over the years I have accumulated quite a few. There are books on Magritte and Dali's surrealism, Andy Howell and Retna's (Marquis Lewis) graffiti, Annie Leibowitz and Alfred Stieglitz's photography, and countless textbooks on art from the European Renaissance and ancient Rome. Ironically, the one I find most inspiring and influential is not of an artist but of the mathematician Benoît Mandelbrot and his study on fractal geometry. Once you see and understand the equation and how it repeats everywhere in everything, it is hard not to incorporate it into your work. I'm drawn to the tattoo/flash realm of art because it has such a great potential for personal stories. When people put something on their skin that will be there for the rest of their lives, more often than not it's going to be of something that has more significance than artwork they have hanging in their homes. For me, every tattoo I have was put there to provoke a memory. The memories we all have are often communicated through stories. I think of the drawings I do as short stories. I'm continually exploring new ways of telling that story and am always honored when people want the stories I've created permanently displayed on their skin.

Anton
—Moscow, Russia

Anton was born as a citizen of the U.S.S.R. in 1977 and has lived there his whole life. He was always interested in art and learning to draw, and spent his early life learning not to "walk and talk," but instead "drawing everything and everywhere." He later received formal art training, earning a degree in industrial and applied arts from Moscow State University. In what he attributes to the "will of fate," Anton met Alex Chinaman, seen by many as one of the oldest and most respected Moscow tattoo artists. He apprenticed under Chinaman, working at three of his tattoo studios. Tattoo flash creation plays an ever-increasing role in his life, and he draws it often and everywhere—at work, at home, and on his travels. His greatest joy comes from seeing his tattoo artwork more widely available to those interested in his unique styles and in knowing that the results of his passionate work are being worn by people worldwide.

Archaic Fusion
—Massachusetts, United States

My name is Kristopher Smith, and I grew up outside of Boston, Massachusetts. I've been drawing ever since I can remember, and tattooing for about nineteen years. I've tattooed in many different places all over the world, including New York City, New York; New Orleans, Louisiana; Johnston City, Tennessee; Philadelphia, Pennsylvania; and Prague, Czech Republic—as well as plenty of places in between those! I currently work at my own shop, Coastline Tattoo, in Provincetown, Massachusetts.

Bannigan Artworks
—Oklahoma, United States

My name is Todd Hallock, and, like many artists, I've been drawing for as long as I can remember, and I always knew I wanted to do something creative for a living. I got my bachelors degree with dual majors in graphic design and photography, after which I landed a job in my hometown as an illustrator. As a creative outlet, I started doing my own artwork on the side, focusing on things that interested me—one of these being Celtic art. I've spent hours studying the art in ancient Celtic manuscripts, such as the *Book of Kells*, and the zoomorphic carvings on ancient Viking ships. I set up a Web site through which I could display my art, and started selling it on T-shirts, prints, etc. (www.celticartworks.com). I took the name of my ancestors, Bannigan, as my business name. After requests started coming in to design custom Celtic tattoos, I decided to further look into the tattoo business. I sent out some inquiries to businesses that sell flash art and was delighted when I got a response from TattooFinder.com. Although I am fairly new to the tattoo business and know I have a lot to learn, I am very excited about this new endeavor.

Bob McClure
—Hvidovre, Denmark

I was born in Denmark on December 22, 1968. I started drawing when I was a young child and have continued developing my skill over the years. My interest in tattoos started around the age of eight or nine. My dad and many of his friends were heavily tattooed, and I remember always being fascinated by them. My first paid art job was for a publisher who needed illustrated pictures of a particular soldier. It was on a low budget, but I was happy that I could help out. After that, I started to learn the art of tattooing from a friend. It was so cool, and I remember being so impressed by how he did the lines, shading, and so on. I knew that it was exactly the thing I wanted to do. I also started creating small-scale tattoo designs until a tattoo parlor asked me to make the designs bigger. So I did, and it led me to where I am today. I would surf the internet for inspiration and gather ideas from artists around the world. I was amazed by the quality and quantity of all the artwork, and that just furthered my belief that being involved with tattoos was where I belonged. I entered the Flash2xs.com Free Flash Contest, won, and before long, I had a signed contract with the company. This was a huge accomplishment for me, and I have loved this opportunity from the beginning.

Brian Burkey
—Colorado, United States

Growing up in Denver, Colorado, I got into art after receiving my first tattoo at the age of eighteen. I was so interested in them that I started drawing tattoo art on my own, and within one year, I was doing actual tattoo work myself. I was introduced to the tattoo world by Bobby Rosini and his son James. By 1994 I was working in a shop in Denver called Nick Mart Tattoo. In 1996, I started freelancing again and resumed drawing flash, but it wasn't really until 2003 that I got into drawing flash sets to sell. It has been challenging drawing more commercially because I've been doing some new designs that I wouldn't normally be doing. I like to do my grayscale art with graphite pencils. I work with 2Bs and 3Bs for my darks to get good depth. For my lights, I use a B and F to get nice grays. For my color work, I use Prismacolor Verithins, because the colors come out really crisp and vibrant. It's a little harder but it's not as messy as the softer pencils, plus you can keep a nice point on them. I also work in other mediums, such as painting. Right now I am working in watercolors, which I really enjoy, and find it has some similarities to color tattoo work. I really love working in different styles and with different mediums because doing so constantly presents new artistic challenges.

Chris Cox
—Colorado, United States

Chris Cox was born in Billings, Montana, and grew up in the Denver, Colorado, area. Most of his professional life has been spent in the automotive and construction fields. As a teenager, he became interested in drawing and soon was copying patterns for a tattoo artist. Over time, he began running a tattoo machine himself. As his drawing improved, he started doing reproduction consignments, which consisted mainly of Native American and wildlife art. This created the opportunity to gain experience working with other mediums and materials. Watercolors, oils, acrylics, pastels, and even branding tools have been used on wood, metal, canvas, paper, leather, and skin. Drawing flash has provided the freedom and ability to explore variations of both traditional and nontraditional subjects. He is currently enjoying the rise in popularity of the older forms done in the many styles of today's artists. Chris explains, "My favorite part of drawing is working with the customer from concept to final form on personal custom pieces. For me, that is what art is about: taking someone's idea and developing it into the reality that is wanted."

Christopher D. Smith
—Maryland, United States

Christopher D. Smith has been tattooing for more than seventeen years. His influences include his children, Charley and Sandy Parsons, Rick Cherry, Mike Malone, Pat Martynuik, Spider Webb, and Friday Jones. You can find his work at the Baltimore Tattoo Museum.

David Floyd
—Colorado, United States

My story starts with the same song and dance but evolves into something rather unique. I have been interested in art since I was very young. I got into tattooing as a teenager in the '80s, and it has been part of my life ever since. I'm from Richmond, Virginia, but I've lived in Jacksonville, Tampa, and southeastern Kentucky as well. Here's where it starts getting interesting. Most recently I stayed in Colorado, where I met an artist named David "Rooster" Walker, who encouraged me to draw flash. Those designs eventually made it to TattooFinder.com and account for my first exposure to the actual commercial tattoo industry. I'm still relatively new to the field but have quickly adapted and even thrived. I am perpetually working on new designs for TattooFinder.com.

David Walker
—Colorado, United States

I've been into art for as long as I can remember and into tattooing since about age fourteen. I've grown in my art and ink over the years—sometimes at the expense and agony of some very close friends—thanks, guys! My influences vary from my dear friend ZEB1, Guy Aitchison, Paul Booth, Philip Leu, and countless others. I'm not sure how to define my style—I guess if I had to call it anything, it'd be low-brow, greasy good shit—but I prefer to let it just speak for itself! But I try not to limit myself to any one style. I'm a gearhead, so of course I dig the new-school greasy stuff. I also dig Asian, traditional, and dark art. I guess as long as it's good, clean work, people can call it whatever style they'd like. Enjoy!

Demon Dean
—Virginia, United States

My full name is Dean Phillip Baumgartner (loved that one in school). I was born and raised in Minnesota, starting back in 1963. I began drawing when I was about ten years old, with inspiration from my uncle. I took art throughout school and then joined the military for four years, where I served as an illustrator. I was stationed in Hawaii. While I was there, I started drawing tattoo designs for my friends. When I went to the shop to get my second tattoo, I met the person who would be my teacher and friend (Johnny Anderson) for many years to come. I think it was after I apprenticed and became a tattoo artist that I was really influenced by art. What a privilege to put something I created on someone's body! My major influences back then were Jack Rudy, Gill Montie, Kari Barba, the Dutchman, and Mike Malone. Today, they are Paul Booth, Edward Lee, Aaron Cain, Hollywood Higgins from Rocksteady Tattoo, and many other TattooFinder.com artists! I've always been inspired to draw flash, but when I saw what Edward Lee could do, I was truly floored. I decided to enter the Flash2xs.com Free Flash Contest to see if I could win some flash from him, and I did! My goal now is to grow as an artist and as a person. I am honored to be part of the Flash2xs.com family, the

TattooFinder.com Web site, and I hope to be of some contribution to the flash world.

Douglas Heuton
—California, United States

I was born on October 21, 1966, in San Francisco, California. I am currently being held hostage by the state of California. I always enjoyed doodling growing up, and it seemed even more enjoyable when I did it during class. As a kid, that got me into a lot of trouble! Then my less-attractive identical twin brother (Edward Lee) and I discovered the tattoo section in the old *Biker Lifestyle* and we were hooked. Unfortunately, I landed my ass in prison in 1986 and have been locked up ever since. The only good things to come from that were getting to know Rachael Bardach, cofounder of TattooFinder.com, who brought me up to a better place and helped me to find my true love of art. Art has brought a lot of patience and resolve to my life.

Edge
—Split, Croatia

I first became interested in art when I started reading comic books at the age of seven, and that interest has never stopped. Artistic development is a process that can last a lifetime if you allow it to become part of you. For me, it's sometimes not easy to find inspiration, while at other times inspiration comes to me in a second. Something I've realized through the years is not to think when I create art. Usually creativity will hit when I allow my arms and mind to be free. I love to draw most after midnight while my family is sleeping! I put on my earphones and am ready to go. Pencil, music, paper—and that's it—nothing more. When I am not in the mood to draw tattoo designs, I don't push it; it's best not to pressure myself to do so. I just set that medium aside and take some oil or acrylic and create something on canvas. I also like to connect and share ideas with other artists. Presently, I am in love with Polynesian tattoo art and would love to live a few months with people from New Zealand, Samoa, and Tahiti. Family is important to me, and a huge source of inspiration is my son. He inspires me and gives me strength when I'm not in a good mood or if I'm feeling down. It's amazing to me to view art as children see it. For them, it's all about fun—and life itself should be fun. And yes, he has started to draw recently, and that makes me so incredibly happy! I thank my wife and my son (my two biggest supporters), my brother and parents, and everyone else who believed in me through all of these years.

Edward Lee
—Colorado, United States

I started drawing flash in the '80s. I mostly sold the originals to shops in the Bay Area, where we hung out. A friend showed me how to make a jailhouse gun—a homemade tattoo machine. Boy, after that, it was on. Somewhere around 1983, and still in the Bay area, a tattooist named Baron saw some of the stuff I was doing with my toy machine. He handed me a real machine, threw his leg up on the chair, and told me to do something. I freehanded a bird on his leg. He asked if I wanted to work for him—and shortly after, I agreed. In 1987 I went to Wyoming to work for Greg Skibo, who for me was a very good influence. He gave me a whole new perspective on professional tattooing. In 1990 I went to work for Mickie Kott, in Denver, Colorado. Mickie, too, has been very inspirational. While working for Mickie, I started drawing under the name "Edward Lee." My wife then, Rachael Bardach (cofounder of Flash2xs.com) started marketing my flash, and with the help of her brother Lou Bardach (also cofounder of Flash2xs.com), we took it all online in 2001. He and Rachael have done a great job—they're like a second family. My inspirations? Ed Hardy, Jack Rudy, Greg Irons, Kari Barba, Eddie Duetche, Guy Aitchison . . . too many to name; it would never end. Artwork should always be inspirational. That's hopefully what our designs on TattooFinder.com (and in this book) are to you. That would mean more to me than anything else.

English Jonny
—Michigan, United States and England

Jonathan Pinfield-Wells comes by his nickname quite honestly. Born in England, "English Jonny" came with his family over to the Colonies at the age of twelve. He describes drawing as a lifelong passion and had a knack for it as a child. His family eventually settled down in Michigan. Out of high school, he went to work in the graphic-design field. After five years, he felt the job didn't allow for the creativity he needed to further his artistic skills, and so he decided to pursue tattooing. His apprenticeship was under master tattooist Dan Collins at Bluz Tattooing in Waterford, Michigan. He also cites tattooist Matt Hockaday as "an amazing artist and painter who influenced me greatly in my early tattoo years." Three years later, Jonny met tattooist and artist Gentleman Jim, who was influential in teaching him the arts of "dealing with people" and the deeper workings of tattoo parlors. It was Jim who introduced Jonny to the Cherry Creek Family, the first distributors of his artwork. Jonny remains in Michigan today, where he has a beautiful wife and has two wonderful sons.

FISH
—Colorado, United States

Michael Fishkin simply goes by the name FISH. He has been tattooing and creating tattoo flash for many years. He always loved the tattoo art style and describes it as "the sickest stuff I have ever seen." He learned his flash style primarily from magazines, emulating other artists' styles in order to develop his own. FISH believes every day is an opportunity to learn, whether that's a new color scheme or a new "trick." One goal for his tattoo artwork is to incorporate a sense of motion, for it to flow, move, and look natural, and to avoid being flat or static. He feels tattoos express people's ideas, dreams, and fantasies in overt ways that enable others to better understand each other. Tattoos are a way to express one's deepest desires without the use of words. As he states, "With art and tattooing, you get the rare chance to affect people's emotions—to make people feel . . . to give them a smile, a memory, without saying a word. Evoking emotions is why I do what I do. I love to witness people's feelings change through the tattoo process; how they forget life for a moment and simply feel. That is what makes art and tattooing so special to me. Tattoos are a piece of us."

Friday Jones
—New York, United States

Friday Jones has worked with clients ranging from Angelina Jolie, Janeane Garofalo, the Neville Brothers, Robbie Williams, and Angie Harmon; she is known for providing an overall experience that combines fine art, detailed craftsmanship, and personal, as well as spiritual, components that transcend how tattoo art has previously been seen. More than a tattoo artist, Friday's designs continue to win many awards and are showcased in art galleries across the United States. Her art has also been featured on the cover of Robbie Williams' 2002 *Escapology* album, as well as the Celtic Warrior Axe designed for Fender-Jackson guitars. Friday began her journey into tattoo art with an apprenticeship at the prestigious Inksmith & Rogers studios in Florida in the early 1990s, which she completed while simultaneously earning a bachelor of science degree in philosophy and art at Jacksonville University. A member of the National Tattoo Association since 1994, she was selected at the organization's annual convention in April 2009 as the youngest on a panel of six (along with Ed Hardy) that roasted the legendary San Francisco tattooist Lyle Tuttle (who inked Janis Joplin and is the only tattooist ever to appear on the cover of *Rolling Stone* magazine). Friday maintains studios in New York and Los Angeles.

Fritz
—Nebraska, United States

My history of drawing flash has been relatively short. I started in 2006, and after several years of rendering patterns by various artists (e.g., Paul Booth, Guy Aitchison, Edward Lee, etc.), I figured it was time to branch out and find my niche. Because of the amount of exposure TattooFinder.com gets and the caliber of artists that the company represents, I'm honored to be associated with some of the best in the biz. Oh, yeah . . . the money's good, too! I would describe my design style as versatile. I hope to eventually have at least something that has appeal to all social classes and groups. As for me personally, though, I dig the dark, twisted art. I try to give a lot of myself and my feelings to the art I create. My heart is in darkness—where no image is off-limits.

Furmanov
—Almaty, Kazakhstan

My name is Sergey Furmanov. I was born in Kazakhstan (part of the old U.S.S.R.) and still live here today. I have been interested in tattoos since I was fifteen or sixteen. Before then, I used my drawing skills to create artwork of many different types and styles. After becoming interested in tattoos, I started to create tattoo designs for my friends, which they seemed to really like. In 2002 I began tattooing. It was just a hobby of mine at first while I was working as an IT specialist and studying at university. I worked out of my home and started by tattooing my friends only. They were happy with my work and asked me why I didn't tattoo professionally. I decided perhaps it was a sign that I should work as a professional tattoo artist in a studio. Now tattooing is my profession, my hobby, and my passion in life. At the present time, I prefer to work in the Oriental and old-school styles. Some of my works can be seen at www.FurmanovTattoo.com. I am very honored to be working with Flash2xs.com and the other very talented artists. Thank you for taking a look at my designs that are included in this book, and I hope you enjoy my work!

Gail Somers
—Idaho, United States

The legendary artwork of Gail Somers is a longtime favorite of tattoo artists and tattoo customers alike. Her enormously popular tattoo designs first debuted in *Tattoo Magazine*, causing quite a stir—and the career of "the Rocky Mountain Recluse" was born. Gail brings a unique style and extraordinary coloring to her art. Whimsical characters, mischievous fairies, playful dragons, vibrant florals, colorful butterflies, and tasteful tribal designs are all part of Gail's amazing pallet of exceptional tattoo designs. Gail's fun-loving and intriguing approach to the world of fantasy has created an ever-growing demand for her incredible art. Over the years, her beautiful designs and intense colors have firmly established Gail Somers as one of the best and most prolific flash artists in the industry.

Gary Davis
—Brisbane, Australia

Internationally known Australian artist and tattooist Gary Davis brings more than forty years of artistic experience and excellence to his remarkable flash art. Highly prized all around the world, Gary's intense colors, flowing style, and variety of designs have earned him a respected and permanent place as one of the true legends in the tattoo industry. Hailing from Carindale Brisbane, Australia, Gary's considerable artistic talents go well beyond tattooing and tattoo design—he is also an accomplished painter, illustrator, sculptor, cartoonist, and graphic designer.

Gentleman Jim
—Michigan, United States

My given name is Jim Skaja, and I have been tattooing since 1990. I can't remember a time in my life that hasn't revolved around art. It wasn't until I met Rand Johnson, from Cherry Creek Flash, that I finally understood art and what I was capable of drawing. Rand and his lovely wife Kay took me and my family under their wings and refined my skills to what they are today, and for that, I am eternally grateful! Tattooing and drawing have taken me across the country twice over. I now reside in Michigan with my wife, Sarah, and daughter, Tori. I have semiretired from tattooing and am currently pursuing other tattoo-related opportunities. I would like to thank Sarah for all of the support she has given me in all my artistic endeavors. I would also like to thank all the great people who support our lifestyle. "Gentleman Jim is one of the most creative and prolific artists the tattoo industry has produced. His mastery of art—both on paper and on skin—is very well known and highly respected. As a flash artist, Jim's hot-selling designs and sets are legendary. As a tattooist, Jim's work is simply amazing—his color work is impeccable, and his black-and-gray realistic tattoos and portraits rival fine photography."—Rand Johnson, Cherry Creek Flash

George
—St. Petersburg, Russia

George was born in 1968 in Sevastopol, Crimea. His real name is Sergey Bardadim. The name George came from his childhood nickname "George Best Buddy." George did his first tattoo at the age of seventeen using an ordinary sewing needle and thread—a primitive tattoo method often used in Russia at the time. And after many friends asked him to tattoo them, he built his first tattoo machine. It consisted of a "Sputnik" spring-powered shaver, empty ball-pen cartridge, and a sharpened guitar string. With the help of this device, George started experimenting with tattoos. Numerous experiments in building tattoo machines helped to compensate for the shortage of information available, and the practice gave him considerable experience in tattooing. For a few years, George worked as a guest artist at tattoo shops in St. Petersburg (Russia), Austria, and Germany. During those years, he started drawing his own tattoo designs and collected them as tattoo flash sets. In 1998 he entered the Association of Professional Tattoo Artists (A.P.T.A.), an organization based in the U.K., and in 2001 he joined the Alliance of Professional Tattooists (A.P.T.), an American organization. Having attained international expertise, George regularly attends the largest tattoo conventions in Europe, such as in Berlin, Frankfurt, Milan, and London. He additionally travels regularly for guest spots in tattoo shops all over Europe. While George's goal is to make sure his customers get whatever type of tattoo they want, he prefers doing custom work and says involving the customer in a detailed discussion of the work is an important part of the tattooing process.

Grapes
—Indiana, United States

I was born Robert Karl Grapes on September 30, 1976. According to my parents, I used to get into all kinds of trouble for drawing on walls, tables, and even using clam shells to draw all over our neighbor's car! I won art contests frequently through church and school and always wanted to make a career from my talent. After graduating from high school in 1995, I went to Murray St. University, and soon after decided that I hated school and dropped out. About six months later, starving and thirsty, I tried my salesmanship skills at a shop in Stevensville, Maryland, called SkinFlicks. It was the first time I'd been in a tattoo shop and didn't know what to expect. The owner was impressed and, thankfully, offered me an apprenticeship. The rest is a long story! My influences in art include H. R. Giger, Boris Vallejo, M. C. Escher, Gerald Brom, Ricky Carrelero, Dorian Cleavenger, Frank Frazetta, and other graffiti artists. My influences in tattooing include Aitchison, Booth, Cain, Litwalk . . . the list goes on. I've worked in only one convention but have been lucky enough to look over the shoulders of a couple of awesome craftsmen and soaked in as much info as I could. When it comes to tattooing and art in general, I'll never stop learning! Thanks to all the artists and staff of Flash2xs.com for their time and trouble. I hope to build a lot of friendships and gain new knowledge from this experience.

Hudson Assis
—Rio de Janeiro, Brazil

While I've always had an interest in art, my artistic pursuits really began in 1987. I was seventeen years old and creating drawings for T-shirts and jackets. It wasn't until 1997 that my interest in skin art really started. Tattooing was popular at the time, but I lived in a rural area of Brazil and only knew two tattooists. One did all his tattooing manually, mostly lettering and words. The other had what everyone was looking for: an electric tattoo machine (very new in my area at the time). I made my own motorized machine and began tattooing with India ink. This wasn't the best tattooing I ever did. I had no idea what I was doing and no professional tutor. It wasn't until 1991 that I was first able to work with a professional tattooist, Pepeu, and we soon opened our own shop, Skin Art House. From 1992 until now, I have worked at many tattoo shops and some conventions. My primary goals have been to learn as much as I can from very talented people and to simply create beautiful tattoos. I have been very lucky to find wonderful friends and mentors on my journey, including Wagner Gorni, Marcos Davies, Diego and Klaus (in Argentina), Javier and Maximo Lutz, Pablo Barada, Edu, Mike Stefano, Fonseca Luiz, and Henrique Mattos. I am also very happy to be working with TattooFinder.com, which has allowed my tattoo artwork to be seen and worn beyond the borders of my country, and by tattoo enthusiasts around the world.

Inkee

—Ohio, United States

I am William "Inkee" Blanchard. The nickname "Inkee" was stuck on me back in the mid-'80s because I always seemed to have a smudge of color on my face. I didn't much like it at first, but I got used to it. Now it's all I answer to. I first drew flash for Superior back in 1994 and got with the Flash2xs.com company before TattooFinder.com existed. I've tattooed all over the United States, both "underground" and in shops, from Michigan to Texas—Virginia to California. I'm mostly into doing up a new twist on Celtic designs and I like doing colorful feminine designs, too—I LOVE the bright colors. I'm not much for drawing just to impress others who draw; I prefer to draw mostly what I think that average people will want to wear forever and what they can actually afford to get. I hope you like the work I have in this book and on the TattooFinder.com Web site. I'm always adding new designs!

Ivan Keel

—North Carolina, United States

My name is Ivan Keel, and I've always been attracted to the creative side of life. I began filling time with art while growing up in Wisconsin. After high school, I went to college for a few years, exploring the field of graphic design. The industry was rapidly changing with computer advancements at the time, and my education was quite scattered. After a couple of years, I took a leave, loaded up my Jeep with some plain black tees, drawing supplies, and a sleeping bag, and headed south. I eventually found myself in Daytona, and after visiting a few shops in the area, I drew up my first couple sets of flash. It was about this time that I began my relationship with TattooFinder.com. Selling online gave me much more flexibility and saved a ton of gas money. I eventually even got enough money to finish up my degree back in Wisconsin. Out of school, I ended up working in advertising in North Carolina, but eventually moved to Los Angeles. There, I worked on a couple of films creating artwork and design. I even got to work for one of America's greatest contemporary playwrights and with an Oscar-winning cinematographer. I was also working as an illustrator for a small L.A. fashion house—another treasure trove of creativity with fresh approaches. Eventually, I had enough of L.A. and headed to the beaches of the East Coast again. I currently work at a small design outfit in Wilmington, North Carolina. I live in a historic home built in 1818 and enjoy a quiet life of drinking too much and making art in many forms. In terms of my work as a tattoo design artist, I feel my role is to give inspiration—to help fill the need we all have to express our creativity. My goal is to help pull out the image on the tip of your tongue.

Jerry Goodwin

—Texas, United States (1944–2008)

Jerry's last published autobiographical statement: "Howdy folks, my name is Jerry Goodwin, artist of Zoo Flash. When I'm designing tattoo flash, my head is above the clouds and into the heavens for I am (as the saying goes) on cloud nine. I was born on March 22, 1944 in Maud, Texas. Yep, that's right, Maud, Texas . . . ever heard of it? Nope? Well, it is a nice little old sleepy farm town close to Texarkana, Texas, and to this day if you are passing through on a horse and blink your eyes you will miss it, ha-ha! During most of my childhood, I lived in Santa Fe, New Mexico. Back then it was like the old stagecoach days with no fences. Why, you could almost go anywhere you wanted and it was grand . . . just pull off the highway and take off cross-country. Sorry to say it is not that way anymore and I miss that freedom. I loved the New Mexico country, but it was a rough time back during that era. There weren't a whole lot of opportunities available in Santa Fe, or, as a matter of fact, in the whole state of New Mexico. So at the young age of twenty-two, I left New Mexico and ventured to Dallas, Texas, looking for better opportunities. I thrived to become a commercial architect and practiced in architecture for twenty years. Throughout my life, in my spare time I doodled with artwork, did a few drawings and sculptures here and there on the side, but never did really get into it. On certain occasions, when people saw my artwork, they made comments that I should be a tattoo artist, but it went in one ear and right out the other. Heck, I was into architecture and going to make it big no matter what it took. I never did make it big in architecture. I guess I should have listened to the suggestions and been a tattoo artist, ha-ha! So here I am to this date, single, retired, and residing in Alba, Texas, at Lake Fork, designing tattoo flash. I give thanks to Flash2xs.com for helping me and giving me this great opportunity to share my God-given talents. I would like to close this bio simply by saying that I believe our talents, visions, and ideas come from God. If you choose and select any tattoo design from any artist, be proud of your selection. When you wear it, wear it with a smile with your head held high (like mine on cloud nine). Know that you have chosen a divinely inspired creation. I thank you for reading this short bio and hope you enjoy my designs, for God gave me the visions as he guided my hand."

Joe Butt
—California, United States

Ever since I could hold a crayon, I have been drawing. All through my childhood, I was that kid in class who was just drawing. I never suspected that I was practicing my career at such a young age. Even back then, I was drawing skulls and dragons and naked women. It wasn't until the age of seventeen that a tattoo machine found its way into my hands. Since then, tattooing has dominated my artistic landscape. Although I do still work in other media (acrylics, oils, digital, and sculpture), I often find myself thinking, "I wish this was a tattoo." It's become the easiest way for me to achieve my artistic visions. After tattooing all over the world, and winning a few tattoo contests, I am still in love with the needles. I am still striving to improve and learn. I am still humbled by the greats—Hernandez, Aitchison, Booth—that list goes on and on. Now married and pushing middle age, I live in Northern California, just between the redwoods and the grape vines. I live in the town where Lyle Tuttle grew up. Yeah, I've hung out with him, no biggie. I love being a contributor to the TattooFinder.com lexicon. I stand among the greats, and by proxy, I am tattooing the world. Children are growing up and seeing my tattoos on their parents. That's monumental. I am changing the world; I am leaving a mark on mankind. I am honored to be a part of the art that lives. Thank you!

Jonathan McGinnis
—Texas, United States

My name is Jonathan McGinnis; I am an artist and employed as a graphic designer. I am originally from Kansas City, Kansas; however, I currently reside in Texas. I have been drawing since I was first able to pick up a crayon. I have always admired tattoos and tattoo-inspired art. While I was in college, my younger brother became my inspiration for drawing tattoo flash, as he began to acquire tattoos. As a freelance artist, I use many mediums for my art, but I am partial to graphite and Prismacolor markers. It is with the Prismacolor markers that I create a specific type of drawing called "automatic drawing." An automatic drawing brings out your subconscious. This type of drawing is spontaneous, free flowing, and contains no "preplanning." I began to notice the similarities in my work to tattoo designs. The automatic drawings soon lead me into the world of tattoo flash. When I design tattoo flash, I draw upon my imagination to create designs, keeping them simple, but with a unique twist.

Lee Little
—New South Wales, Australia (1968–2009)

Lee's last published autobiographical statement: "G'day fellow tattooist and tattoo enthusiasts! I was born in Newcastle, Australia, in 1968. I started my tattooing apprenticeship at the age of eighteen, with Les Lee at Bankcorner Tattoo, Newcastle. At the time, there were only two tattoo shops in the entire area, so we kept very busy. As evidence for the growth in popularity of tattoos locally, there are now over twenty shops in the Newcastle region. I started my own shop in 1996 and then went on to establish Newcastle Tattoo Studio in 2001. I now enjoy working in my own private studio with select clientele established through years of experience. I've been drawing tattoo flash for at least as long as I've been tattooing. My designs are all easily tattoo-able, and I created them specifically to withstand the test of time (based on my knowledge and experience from tattooing). I have a passion for many art forms, with experience in graphic design, signage, digital art, airbrush, business identity (logos), charcoal, decals, murals, graffiti, etc. I set high standards for myself in my art, approaching it through hard work and determination. I'm always trying to do better—never resting on "that'll do"—and instead striving to evolve in times of constant change and fashion. My other interests are motorcycles and trail riding with my buddies from trailmates.net. It's my escape from the rat race that life dishes out and a great way to rest my oftentimes overloaded imagination. All my love goes to the cook, Karin, and our two children, Karlee and James. Without them, my inspiration may have never evolved."

Marc Lapierre
—Massachusetts, United States

My name is Marc Lapierre. I hail from western Massachusetts. Right around the same time I learned my first words, I was drawing my first pictures. I've always been into drawing cartoons, comic books, and things of that nature. More than fifteen years ago, I self-published my first comic book, while still in high school. Today, I'm working as much as I can as a freelance cartoonist and graphic designer. Just like in my youth, I draw pretty much whatever people ask me to draw; only now I charge for it! (Man, I wish I had thought of that when I was thirteen.) About ten years ago, a friend asked me to draw her a picture of a teddy bear on some clouds. That was the first time it occurred to me that this could be another outlet for my creativity. Since then, I've been designing tattoos on the side for friends, family, and anyone with a few bucks to throw my way. The more requests I got for custom designs, the more attracted to the medium I became. I love the creative freedom that is afforded to me when I'm working on designs. The more I designed, the more I wanted one. Four years ago, I finally came up with a design for myself and got it done. If I had to sum up my style in one word, it'd have to be "fun." I like to keep my designs bold, sharp, and colorful. My typical design recipe is to take some traditional themes, add equal amounts of comic book flair and rock 'n' roll style, throw in a dash of humor, and stir. I also enjoy drawing tribal-type stuff and other abstract type designs, but I get the biggest kick out of devils and pin-up girls. They're just cool!

Mark Strange
—Florida, United States

Mark Strange was born in central Indiana in 1969—the land of corn and soybeans. His father was an engineer, and his mother was a cabinet-maker who also painted with oils and acrylics. Mark was artistically inclined from a very young age. Drawing from the time he could hold a pencil, he moved on to painting with whatever he could get his hands on (Mom's oils and acrylics, usually). As he grew, his artistic experimentation progressed, and by age ten or eleven, he had moved on to clay sculpture and metal fabrication. During this period, he was exposed to the tattoo industry on an almost daily basis through a close family friend. By 1986, after years of observation and helping at the studio, he started to entertain the idea of tattooing. In 1991 he took on learning the trade full time. By 1996 he was attending several tattoo conventions a year and producing commercial flash. His goal when designing is to create designs that are simple and easy to tattoo but have the look of a "custom" design. Mark works an average of seventy hours a week but spends most of his down time immersed in various art projects other than tattooing, including handcrafting tattoo machines. In his own words, "It is true what they say . . . this profession will consume you!"

Marty Holcomb
—Ohio, United States

With more than thirty-eight years in the professional tattooing business, Marty has done thousands of custom-designed tattoos and has won numerous awards for his art and tattooing. He is an accomplished painter and designer, as well as a world-renowned tattoo artist. In 2001 his book, *Silent Symphony—The Art of Marty Holcomb*, was published, showcasing his paintings. In the last ten years, he has done approximately 15,000 tattoo designs, most of which are in publication and distributed worldwide. He is currently tattooing again in Columbus, Ohio, and is working on some new flash for TattooFinder.com. Marty's original art, such as paintings, drawings, and even original flash (these are the originals, not copies), can be purchased through his Web site at www.martyholcomb.net.

Matt Roland
—Georgia, United States

Growing up, I was always the kid with his nose in a sketchbook, comic book, or art book. Most of my schoolwork was covered in doodles and scribbles in the margins. I began my tattoo career with a formal apprenticeship in 1995 in Augusta, Georgia after leaving behind five years of corporate cubicle life as a data processor for a large insurance company. The need to find a way to be creatively successful had finally taken over and that necktie was slowly becoming a noose. I currently own and operate Tribal Urge Tattoos in Augusta, and feel blessed to be a part of this wonderful industry. I believe that my artwork speaks for itself, and TattooFinder.com helps it be heard!

Melanie Paquin
—Quebec, Canada

I was born in Quebec, Canada, with a pencil in my hand. As a child, I took many art classes, both because I truly enjoyed art and because they often got me out of gym classes! As a kid, I drew on everything—clothes, shoes, desks, even friends! While art was never encouraged as a career growing up, it was always encouraged as a pastime, so I kept at it. When I graduated from secondary school, I enrolled in college for fashion design and graduated. My tattoo art started around the age of sixteen, drawing tattoo designs mainly because I couldn't find a design I wanted tattooed on me. Friends soon started asking me to draw tattoo designs for them, and I realized I might be on to something. I wanted to tattoo, but after a lot of rejection and bad experiences, I gave up on it. It is hard to decide to change career paths once you have a mortgage, but sometimes you just have to take a risk and follow your passion. I've done that with my tattoo artwork, and now I'm ready to do that with tattooing, too! I finally started my tattoo apprenticeship in 2011 at Tatouage Magnolia! I feel extremely honored to be part of the Flash2xs.com family and work with such talented artists. *Un merci spécial à toute ma famille et amis pour leur support continu.*

Paddy
—County Cork, Ireland

My name is Paddy Bullman. I was born in a small town called Youghal in the county of Cork in the south of Ireland. I can't really say I have an occupation. Of course, I am a tattoo artist now and most people would consider that an occupation, but I don't—I regard it as a way of life. During my life before I started tattooing seriously, I tried a lot of different professions. In my earlier years, I was a sailor at sea, going off to work on ships at the age of sixteen. Since then, I have moved around a lot. The last twenty or so years I spent most of the time living in Sweden. Tattooing I have done all my life, though naturally enough not full-time at the start. At the age of fourteen, when I was a child living in Ireland, there was one tattoo artist in the whole country. He was in Dublin, 350 miles away. He might as well have been on the moon, so I had to do things for myself. My first tattoos were done on my fourteen-year-old buddies using a sewing needle wrapped in cotton, dipped in Indian ink and hand-hacked into their tender young skin. The resultant masterpieces often caused strained family relationships and pink roses looking more like cabbages. Well, we all must start somewhere. I have become a lot better at my work through the years and covered up the old masterpieces on my old friends. My hobbies are reading, astronomy, cosmology, physics, and motorcycles. Some of my heroes are Stephen Hawking, Albert Einstein, Mahatma Gandhi, and all other people willing to spread knowledge and make big sacrifices to try and make this world we live in a better place.

Payaso
—Colorado, United States

My name is Israel Chavez. I was born in 1977 in Grand Junction, Colorado, and remain in Colorado today. Mr. Payaso (my pen name, meaning "the clown") represents the many hats I've worn in this life. I have spent considerable time inspired by my creative motivations, developing my own unique style of art. My style falls within the realm of "hip-hop street art" but without any gang influence. In 1990 I started to bring my style to the tattoo world. I primarily work on paper in black and gray—I'm not a big fan of color. I also enjoy doing larger-scale murals. In 1997 I created my own art label, Los Unicos, meaning "the Only One." The term Loyalty United (L/U) represents me and my work, as we are both true to one another. What's the L without the U? I've always enjoyed sports, playing baseball and basketball throughout school, and still love watching games today. Presently, I'm focused on growing my clothing line under my L/U label. It is my mission to bless the hip-hop world with this real street heat. I believe in myself and I know that if I expose this distinct style of art, it will be successful.

R. Shane "Endorpheus" Hall
—Idaho, United States

As a kid, I started drawing tattoos on my classmates with ballpoint pens, markers, paint, mustard, ketchup, liquid paper . . . whatever would leave a mark. I got my first piece at Sunset Strip Tattoo, in Hollywood, California, when I was twenty-one, and knew then I wanted to be a tattoo artist. I have worked at Warm Art Tattoo, War Paint Tattoo, and Slavedragon Tattoo. I have had the privilege of learning from some very incredible artists. When I was a "noob" tattoo artist without these influences, my goal was to challenge myself with an inexhaustible supply of complicated, over-detailed designs. As time goes along in this profession, you come to find that simpler, well-placed designs are much more visually appealing and hold up better over the years. I think the role of the flash artist is to create designs with real human beings in mind . . . hard-working people with their own stories and their own dreams. As long as there are people who want to get tattooed and don't necessarily have the imagination or art skills to create their own designs, our role will always be to lend them our skills. I'm still working very hard with my band "Foolsbane" to record and tour. We are working on our third album, and our goal is to take it on the road. I would love to have another Harley-Davidson, a Camper/RV, and the time to enjoy it all. I'd like to spend more time with my parents. Overall, I'd like to leave things better than I found them. I am humbly thankful and relieved to be involved with such a flexible craft, my awesome clientele, and among all the artists here at Flash2xs.com/TattooFinder.com.

Rand Johnson, Cherry Creek Flash
—Minnesota, United States

Rand Johnson has earned his way (and paid his dues) through art for almost forty years—working as a graphic designer/illustrator for ad agencies, design studios, marketing groups, and publications. A keen interest in tattooing eventually led to an abrupt career change in 1993. Rand traded in his pens, brushes, and paper for tattoo machines, ink, and skin—and opened the Cherry Creek Tattoo Studio in rural Minnesota. His reputation for fine artwork and attention to detail spread quickly, putting his remote studio on the map and keeping Rand very busy. His natural talents in art opened many doors in the world of tattooing. Many of the industry's top artists willingly answered his endless questions and candidly offered their experience, advice, and critiques. Rand sees tattooing as a tight-knit community and expresses an enormous debt of gratitude to "the professionals who had spent their lives paving the way for a newcomer like me." Perhaps due to the limited amount of flash available back then, or simply due to his background in commercial art, Rand found himself custom drawing most of the tattoos he did. It didn't take long for quite a pile of designs to accumulate. That's when the career he thought he'd left behind—graphics—married his new love—tattooing—and Cherry Creek Flash (www.CherryCreekFlash.com) was born. Today, Rand spends most of his time drawing flash and marketing the art of other aspiring artists.

Ray Reasoner
—Michigan, United States

I love art in many forms but tend to stick to drawing. My drive to draw landed me a contract with Flash2xs.com in late 2003. I have been learning more every year since then. It is almost creepy how the more I learn, the less I know. I have many influences. There are so many people that have given to the tattoo industry through their art, technology, dedication, and business ethics that I cannot name them all. I'll start with Filip Leu, Paul Booth, Tom Renshaw, Deano Cook, Sailor Jerry Collins, Lyle Tuttle, Jack Rudy, Shane O'Neil, Endo, Joe Capobianco, Mike Cole, Bert Grimm, Bob Tyrrell, Tramp from Detroit, Jay Morton, Lou Bardach, Robert Pho, Guy Aitchison, Ed Lee, Rand Johnson, Mario Barth, Jay Wheeler, Kari Barba, guys from the Texas Custom Irons forum, Paul Rogers, Percy Waters, Sam O'Reilly, and Thomas Edison. I would like to also specifically say thank you to C. W. Eldridge and Don Ed Hardy for making my learning of our history more accessible. My biggest influence is that hairy guy with the burned stick in a cave somewhere a very, very long time ago. Not only can I relate to his body-hair coverage, but without that beginning there is no now, and I would like to go from now to the future of this great industry. I hope that you enjoy the level that I am currently at—and go get some ink! Life is a highway, and I am currently stuck in construction.

Rembrandt
—Arizona, United States

Rembrandt was born on February 3, 1964. He has traveled and lived all across the United States. He was drawing before he could walk or talk and will still draw on anything (even moving things, if he can catch them). Although he sketched more than he studied in school, he still managed to graduate from Catalina High School in Arizona. His college career consisted of general studies, including an art class that he ended up teaching. Rembrandt began tattooing in various shops in California and Arizona, where he learned the fine art of putting needle to flesh (and started to sell his flash). He opened shops in Tucson, Arizona, and in the Woodlands, Texas, but has since closed his doors on each. Rembrandt fought a battle with throat cancer and won. He says his art brings him the greatest solace in his life, always seeing him through the darkest storms. Rembrandt credits his artistic inspirations from the tattoo world as Paul Booth, David Bolt, Aaron Cain, and Edward Lee. Other artists more generally include H. R. Giger, Frank Frazetta, Hajime Sorayama, and Boris Vallejo. Rembrandt has won many awards at conventions all over the United States. He has had the opportunity to have his work exhibited in various galleries and in several magazines, including *Tattoo Flash*, *Savage*, *Skin & Ink*, and *Eros*. He has created illustrations for poetry magazines and done commercial mural work. He loves art of all forms, but creating flash and tattooing are his biggest passions.

Rob Sacchetto
—Ontario, Canada

Tattoo artist Rob Sacchetto was born and raised in the northern mining community of Sudbury, Ontario. He has spent some twenty-five years dedicated to the visual arts and has worked in a variety of mediums, including illustrated film, television, comic book illustration, and concept design. He also transforms people into genuine zombies, complete with gaping wounds and rotting skin, through his site, www.zombieportraits.com. A self-described horror fanatic and comic-book geek, Sacchetto zombifies people from across the globe using ink and watercolor. Since launching his site in November 2006, Sacchetto has sold over 2,000 original zombie portraits around the world, as well as written and illustrated *The Zombie Handbook: How to Identify the Living Dead, Survive the Coming Zombie Apocalypse* (recently translated to Spanish), and *Zombiewood Weekly: Celebrity Dead Exposed*. Along with selling a line of products on his portraits Web site, Rob's products can also be found at major bookstores in both the United States and Canada. His work has been featured in the documentary *Zombiemania*, where he zombified himself along with the other interviewees for the film. Never having enough on his plate, he launched a daily blog, www.zombiedaily.com. To date, his has over 1,000 original postings, paintings, and pieces for fans to check daily.

Ronn Wyman

—Colorado, United States

Hi, my name is Ronn. That's right, 2 Ns. It's not short for anything, and I don't have any clever nickname, either. I am currently doing a hitch in the Colorado Department of Corrections for the crime of self-defense. About seven years ago, I took an interest in Odinism, and I really liked the skill and intricacy of the Celtic and Norse artwork that was done back in the day. I also really admired the moral and ethical values of my pagan ancestors and have tried to live by their standards as best as I can. Anyway, I got some books and started practicing the knot-work patterns and made some armbands for myself. Of course, the other guys on the yard saw my work and started asking me to do some patterns for them as well. A friend convinced me to send some work to Flash2xs.com, and so I did my first sheets, sticking to what I feel is a traditional Northern European tribal style. One of the things that is nice about these knot-work patterns is that they work equally well for both dudes and chicks. The patterns are also intriguing to look at, and they draw a lot of comments from people.

Sam Sheinin

—Calgary, Canada

I was born in Calgary, Alberta, Canada, and from a young age, I was always found drawing. My earliest drawings as a kid were those of Kiss, the Hulk, and characters from classic horror movies, like *An American Werewolf in London* and *The Thing*. I have taken fine art, classical animation, and numerous art classes, but the only thing that kept my interest in art for the past seventeen years has been tattooing, and I have been both honored and humbled to have the opportunity to work next to some of the industry's finest artists. I've owned and operated my own studio, Lucky Strike Custom Tattoo (www.luckystriketattoo.ca), for the past five years, and it has become highly recognized as Edmonton's premier custom tattoo studio, with award-winning tattoo artists, loyal clientele, and top-notch guest artists. I enjoy drawing many different styles of flash, and I'm mostly inspired by the classics, such as Sailor Jerry, Paul Jeffries, Dave Shore, and Johnny "Dutchman." I hope my work provides some level of inspiration for artists and the public alike, whether you're drawing something up or looking for an idea for a new piece.

Shane Hart

—Kansas, United States

I began my tattooing career in 1989, with an apprenticeship to Gary "Professor Inkslinger" Barber of Olathe, Kansas. He was reluctant to teach me because I was only sixteen at the time, but he did anyway. In 1994 I met East Coast Al and went to work at his studio in Kansas City, Kansas. It was during this time that I was introduced into the National Tattoo Association and met Rand Johnson of Cherry Creek Flash. Creek would later be the primary distributor for much of my flash, along with National Tattoo Supply and TattooFinder.com. After several years of tattooing with East Coast Al, I felt that it was finally time to have a studio of my own. In 2000 I opened Shane Hart's Studio of Tattooing in Lawrence, Kansas. Two short years later, I hosted a one-time tattoo expo at the Adams Mark Hotel in

Kansas City, Missouri. Around that same time, a good friend turned me on to product design and I closed my studio in 2004 to pursue this field full time. I was also blessed with regular guest-artist spots at several Kansas City tattoo studios during this three-year period and had a short stint on the Board of Directors of the Alliance of Professional Tattooists. In 2007 my family and I decided to move to Colorado. This allowed me to pursue working with Rich Ives at Steel City Tattoo in Pueblo on a collaborative project to create an "institute" to pass our tattooing theory and methodology on to fellow tattooists. We have since returned to Kansas, and I am also still currently doing illustrative, custom tattooing.

Shane O'Neill
—Delaware, United States

Shane O'Neill is a talented, self-taught artist excelling in all mediums, but his true calling lies in the art of tattooing. He credits his brother with motivating him to learn how to tattoo, and he began tattooing in the spring of 1997. Shane's experience as a professional illustrator seemed like a natural transition into tattooing. He has a bachelor's degree in fine arts from the Philadelphia University of the Arts. Shane has tremendous respect for his personal influences: artists like Tom Renshaw, Paul Booth, Jack Rudy, Brian Everrett, and Bob Tyrell. Shane specializes in realism, portraits, wildlife, and horror. He also has his own line of flash available for purchase. Shane travels around the country and internationally to tattoo conventions. While attending these events, you can find him teaching seminars and producing some of his best work. Shane has been featured in many magazines and has won countless awards for his tattoos, including being crowned "Ink Master" of the Spike TV's tattooing competition series' reality show, *Ink Master*. He has achieved far more than he imagined and truly appreciates all the recognition. You can find Shane at August Moon Tattoos in Bear, Delaware, or visit his Web site at www.shaneoneilltattoos.com.

"Thanks to everyone for all your support!"— Shane O'Neill

Stevie Soto
—California, United States

I was born on July 3, 1979, in the city of Orange, California. I grew up in Anaheim, California, and I've lived here ever since. As a kid, I wanted to be a baseball player or an artist. I was always interested in tattoos, and luckily my passion is now my work. Growing up, the gangster element was always around, so naturally I was exposed to some ink. I did attend three years of community college, mostly taking art classes. In 2001 I began to learn the craft of tattooing and started to create flash, which has since become very popular. I worked very hard for many years and now I find myself in a great place in life. I own and operate Goodfellas Tattoo Art & Design Studio in the city of Orange, California. I'm happily married and have a son and three daughters. When I'm not tattooing or creating art, my hobbies include hanging with my family and training in Muay Thai.

Suspek
—Colorado, United States

Mickey Drogsvold (aka "Suspek") was born in Phoenix, Arizona, and now lives in Colorado. Like other artists, he describes himself as being born "with pencil in hand." His early art pursuits often got him into trouble, such as the time he created a bootleg comic book in school, as well as his involvements with graffiti, for example. In 2004 he started drawing tattoo flash with the hopes of landing an apprenticeship. He drew a design for a friend and went with her to the shop where she was being tattooed (bringing his portfolio of art with him). This got him an apprenticeship in 2005 under Mike O'Neil and Rachael Bardach, then owners of Main Street Tattoo. While his art helped get him in the door, he still spent a lot of time "hanging out in the shop until they gave me a job." He worked there for many years and says he's learned a lot from the rest of the gang. He was brought on as an artist with TattooFinder.com in 2006, which afforded his art worldwide exposure. He prefers to draw in black and gray, because he "sees life more in black and shades of gray." His artistic influences are M. C. Escher, H. R. Giger, and "every graffiti artist who has ever picked up a can." His current goals are to develop his tattooing and flash skills and to expand his talents to other mediums. He sees the passion the world has about tattoos as a natural part of wanting to "fit into the tribe, same as back in the caveman days . . . just more individualized now."

Swan
—Colorado, United States

I was born into a single-parent home, so I was hungry for praise and attention from the start. From age thirteen, my grandmother nourished me with creativity through pen and pencil. This is where I learned to have confidence and ingenuity—beyond any lessons I gleaned from books. What inspires me to draw? Drawing fills places inside me that people and things don't seem to very well. I prefer to connect to other people through my own little world, and yes, its total escapism. I love using colors in my artwork, yet I don't see us yet fully manipulating colors to the extremes we can on skin. While black and gray has its own tonal sepia of values, I love what places we can reach through provocation of color stimulus. I don't have a specific physical environment that enhances my creative juices, but I do have triggers that inspire my soul to get past the dirtiness of life. Triggers for me include a perfect sentence by one of my children, or the slamming background base chords from a Bob Seger song, or thinking of people I've lost, or that I'd like to meet. I create art that then, in turn, has a life of its own. Art has brought people and their stories to me and has given me an opportunity to visually recreate a special life event for them and put that to skin. To me, a tattoo is like a map for people to connect. Thanks for your interest in my work.

Terri Fox
—Oklahoma, United States

I was born in '54 and raised in the Syracuse area of New York. I hung out there until '72 and then traveled the United States. Eventually, I settled in Oklahoma, where I raised four great kids in the country lifestyle, and most of us still live there to this day. These days, I'm blessed with the complete joy of my grandkids—eight so far. Inspirations for my art came at a few stages in my life. As a child, I was impressed by the paintings my grandfather Fox created on the walls of his home during a time when they couldn't afford to buy pictures (something I did later in my own home). My mother, father, kids, and grandkids, and many other relatives, share a love and talent for art. I can't imagine life without it (or music). It was actually the support and encouragement from my kids that finally gave me the initiative to start designing tattoos. I also tried to learn the art of tattooing to better understand creating tattoo flash, but I quickly learned it wasn't my cup of tea. I also enjoy wood carving and I create wooden game boards . . . some from my own imagination; many done as custom-personalized designs. My true passion in art is sculpting (earth clay and polymer), and I eventually want to start sculpting pieces inspired by some of my tattoo flash. All in all, I embrace each new day as a chance to make my own little corner a pleasant and loving place to be. If my energy makes its way out into the rest of the world, I hope it brings others happiness as well. Much peace, love, and light to all.

Terry Riley
—Washington, United States

I have been making a living with my art since 1984 and have caricatured more than 120,000 people. My cartoons and caricatures have appeared in many nationally and internationally published magazines. Titles such as *Omni*, *Hustler*, *Chic*, *National Lampoon*, and others have published my work. My corporate clients have included Coca Cola, American Airlines, MetLife, and many others. For the past three years, I was the feature caricaturist at Sunset Celebration attraction in Key West, Florida. Through all of that, I have always drawn fantasy art for myself, and drawing tattoo designs is a great bit of fun.

Index